D0366919

Best Walks in the Chilterns

Roy Woodcock

Best Walks in the Chilterns

Constable · London

First published in Great Britain 1998
by Constable and Company Limited
3 The Lanchesters
162 Fulham Palace Road
London W6 9ER
Copyright © 1998 Roy Woodcock
The right of Roy Woodcock to be identified
as the author of this work has been asserted by him
in accordance with the
Copyright, Designs and Patents Act 1988
ISBN 0 09 476520 0
Set in Palatino 9 pt by
SetSystems Limited, Saffron Walden, Essex
Printed in Great Britain by
St Edmundsbury Press Ltd
Bury St Edmunds, Suffolk

A CIP catalogue record for this book
is available from the British Library

Contents

Illustrations

List of Maps

Acknowledgements

I am grateful to many people who responded to my letters and phone calls whilst I was seeking information, especially:
Simon Melville and Keith Payne of English Nature; Trevor Lindley and Julia Sutton from County Hall in Aylesbury; Nigel Snell of the Red Kite Reintroduction Project; Daniel Larkins at BBONT; Christine Preston of the Chiltern Society; Dr Helen Read, ecologist in Burnham Beeches; Keith Wallis, District Manager for the Forestry Commission; Peter Whittle, Estate Officer for the Wormsley Estate, and Verity Walker from the Regional Office of the National Trust at Hughenden. Also thanks to the many librarians who answered my queries in Worcester, High Wycombe and Princes Risborough libraries.

Introduction

Broadly speaking, the Chilterns are located in Hertfordshire near Tring, Marsworth, Aldbury and Ashridge; Oxfordshire from Goring and Nettlebed to Watlington, Chinnor and Thame; Bedfordshire near Dunstable, but mainly in Buckinghamshire from Burnham Beeches to Hambleden in the south and as far north as Princes Risborough and Wendover. To define them more precisely than this, however, is slightly more difficult.

Their eastern boundary is to be found where the chalk dips beneath the rocks which make up the London basin, at the line of towns between Rickmansworth and Watford, but this margin is confused by the fact that large areas of the Chiltern chalk are concealed beneath thin deposits of more recent rocks, drifts and Reading Beds.

To the west, a scarp slope forms an obvious boundary, yet many of the villages at the foot of the scarp, such as Watlington, Great Kimble and Monks Risborough, merit inclusion with the Chiltern region. Their old parish boundaries certainly extend well out on to the lowland plain of Oxfordshire or Buckinghamshire as well as up the escarpment.

At the southern boundary the River Thames makes a good dividing line, although the chalklands continue southwards as the Berkshire Downs. About fifty miles north of the Thames the northern boundary is less decisive but the main mass of the chalk hills decrease in height and the scarp becomes less significant close to Dunstable and Luton, so the M1 makes a useful modern boundary.

Beyond the downland near Dunstable and Whipsnade there are isolated outliers such as Sharpenhoe Clappers, and further north still the chalklands form the East Anglian Heights extending all the way to the North Norfolk coast.

In spite of difficulties in defining the area, its distinctive and yet diverse characteristics are very clear. Now officially designated an Area of Outstanding Natural Beauty this ever-changing patchwork of hills, valleys, beech woods and chalk downs is crossed by a network of narrow roads, footpaths and bridleways and scattered with old forts and monuments, flint churches and many interesting villages and isolated hamlets which give the impression that time has stood still.

Just as the landscape of the Chilterns is quite distinctive, there are also characteristic sounds of the Chilterns, with the wind on top of the downlands, the calls of sheep, buzzing of flies and chirping of the crickets, and in the beech woods the noises of wind-blown trees swaying, the calls of the jay or green woodpecker and the crunching of the beech mast.

The Chilterns are home to over 100,000 people and provide a living for farmers and foresters as well as urban inhabitants. They also provide recreation and fresh air for thousands of visitors every weekend, when they can become very crowded, but even in midsummer it is possible to find quiet walks mid-week.

Although benefiting from the mild south-eastern weather, the exposed higher parts of the Chilterns can feel very cold, and snow will linger there for several days longer than on the surrounding lowlands. In some weather conditions the valleys and woods provide shelter, particularly if walking in bitter or windy weather but also to be appreciated on the occasional hot and humid summer days, especially in August.

Geology and Geomorphology

The Chilterns are formed from just a small part of the chalk which extends from Dorset to Yorkshire. The chalk was created by the accumulation of calcareous mud on the bed of the sea, more than 100 million years ago. At that time the sea was warm, averaging 20°C, and accumulations on the sea bed contained a few shells, but more frequently just small remnants of echinoids, crinoids and crustaceans. But the main component, often as much as sixty per cent, is calcareous algae such as coccoliths. Much of the chalk contains flint which was formed later, as a secondary deposit, probably resulting from groundwater dissolving silica from sponge skeletons and being reprecipitated as flint nodules.

Some 40 million years ago, at the time that the Alps were being formed, the calcareous mud was uplifted by earth movements. Since then there have been millions of years of erosion in which the landscape has been shaped and changed, and a period of higher sea levels when superficial deposits were laid down on top of the chalk. These deposits are geologically younger than the chalk, and cover much of the Chiltern plateau and create acid or neutral soils, in contrast to the alkaline soils of the chalklands. The cover of these superficial deposits is generally a metre or so in thickness, but up to 5 m has been measured at Ibstone and other locations. The material is derived from the chalk and younger rocks deposited on top of the chalk. Many of these deposits were created in glacial and periglacial conditions when rocks were broken up by changes of temperature and freeze-thaw activity. The Chiltern chalklands are not typical of other chalk areas in southern England, because of this cover of drift, and because more than twenty-five per cent is forest-covered. This helps to create the unique character of the Chiltern landscape.

The chalk of the Cretaceous period is divided into three sections, Upper, Middle and Lower.

Upper Chalk is softish, with many layers of flint, and is up to 90 m (300 ft) in thickness.

Middle Chalk is much harder, with a few flints in some of the layers. At its base it also contains Melbourn rock, which is hard, and often forms distinctive features, such as a subsidiary scarp below Ivinghoe Beacon, seen especially half a mile west of the Beacon, near Crabtree Cottages.

Lower Chalk contains both white and greyish chalk, and amongst its variation is Totternhoe stone which is a hard chalk, and the chalk marl, which is good for making cement. Totternhoe stone is to be seen near the village of that name west of Dunstable where it has been quarried, but it also forms part of Sharpenhoe Clappers. Occasional bands of harder chalk in the Lower Chalk cause breaks of slope, and sometimes create springs.

The layers of chalk are similar to a pile of books, with the youngest layers of the Upper Chalk on top. The Middle is exposed in places on the plateau, and together with the Lower is exposed in the valleys and on the scarp, where it is possible to see below the top layers (the top books of the pile). The Lower is generally at the bottom of the scarp.

The Upper Chalk is the most widespread, but is often covered by a layer of younger, superficial deposits. These were associated with the times when the land was lower than at present during the interglacial periods, enabling marine deposits to be laid down on top of what are now the Chilterns. There are also some glacial deposits, material carried and then dumped by ice during the glacial phases of the Ice Age. These are particularly noticeable on the lower parts of the dip slope.

Amongst these superficial deposits are the boulder clay, which often supports woodland, for example at Whipsnade and Ashridge; there are crag deposits near Berkhamsted; gravels on the higher ground of South Hertfordshire; sands, loams and gravels of the Reading Beds west of High Wycombe and in the Hughenden Valley; clays and sands on some Buckinghamshire hill tops. The widespread nature of the drift cover gives different scenery from that to be found on the chalk.

The cutting of the M40, excavated in the 1970s, shows horizontal bedding of the Upper Chalk, with superficial Pleistocene deposits of clay, silt, flint and sarsens in a cap on the top.

The chalk is soft and can be easily cut, but contains hard flints in places. These can be seen in the fields and on the footpaths, and they have been widely used in walls and buildings. Flint has often been used in churches, together with clunch, which is a chalky marl. Clunch is easy to carve, but weathers badly, and so is only suitable for the insides of churches. The stone needed for quoins was imported from places like Totternhoe quarry. Hambleden and Bradenham are two outstanding villages for their examples of flint buildings. Barns will often have flint and brick ends, with low side walls of flint, and weather boarding sides, especially in the large Buckinghamshire barns. Flints in the fields have often been a nuisance, and there were times during the nineteenth century when the local people picked up the stones by hand to sell to highway authorities, as this improved the quality of the fields as well as earned them some money. The flint seems inexhaustible, as more and more keeps appearing. Important sites for extracting flints were near Nettlebed and Ivinghoe.

Puddingstone (Walk 15) is an unusual rock, a form of conglomerate which means that many small pebbles have been cemented together. Lumps have been exposed in fields by the plough in several places. Many have been found near to Chesham and Hemel Hempstead.

Greywethers or sarsen stones (see Walk 18) have also been found in several places, notably the Hughenden Valley, and the village of Bradenham used to be the centre for cutting sarsens. Some were probably taken from here along the Ridgeway to Avebury.

West of the chalklands, out on the plain, are the sands and clays of the Greensand period. Some of the clays at the foot of the scarp have created springs (e.g. Pyrtle – see Walk 8 on pages 148–49) and hence become suitable sites for settlements.

The shape of the Chilterns, its geomorphology, can be described as a cuesta, meaning a hill with a steep edge (scarp) on one side, and a gentle slope (the dip slope) on the other side. The chalk was tilted by earth movements millions of years ago, and the western side was pushed up and formed the escarpment (scarp) which faces Oxfordshire. The scarp is perhaps the most distinctive feature of the Chilterns and is often clothed with beech woods. The gentle side is the dip, sloping down eastwards towards London. The scarp reaches a highest point of 267 m (875 ft) in Wendover Woods from which there is no view, and the highest viewpoint is Coombe Hill (grid ref 8406) near Ellesborough with a height of 254 m (832 ft). Note that there is a second Coombe Hill near Wendover Hill (grid ref 8909), and there are many other coombes in the Chilterns (see Walk 6). Coombes are small steep-sided dry valleys, and are probably the result of freeze-thaw action creating a semi-frozen sludge of rocks and soil which slid downhill.

The scarp is cut (scalloped) by coombes and dry valleys. Rivers rise in springs at the foot of the scarp where the spring line settlements have developed, but the main river valleys are on the dip slope, as most of the drainage flows eastwards. Most of the valleys are now dry, although rivers still flow in a few of the main valleys.

The Ice Age lasted for about 2 million years, and included several glacial as well as warmer interglacial periods (some of which were warmer than the present day for thousands of years). It is possible that some of the Chiltern valleys were full of glacial materials at the end of the Ice Age, and the rivers would flow on top of these deposits. As they were removed by post-Ice Age erosion, the chalk beneath was exposed, and this enabled the rivers, which had formed the valleys, to disappear underground into the porous rocks. Another possible explanation of the presence of the dry valleys is the effect of permafrost which existed during colder times in the past, when the ground was frozen solid, as in the present-day tundra. The summer thaw produced water and rivers would flow on the surface and erode valleys. When the permafrost melted with the warm up of the climate, the rivers could sink into the porous chalk. A third possible explanation of the dry valleys, is simply that the water table has become lower. A fourth is that overuse by man has lowered the water table, and this has certainly been happening in recent decades. A final suggestion is that the removal of the forests quickened the throughflow of water and this lowered the water table.

Many of the dry valleys are asymmetrical, with a steeper slope facing west or south, possibly because of the effects of the afternoon sun warming the icy slopes at the time of formation. The steeper slopes generally contain the coombes (see above) and hangers (see Walk 1).

The ice reached as far south as the Chilterns, and melt-water cut channels through the hills, creating gaps, in which gap towns have grown up – Tring, Wendover, Princes Risborough and Goring. Gaps are followed by routes, the A41, M1, and the Grand Union Canal. Melt-water also helped to enlarge existing river valleys on the dip slope, and although most of the valleys are now dry, there are still a few rivers draining south-eastwards on the surface, although the starting point of the river may change with the seasons, as the water table fluctuates up and down, and some rivers are only winterbournes (a bourne is a stream). The rivers are the Ver, Glade, Bulbourne, Chess, Misbourne, Wye and Thames, though only the Glade, Bulbourne, Chess and Misbourne cross the main part of the Chilterns. In addition to these rivers in the main valleys, there are also the Hambleden and Hughenden streams.

Vegetation and Fauna

Landscape is dependent on the geology and geomorphology, but is also affected by vegetation. Compare the light green of the beech woodlands in May with the barren look of winter or the browns and golds of the autumn. Each season will give differences, although the Chilterns can be described as an area with walks for all seasons, with the blue of bluebells in spring, the greens of summer and the browns of autumn. There are also the seasonal changes of farm fields.

The woodlands are beautiful, contain interesting wildlife and provide shelter from cold, strong winds and occasionally heat but they can create problems whilst walking, as all sense of direction can be lost. There are often many paths, including some which do not appear on maps, and it is advisable to carry a compass to check which direction you are walking in.

The famous beech woods of the Chilterns have not always been a major part of the landscape. After the Ice Age, tundra, then birch, pine and mixed forests with oak, elm and lime grew as the climate warmed up. In the eighteenth century the main demand was beech for fuel and oak for the navy and for building houses, but now that has ceased the woodlands are likely to revert to being more mixed. Sycamore were introduced into England in the fifteenth and sixteenth centuries and are now very common, as they spread rapidly. There are areas of juniper, for example near Chinnor, and a box wood has survived near Kimble. Ancient woodlands will often show signs of pollarding (see Walk 19 and later in this Introduction) but other indicators of ancient woodland include several small plants which take many years to establish themselves; bluebells, dog's mercury, lily of the valley, wood anemone or the wild service tree.

The ecology of beech woods is quite distinctive. They have a dense layer of foliage in the summer, which cuts off seventy to eighty per cent of the light. This is why the woods are so shady and dark, and have little undergrowth in the summer. Only shade-tolerant plants can survive, for example yew, holly and spurge. Some brambles establish themselves, but they do not always manage to produce flowers.

In spring the woods are open and clear, which is why bluebells thrive in many places, and dog's mercury (a member of euphorbiaceae, the spurge family) is also common. The beech in summer are light green, and in autumn the leaves begin to turn to browns, orange and yellow. As the leaves fall, a leaf carpet develops on the floor. The floor of beech woods is lined with leaves in autumn and winter, and also with beech mast which crunches underfoot. In autumn the woods spring to life again, as light gets in, with fungi being widespread.

Historically much of the beech from the Chiltern woodlands was used in furniture-making. Even in the thirteenth century there are records of the names Turnur, Turnator, which indicate that there were people then who were wood-turning and working with wood. In 1725, Daniel Defoe mentioned the beech woods as being used for making carts for London, and also for chairs. Legs, rails and splats were made from beech, but the seats were elm or fruitwood. Ash was used for the bows and some oak and walnut for special pieces. Bodgers made the legs and stretchers, and only the backs and seats were made in the factories.

Many villages made chairs, mainly Windsors at first, but some had their own local speciality. Chinnor, for example, was famous for ecclesiastical chairs. Chairs were an important source of income to many small villages, but in the larger towns, notably High Wycombe, huge sums of money were earned. High Wycombe sent chairs to St Paul's Cathedral and to many foreign locations. In the nineteenth century High Wycombe boasted that a chair was made every minute throughout the entire year. The growth of the industry can be seen from the figures that in 1841 only 95 people were employed in chair making, but by 1871 the figure had risen to 431. However, by the end of the century, machines were replacing hand tools, and bigger industrial concerns were taking over. Foreign timber was being imported by 1890, as it became cheaper than Chiltern timber. From that time onwards more trees were allowed to grow much larger and this changed the character of many of the woods.

Bodgers often lived and worked in the forests, in the midst of the trees which were their basic raw material. Each bodger would have an area of woodland containing a small stand of beech. The trees would be felled or coppiced and a simple pole lathe would be used to produce the legs and stretchers. Chair-framers in the towns would fit the pieces together, as work-shops were needed to do the assembling and polishing.

After the end of bodgering, woods were no longer cut and controlled, and so they overmatured and management became vital. In several areas conifers were planted but since the 1980s the Forestry Commission has gone in for mixed forests.

There is much evidence of former coppicing in many of the woods, which was formerly an essential part of life. Coppicing provided the main source of timber for fuel, as well as for fencing and baskets. The Chiltern woods supplied London (where the population had been growing rapidly during the sixteenth and seventeenth centuries) with fuel until about 1800, and Henley was the main centre for handling this trade which went down the river. Now there is no coppicing except where the National Trust is restoring the practice, and in Burnham Beeches where the managers are also coppicing again. Coppic-ing helps to open up areas and let in more light, which is better for flowers such as orchids and helleborines.

Coppicing is cutting trees at a height of less than a metre above the ground, but pollarding is cutting at 2.5 metres. Many trees were pollarded in the past. Burnham Beeches and Friths-den are two particular areas where this practice was common. Frithsden is visited in Walk 4 and Burnham in Walk 19.

Frithsden contained an area of beech wood pasture, with grass beneath the trees. Beech probably colonised this area after the retreat of the ice, and so the forests are quite ancient. Pollarding was an idea brought in from the Mediterranean 4–5 thousand years ago, and was a way of obtaining fuel without killing the tree, an early form of conservation of resources. Branches were cut off the main trunks which became lumpy and knobbly, hence the weird shape of many old pollarded trees which have survived in areas of ancient woodland.

Many of the old pollards became top heavy, and so they are

easily blown down when strong winds occur, although the damage is normally very patchy. Also, as some trees die, others will grow, including silver birch, ash, oak, cherry and holly, as well as some beech. These other trees were formerly much more common before the years of all the beech-planting for the furniture industry.

Pollarding will extend the life of a tree, as shown by the 400-year-olds in Burnham Beeches. Two hundred and fifty years would be a more normal life expectancy for a beech. The gnarled and twisted shape of the pollards helps to attract wild life, as small areas of dead and rotting wood can be found in various places on the trees, and these do not harm the tree but provide a habitat for insects and plants.

The chalk grassland areas were probably all wooded until Neolithic man made clearings, finding the chalk soils easier to work than the heavy clays. They practised arable and sheep farming, but after Roman times the arable declined. The woodland spread, but some areas of grass survived. The next major change occurred in the seventeenth century when sheep and cereals were the favoured farming activity, and later there was more ploughing in Napoleonic times. After this period, farming went into depression which did not lift until World War II, when widespread ploughing occurred. The remaining grasslands are very special for their flora and fauna.

Flowers grow in the grassy turf, which is short, partially because it is grazed but also because the soil is low in nutrients. Some plants stay very close to the ground, to conserve water and to avoid being eaten by sheep. Others, like thyme and basil, escape because they are strong-smelling. Some plants have long roots, to survive dry spells in this light soil, for example salad burnet, or lady's bedstraw. Chalk downland is one of the richest of all grassland habitats, and may contain as many as forty different types of plants in a square metre.

Insects also thrive in a rich wild flower environment, and there are many hummocks on old grasslands which are nests of the yellow meadow ant – a sign of a healthy grassland ecosystem. A variety of butterflies can be seen on these flower-rich chalklands, including the marbled white (see Walk 5), five of the seven British types of blue butterfly, dark green fritillary, silver spotted skipper and brown argus.

The chalk grasslands are easily lost and are in constant need of management, or they will quickly turn to scrub. Grassland is invaded by hawthorn, wild rose, dogwood, privet, buckthorn, all of which have berries and are spread by birds. Scrub has been cleared, often by volunteer labour, in order to give the chalkland plants more chance of survival. The survival of small plants is helped by grazing sheep on the land, as they nibble away at the shrubs and bushes. Rabbits are also beneficial in this way. In regions of scrub management, rotational cutting is used, so that different areas are cleared in turn, which not only keeps everywhere under control, but can create a variety of different habitats for wild life. In the Aston Rowant Reserve some juniper scrub can be seen.

There are deer in the woods, especially muntjac and fallow, with a few roe and sika. They are best seen early in the morning or late in the evening. The muntjac are only about 0.6 m (2 ft) in height and after escaping from Woburn in 1890, have been successful in spreading further afield. The fallow have antlers in the autumn.

Badgers are here in small numbers, but are rarely seen. Foxes are quite numerous, as are rabbits who are useful grazers in grassland areas.

Since being introduced from North America near the end of the last century, grey squirrels are plentiful – and becoming a pest. They strip bark which can kill the trees. If you hear a big noise in the woods it is unlikely to be a deer, more likely to be a squirrel hurling itself from one tree to another or from branch to branch.

Birds are widespread and numerous, and many references are made to these in individual walks.

History

Remnants of ancient settlements can be seen in several of the walks, as the Celts built forts which can be seen at Ivinghoe and Whiteleaf. These overlooked the plain below and also the ancient route of the Icknield Way. To the Celts, the word Cilterne meant the hill country, regarded as wild country. Another possible origin of the name is that *chilt* comes from the Saxon word for chalk. Iron Age settlements existed in the Chilterns and some aspects of their way of life can be seen at the Chiltern Open Air Museum in Walk 18.

Romans settled on the dip slope and in the valleys, especially in the eastern part of the Chilterns, notably at St Albans. In the west the Lower Icknield Way was used by them and there are several sites of villas along this route, at Little Kimble, Saunderton and Bledlow. The Chiltern valleys were opened up during Roman times and farming must have continued after the Romans had departed, although scrub and woodland did return to some of the fields.

Settlements grew up at the foot of the scarp, where springs emerged from beneath the chalk. These spring line villages include Monks Risborough and Watlington, and the parishes in this area were established with long and narrow shapes, as at Bledlow, Great Kimble and Pitstone. This gave each parish a share of the fertile lands of the plain, a section of scarp and some of the dip slope, enabling each to grow crops, graze animals and also have woodland for fuel. The narrow parishes often resulted in churches being quite close together.

In Saxon times the Chilterns were still sparsely populated woodland, and often used as a refuge, though most villages, farms and lanes were in existence by the time of the Domesday Survey. More people settled in the lowlands of the Aylesbury Vale, and moved up into the higher areas for grazing and woodland products. The heavily wooded Chilterns were settled late, with most settlements being isolated hamlets in the valleys, with farming taking place on cleared sections of the forest. Fields were usually small and surrounded by hedges, the remnants of the forest. Clearing woodland to convert it into farmland was known as assarting. The woodland provided fuel, and poles for fencing, but was also a source of income with timber being sent to London via the Thames, as the main source of fuel. Proximity to London has always affected the Chilterns, and the Chilterns were used as traditional hunting territory for Londoners. In later centuries, towns developed along the main routes and later still the Chiltern area developed as a region of small towns with industries.

Life was not easy, and careful use of all resources was necessary. Some of those people scratching a living from the edges of the commons found areas of clay on Reading Beds or plateau gravels where brick-, pottery- or tile-making could take place, and in other areas lace-making and straw-plaiting were developed. In later years there was chair-making, too, all adding to the sources of income.

Fluctuations in agriculture and the decline of these old craft industries, often because of mechanisation or foreign competition, led to loss of income and decline, but the influence of London was becoming greater and greater.

With the arrival of the railway, the Chilterns began to change dramatically, christened Metroland in 1915 when the Metropolitan Railway encouraged walkers to visit the Chilterns. The area subsequently attracted house-hunters, too, and rows of semi-detached houses spread rapidly and at first, unplanned. Clough Williams-Ellis, of Portmeirion fame, wrote about the 'octopus of urban growth' in connection with these settlements.

The population continued to grow throughout the 1930s but the real surge came after World War II. There had been few regulations in the pre-war period, but as rapid development took place after the war, planning controls increased. This was too late to save many areas but, fortunately, there were large estates, such as Wormsley, which were saved from buildings.

The region's links with London changed it from an area for hunting and a source of fuel wood and some food, to a dormitory and also a region for second homes, for what are often referred to as the 'chattering classes'. The bigger towns still have some industry, and they provide schools and recreation for local inhabitants, but have now become more closely linked with London, so the Chilterns are included in wider planning concerns, such as the Green Belt.

The Chilterns were included in the Greater London Plan of 1945, and new towns and motorways have become a part of local life. Parts of the Chilterns were designated an Area of Outstanding Natural Beauty (AONB) in 1965 and this, together with the work of the Chiltern Society, will ensure that the individual nature of the Chiltern region will not be lost.

Many of the original routes through the Chilterns follow gaps cut by rivers: Watling Street – A5 – through Dunstable Gap; the Roman route – Akeman Street – now A41 through Tring Gap; Wendover and Misbourne; Princes Risborough to Wycombe – not such a gap, but there is less scarp here, enabling the link to go through to the Wye Valley and the Thames. These routes mostly trend from south-east to north-west, following the rivers. But this is not true of the Ridgeway or Icknield Way, as these older routes followed the ridge or the foot of the ridge.

Many other old routes have become holloways, used by packhorses and wagons, and some have survived, for example Colliers Lane, which is followed in Walk 10. As the amount of coach traffic increased in the seventeenth century better routes were required. In order to look after these, finance was necessary, and so the turnpikes were born. This funding began in the early eighteenth-century – the Henley–Oxford route was turnpiked in 1736, and one of the old milestones is seen in Walk 15. High Wycombe to Stokenchurch was turnpiked in 1719, and one of the old toll houses from Wycombe is now in the Open Air Museum (Walk 18).

Railways began to develop in the late 1830s and they had an effect on the road traffic, partially because of payments required on the toll roads, and they also affected the canal traffic which had been important from 1800. The Berkhamsted line was opened in 1839, using a cutting through the Chilterns near Tring which was dug in 1837. Other lines followed, High Wycombe to Princes Risborough in 1862, Amersham to Wendover in 1892, and another cutting dug at Saunderton in 1905. Modern lines give fast and regular services to and from London.

When the Chilterns were thought of as a remote and lawless area, a Steward was appointed to supervise them. The Stewardship of the Chiltern Hundreds is a Crown office and, as such, cannot be held by a Member of Parliament. As Members of Parliament may not resign, nor may they hold a civil office for profit, an ingenious escape route was devised in the eighteenth century whereby anyone wishing to leave Parliament could apply for Stewardship of the Chiltern Hundreds. The office is now only nominal, but this was not always the situation, as payment for this post was made in the thirteenth century. Highwaymen and thieves were then a particular problem and a popular contemporary description of the Chilterns said 'Beat a bush and start a thief.' Nowadays the area is more famous for footpaths than footpads.

The Hundreds were administrative areas, which only have historical interest now. They cover most of South Buckinghamshire, and the three Chiltern Hundreds listed in the Domesday Book were Desborough, Burnham and Stoke. Desborough extends from Medmenham to High Wycombe and then to Stokenchurch and Turville; Burnham includes the Chalfonts, Amersham and Beaconsfield; and Stoke Hundred borders the Thames and extends to Eton, Gerrards Cross and Slough.

Grim's Ditch consists of numerous trenches and embankments which are not all connected together and which are found in many parts of the Chilterns. Most commonly there is a raised bank and a small ditch, variable in breadth and depth, but up to 12 m (40 ft) wide and 9 m (30 ft) deep, which would have needed a huge amount of labour to construct. They were probably built by digging a ditch and using the earth to pile up as a mound, the technique used at Offa's Dyke. King Offa certainly spent some time in the Chilterns, and had his court at Berkhamsted for a time. This may or may not be relevant. The different sections of Ditch appear to be from two different periods, as some are very old, with evidence of the Iron Age, but parts have been dated at about AD 800.

Most of the banks and ditches are either parallel to the Chiltern scarp, or at right angles to it – which may be significant. They have a certain amount of rectangularity, but there is a near semi-circular shape from Northchurch towards Wigginton Bottom and Hastoe. A dog-leg stretch passes close to Hampden House. An impressive straight line near here suggests that the countryside must have been open at the time it was made, or how could such straight lines have been constructed?

It is now generally thought that the banks and ditches were boundary lines, possibly boundaries of enclosures or perhaps dividing the common grazing on the uplands from the small plots of land on the scarp. Suggestions that they were for defence or a fire break have also been considered, although they would not have been particularly useful or successful for either.

Agriculture on the Chilterns has been very different from that on the plain, being less productive, though more varied. Generally the soils are less fertile, though with a few rich areas in some of the major valleys. Soils on the chalk are not very good, but the Victoria County History states that although the soils are poor, they 'throw up some very good herbage in a kindly season'. Where the chalk is covered with drift deposits, the soils are often not much better. Clay with flints usually gives a heavy loam, and the boulder clay soils are lighter but still quite stony.

Farming began in Neolithic times, and gradually increased during the Bronze Age. The chalklands in the Chilterns were not typical of other chalkland areas because of the covering of superficial deposits making them much heavier to work. The best areas were often at the foot of the scarp on the edge of the chalk, and here there were springs and the advantage of being on the old north-south routeway.

In medieval times there were three-field villages out on the plain, but up on the Chilterns, land was often controlled by individuals, either by the Lord of the Manor or by tenants. Farming was important in the valleys, with woodland and pasture on the ridges. As early as the thirteenth and fourteenth centuries food was being sent to London from the southern parts of the Chilterns. After the Black Death in 1348–49, however, many farms and fields were abandoned.

In the sixteenth century the farming had become mainly arable, especially wheat, with some barley for malting. Bell pits were often sunk through the superficial drift deposits (generally not more than 3 m thick) to reach the chalk, which was dug up and spread on the fields.

Farming always had to compete with woodland for profitability, and as the price of corn increased, so woodland decreased. Most common arable land had gone by 1800, though areas still remained at the foot of the scarp.

After 1850 corn was so profitable that hedges were grubbed up and chalk pits dug to fertilise the slightly acidic clay soils. The peak period for arable was reached about 1880. At that time, foreign imports from the Prairies and elsewhere became much cheaper, and so farming declined, with more land being converted to grass and some allowed to turn to scrub.

There was a big ploughing campaign to feed the nation during World War II, and some downland and commonland was then ploughed for the first time. More hedges were grubbed up to enlarge the fields, and quite a lot continued to be ploughed after 1945. Mechanisation increased, then came the European Common Agriculture Policy, including set aside, and change continues, affecting the appearance of the country-side as well as farming. With mechanisation and increased efficiency there are fewer farmers and so there are surplus farm buildings. Many have become private houses, though often retaining stables. Many barns have been converted, and recently the yellow of rape or the blue of linseed have appeared in the fields instead of the golden cereals.

Place Names

Place names often give some indication of history or local physical features, and there are many examples of this in the Chilterns.

Hoh means a ridge or shoulder of land protruding from the scarp, as at Sharpenhoe and Ivinghoe.

Dene or den is a valley, generally long and winding, often on a dip slope, as at Hambleden, Assendon, Hughenden and Hampden.

Coomb or coombe or cumb is also a valley, but often on a scarp.

Ham is a village or homestead, as at Burnham or Bradenham, or Studham (village with horses).

Ton also means a homestead, Watlington is the homestead of Wacol or Waecol.

Ley is a grove or open woodland or meadow, as at Hedgerley.

Ora is a slope, as in Chinnor, the slope of Ceonna.

Relevant Organisations

CHILTERN SOCIETY

The Society is a registered charity and was founded in 1965 with the stated aims of stimulating public interest in and care for the beauty, history and character of the Chiltern Hills. This helps to encourage everyone to be aware of the precious countryside resource.

The variety of work undertaken ranges from keeping an eye on planning applications in the area to consultation on government proposals and the County and District Structure Plans. In addition there is physical conservation work, such as repairing stiles, pond clearance and hedge laying – and much more besides.

There are now over 5000 members, and all work is voluntary. The Society has close links with the Chiltern Open Air Museum at Chalfont St Giles, and the Chiltern Woodlands Project Ltd which works for the conservation of the mainly small beech woods in the area. A newsletter is published four times a year and keeps everyone informed about local developments. Groups of members take on responsibility for different aspects of preserving the quality of the Chilterns, whether it be for Rights of Way, Conservation, Rivers and Waterlands or Historic Works and Buildings.

Of particular interest to walkers is the Rights of Way group which waymarks and helps to keep open over 2000 miles of footpaths.

FORESTRY COMMISSION

The Forestry Commission was set up in 1919 with the aim of increasing the amount of timber produced in Britain. In the Chiltern region the Forestry Commission manages 3500 ha (8759 acres), notably at Aston, Wendover, Cowleaze and Hodgemoor. Some 2000 tonnes of timber is extracted from Wendover Woods each year. In recent times aims have widened and the Forest Enterprise section of the Forestry Commission not only manages the woods for timber production, but also for conservation and recreation. Many events are arranged in the woods, such as craft workshops, cycling events along forest trails, guided walks and fun days for children during school holidays. Cowleaze Wood with its famous sculpture trail is visited in Walk 11 and Wendover Woods, where information about wild life is available, are visited in Walk 6.

BBONT

The Berkshire, Buckinghamshire and Oxfordshire Naturalists' Trust is an independent charity which helps to protect local wildlife habitats by looking after 90 nature reserves in the three counties. In recent years BBONT has saved 16 ancient woodlands, 202 hectares (500 acres) of downland and 21 old flower meadows.

The Trust attempts to ensure that local planning decisions pay due consideration to wild life and that landowners and farmers also consider the conservation of wild life on their land.

BBONT studies and records information about local fauna and flora, especially on the nature reserves. These reserves provide habitats in which plants and animals can live naturally, without too much interference from such problems as man, concrete or insecticides. Rare forms of wild life can survive in the reserves, and sometimes spread back out into other parts of the countryside.

BBONT raises money from memberships, fund-raising and occasional donations and grants, but cannot employ many full-time staff. Much of the work is dependent on many hundred volunteers.

BBONT reserves seen on these Chiltern Walks are Chinnor Hill (Walk 10), Chequers (Walk 7), Grangelands (Walk 8), College Lake (Walk 3) and Warburg (Walk 15).

NATIONAL TRUST

The National Trust manages large areas of land in the Chilterns, as well as owning magnificent houses and parts of villages. The largest is the Ashridge estate in Hertfordshire, over 1600 ha (4000 acres) of woodland, commons and chalk grassland, stretching from near Aldbury and Berkhamsted northwards to Ivinghoe Beacon. The estate is a self-funding property and is open to walkers all the year, with many miles of footpaths. Ashridge is visited in Walk 4. Ivinghoe Beacon is included in Walk 5, and on the grassland there is a fenced area for sheep, which are used to help maintain the rich grassland flora.

In Bedfordshire the Trust owns a farm as well as chalk grassland on Whipsnade Downs, where sheep-grazing has been reintroduced to help manage the grassy slopes. In Whipsnade village is the unusual Tree Cathedral which is seen in Walk 2. To the north of Dunstable is Sharpenhoe Clappers, an isolated Chiltern hill, with an Iron Age fort on its summit, and visited in Walk 1.

The Oxfordshire Chilterns include Aston Hill and Watlington Hill, and the Watlington area is seen in Walk 14. Watlington Hill contains areas of both grassland and woodland, which have to be carefully managed but in different ways.

The largest number of NT interests in the Chilterns are found in Buckinghamshire where Bradenham, Hughenden, Coombe Hill, Low Scrubs, Pulpit Hill and West Wycombe are located. Much of Bradenham village, as well as surrounding woodlands, hills and farmland, belongs to the Trust, and West Wycombe is another village largely owned by the National Trust. In West Wycombe (Walk 12) there is also the nearby hill and park owned by the Trust. At Coombe Hill (Walk 7) is an area of grassland with some woods, and on the summit is the Monument which is located at the highest viewpoint (not the highest point) of the Chilterns. Adjacent to Coombe Hill is the wooded area of Low Scrubs, also managed by the NT and walked through in Walk 7.

The National Trust is involved in active management of grassland and woodland areas, often in close consultation with other organisations, such as the Forestry Commission or BBONT. In forested areas most of the replanting is now of mixed species, and not just beech. Control of wild life is another aspect of forestry management, and the rangers keep control of squirrel and deer numbers (especially the muntjac), as they have become too numerous and cause considerable damage to the trees.

Information Boards are provided in several locations, and the NT has strong links with many schools for educational purposes.

AREA OF OUTSTANDING NATURAL BEAUTY

Eight hundred square kilometres of the Chilterns were designated an AONB in 1965, with a further 33 square kilometres added in 1990. The AONB does not include the entire Chilterns region, as the suburban areas of the eastern margin are excluded. It does, however, contain the core of the Chilterns and the escarpment, extending from Goring and the Thames northwards to Dunstable, with a separate isolated area north of Luton.

The AONB aims to conserve and enhance the natural beauty of the farms and woodland, to consider the needs of rural industries and people, and at the same time to cater for recreation.

BUCKINGHAMSHIRE COUNTY COUNCIL

The County Council manages several areas of rural landscape for the enjoyment of the public. There are 5 Country Parks, 15 Picnic Sites, over 400 ha (1000 acres) of woodland and 2,500 miles of public rights of way.

Amongst these locations are Pitstone Hill (see Walk 5), an area of downland which includes a Site of Special Scientific Interest (SSSI); Pavis Wood and part of Cholesbury Camp (see Walk 6); Bacombe Hill and Coombe Hill Monument (see Walk 7); the Rifle Range and Grangelands Nature Reserve and Whiteleaf Hill (see Walk 8); and the Hampden Monument and Cockshoots Wood Picnic Site (see Walk 9).

ENGLISH NATURE

English Nature was created in 1991, when the Nature Conservancy Council was dissolved to create three regional bodies in the three countries of Great Britain.

English Nature is responsible for advising the government on conservation of nature, including wild life and natural features. It promotes conservation, both by direct and indirect means, often through other people and organisations. It creates and manages National Nature Reserves, and identifies and designates Sites of Special Scientific Interest. There are 63 Sites of Special Scientific Interest in the Chilterns, and 3 National Nature Reserves. The SSSIs and National Nature Reserves are protected in law.

English Nature works with similar organisations in Scotland and Wales, through the Joint Nature Conservation Committee, which was created in 1991.

Choice of Routes

The choice of twenty routes for this book was inevitably personal, based on knowledge of what seemed to be the most interesting and outstanding features of the Chilterns, together with an attempt to cover a wide range of countryside. Landscapes, the history and the buildings were all part of the attractions. The book aims to give information about all the local features which can be seen on the walks, as well as detailed route descriptions. For the former, see the numbered headings at the end of each walk.

Ordnance Survey maps will be helpful.

The 1:50 000 Ordnance Survey Landranger maps show the routes of the walks. Although on their own they do not provide sufficient detail they should be adequate if used with the detailed instructions given in each walk.

The 1:25 000 Ordnance Survey Explorer maps, which have replaced the Pathfinder maps in various locations including the Chilterns, are better to have on a walk, although obviously they do not cover as much ground so would prove more expensive.

Walks 3, 4, 5, 6, 7, 8, 9 and part of walk 10 are on Explorer 2 Chiltern Hills North.

Parts of walks 10, 18, and 20, most of walk 17 and the whole of walks 11, 12, 13, 14, 15, 16 and 19 are on Explorer 3 Chiltern Hills South, a double-sided map which covers a large area.

The Chilterns are covered with a large number of footpaths, mostly well signposted thanks to the work of the Chiltern Society, although this can be confusing in woodland areas where there are many extra footpaths which are not shown on Ordnance Survey maps.

It is worth carrying a compass in case of problems of direction-finding in some of the Chiltern woods.

Walking is meant to be an enjoyable activity, so the speed of the walk should be as fast or as slow as you wish. There are those who rush at 4 mph, which is too fast for me, and others average 2–3 mph but for my choice, if there are birds to look at, churches to visit, the sun is shining and there is no hurry, the average speed might be more like 1–2 mph.

Walking boots are advisable, especially in wet or wintry weather. The exposures of chalk can be slippery on the paths because, although the rock is porous and should drain quickly, it retains a wet and greasy surface layer after rain. Although wellington boots might be suitable on flat ground, they are unsuitable on slopes and on flinty areas, as are trainers.

The Country Code
Enjoy the countryside and respect its life and work.
Guard against all risk of fire.
Fasten all gates.
Keep your dogs under close control.
Keep to public paths across farmland.
Use gates and stiles to cross fences, hedges and walls.

Leave livestock, crops and machinery alone.
Take your litter home.
Help to keep all water clean.
Protect wildlife, plants and trees.
Take special care on country roads.
Make no unnecessary noise.

Advice is to:
Leave only footprints.
Take only photographs.
Kill only time.

THE BEST WALKS

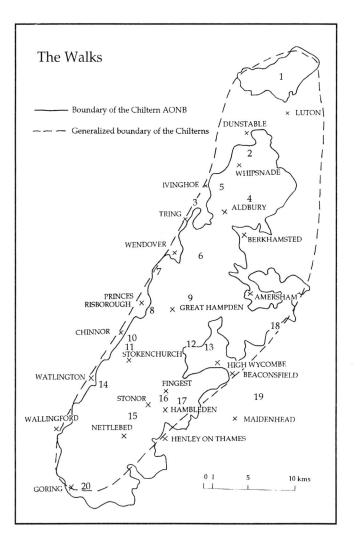

The Walks

— Boundary of the Chiltern AONB

– – – Generalized boundary of the Chilterns

1

× LUTON

/ DUNSTABLE
×

2

×
WHIPSNADE

IVINGHOE × 5

3   4
× ALDBURY
TRING ×

× BERKHAMSTED

WENDOVER
×   6

7

PRINCES   9
RISBOROUGH × × GREAT HAMPDEN
8

× AMERSHAM

CHINNOR ×   18 /

10
11   12 13
STOKENCHURCH
×   × HIGH WYCOMBE
WATLINGTON × 14   ×× BEACONSFIELD

FINGEST
×
STONOR 16 17   19
WALLINGFORD × 15 × HAMBLEDEN
×   NETTLEBED   × MAIDENHEAD
×
×× HENLEY ON THAMES

0 1   5   10 kms

GORING ×— 20

Bedfordshire – near Luton and Dunstable

Walks 1 and 2 are to be found near Dunstable, which is easily reached from the M1, A5 or A505. There are good bus links with London and with Luton, which also has a train service. The towns of Luton and Dunstable meet close to Exit 11 on the M1, but both are ancient towns in their own right.

Located near a gap in the northern hills of the Chilterns, Dunstable grew as a market town, on many important routeways. Watling Street crosses the older route of the Icknield Way here and the Romans developed their town of Durocobrivae at this meeting point.

After a period of decline, Henry I founded the town of Dunestaple here and a market for the surrounding area was created. Henry built himself a house nearby and came here with his court to celebrate Christmas in 1122. In 1132 Augustinians built a priory near the royal residence, and they provided a hostel for travellers.

The church of St Peter has a very wide Norman nave which has survived since 1150. The north west door has fine thirteenth-century ornament, and the square red marble pulpit is Victorian. An old door with bullet holes has been preserved. Henry VIII frequently visited or passed through Dunstable, and Anne Boleyn, Catherine Howard, as well as Catherine Parr all came here with him on different occasions. Henry VIII officially ended his marriage to Catherine of Aragon in Dunstable Priory, the only remnant of which is the Priory Church in Church Street. One of the church's stained glass windows shows both Henry I and Henry VIII, and the initials H and C are to be seen with a broken lovers' knot at the bottom of the window.

Just like Luton, Dunstable has had a car industry and ancient links with hat-making. Dunstable bonnets were sent all round the world.

Walk 1 – Sharpenhoe Clappers

Located on OS Landranger 1:50 000 sheet 166 and OS Pathfinder 1:25 000 sheets 1072 and 1048.
Length of walk is 7 miles.
Time required is 3 hours.
Terrain – a gentle stroll for most of the distance, with one steep climb near the end of the walk. Some of the paths can become muddy.
Starting point is at the National Trust car park, grid ref 066296. The walk can also be joined by walking from Sundon Hills Country Park, which can be reached by bus from Dunstable.

To reach the starting point leave the centre of Dunstable driving north on High Street North and turn right for Houghton Regis. At a large traffic island take the left fork towards Sundon and Streatley. Pass over the M1, go through Lower Sundon and on to Streatley, then turn left for Sharpenhoe.

Sharpenhoe Clappers rises to a height of 160 m (525 ft), and is capped by the Clappers Wood. This hill is at the northern end of the Chilterns and the northern edge has a steep slope overlooking the village of Sharpenhoe. In winter months the trees look like thin spines on the skyline and give a bleak and bare appearance, but in summer there are green beech woods, hedges, and undergrowth, rich in wild life.

The walk goes from the Clappers car park, through fields and woods, passing the edge of Sundon Hills Country Park and the village of Upper Sundon, and round to the final steep ascent up to the Clappers. A circuit of the hill completes the walk.

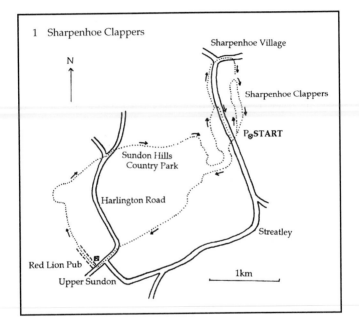

1 Sharpenhoe Clappers

N

Sharpenhoe Village

Sharpenhoe Clappers

P⊗ START

Sundon Hills
Country Park

Harlington Road

Streatley

Red Lion Pub

Upper Sundon

1km

From the car park cross the road and go over a stile, following the sign for the Icknield Way (1). Cross this field and then veer to the left along the field boundary marked by a line of trees. This margin soon bends round to more trees at the top of a very steep slope. Radio masts can be seen across the field to the left. At the hedge there is a path going off to the left, but our route is slightly right into the woods, on to the Bunyan Trail, sponsored by Scholl Consumer Products, and following a yellow public footpath sign, which is still the Icknield Way. The path runs just inside the edge of the wood, with an open field to the left, and a steep hanger (2) down to the right.

Dog's mercury lines the floor of these woods, and is the first greenery coming through in the spring. At a junction of footpaths where one goes steeply down to the right, turn left along a field margin, still following the sign of the Icknield Way. The edge of the wood has been recently cleared here, but it is rich in bluebells and a delight to see in April and May. Follow the edge of the wood past several bends, until there is a view of a radio mast, the embankment of a small reservoir and a farm straight ahead. Do not walk on to these, but turn right, to pass a wood on the left of the path. At the end of this wood, the Icknield Way and Bunyan Trail both turn right (3), but we go straight ahead on to a long open stretch, with a hedge to the left of the path.

After half a mile of straight path, walk out on to a narrow road (Harlington Road) which leads into the village of Upper Sundon. Go into the village as far as the Red Lion and then turn right along a track between hedges, then through a gate and descend across the middle of an open field. When the track ends, at the sewage farm go right through a small gate and cross the field to another small gate at the far left corner. This leads to a path through the small patch of woodland. There is an old quarry to the left, and an open field to the right. At the end of the wood, turn left along a field margin. Turn right at

the corner of this field and continue for nearly 100 m, as far as a path turning right alongside a narrow line of trees.

The village of Harlington with its tall church tower can be seen over to the left, and the steep slope of the chalk scarp can be seen to the right. At the group of barns, turn right, and then left, to pass along the right side of the buildings. Walk along the left side of a small stream where a few willow trees grow in the damp environments. Approaching the end of this field the trees on the top of Sharpenhoe Clappers can be seen straight ahead. At the road turn right, and after 20 m turn left along the narrow road, with a narrow stream on the left side. When the road bends left, turn right at a gate, to follow the public bridleway. Skylarks and pipits are likely to be heard along this section of the walk. This is a clear track across open fields, and bends left passing near some new planting and two small ponds. A footpath goes right from here, across a field and up to the scarp, but keep straight ahead along the track.

The track ends in the corner of the next field, and one footpath goes straight ahead, but take the right turn over a narrow footbridge, and walk alongside the hedge on the left and a small stream, which is fed from a spring, one of many in the Chilterns. Once past the spring the path is rising slightly, but at the foot of the very steep slope turn left. There is also a path going straight on up the slope, into the Country Park, but ignore this. The narrow path by the fence has the open field on the left and the wooded slope on the right. Follow this to the end of the field, then turn left, still with field on the left and slope on the right. Continue on this path which opens out to a broad track, and leads through to a small gate and the road, near a house called Moleskin.

Sharpenhoe Clappers

This is the place for decision-making, with two alternative routes possible.

EITHER: A Turn left in order to pass the pub in the tiny village and then walk up the steep end of Sharpenhoe.

OR: B Walk up the narrow road and then complete a circuit of the Clappers hill top.

A If you wish to visit the village, or the pub, turn left at the road and walk down to the road junction. Turn right past the Lynmore Inn, which was built in the early 1800s and formerly contained a blacksmith's shop and was called the Horseshoe. At the layby on the right side of the road is a footpath leading along a field margin to the foot of Sharpenhoe Hill. From here a steep stepped path leads up a well wooded slope to the northern end of Clappers Wood. At the top a path leads along the right (western) side of the hill and back to the car park. If preferred, a circuit of the hill can be made to look at the interesting wild life.

B At the road turn right and walk up the hill. This is a steep climb, and still quite a marked scarp, even though it is the northern end of the Chilterns. Half way up the hill it is possible to get off the road on the left hand side, and follow the path into the car park.

If the latter is chosen, once in the car park take the path leading past the information board (6). Follow the surfaced path and just before reaching the gate which leads on to open grass-land, turn left and follow the path into the woods, where a variety of bird songs will be heard in spring and early summer. Go up a few steps on to an open grassy area, and down to the left on the slopes there are rabbit holes. Walk straight on into the woods and reach the concrete memorial to the brothers of W. A. Robertson who were both killed in action (4).

Crunching on the beech mast, walk to the far end of the wood, to look down on Sharpenhoe village (5).

At the end of the wood and at the top of the steep north-facing slope, turn right and then right again to return along the margin of the wood. Just before reaching the Robertson Memorial go through a gate out on to a delightful expanse of grassland and bend round to the right near the edge of the grassy downland, to retrace steps to the car park. (6)

(1) The Icknield Way is named after the Iceni, an ancient British tribe, of whom Boadicea was the Queen. The old route extended from East Anglia southwards into Wiltshire, and was in use in Neolithic times about 6000 years ago. It became used more frequently in the Bronze Age about 2000 BC and has several pre-Roman sites along its length. Over the centuries there have often been two routes, an upper and a lower – the Romans used the lower. The lower is slightly to the north of the upper, and is on lower ground which might have become wet and muddy in the winter, though an easier route in the drier months. The upper followed the chalk ridge and remained much drier in winter, although it was often on the hillsides, rather than on the hill tops as these had dense vegetation. Medieval travellers on this route would have had to contend with thieves and highwaymen, for which the Chiltern area was noted. The Icknield Way claims to be the oldest road in Britain, though it is not a true road, but more a mass of tracks and lanes, following the trend of the geological structure of the land. It was often a very wide track, more than a mile, and was used as a drove track, but became narrower as local farming improved and more land was needed. The lower Icknield Way has stretches of road on it today, but the upper Icknield Way is only followed by paths or bridleways. The modern Icknield Way footpath follows the original route as closely as possible. It has a Neolithic axe as its symbol and uses red arrows to denote byways, yellow arrows for footpaths and white arrows for permissive paths. It extends for 120 miles from the northern end of the Ridgeway at Ivinghoe Beacon, to

the southern end of the Peddars Way, passing through the Sundon Hills Country Park and Sharpenhoe Clappers on the way.

(2) A hanger is a steep slope with trees clinging to it to create a dense area of woodland. Hangers are often located on scarp slopes in chalklands as in the Chilterns, North or South Downs, and perhaps most famously of all at Selborne in Hampshire, the home of Gilbert White the great eighteenth-century naturalist. The trees appear to hang on the slopes, often in a steep semi-circular hollow. This curved shape of the steep slope is because hangers are usually within coombes, those steep hollows shaped like giant armchairs on the steep slopes of scarps. These have been formed by erosion over thousands of years, but are mainly the result of frost action, and the freezing and thawing of tiny drops of water. This action, repeated millions of times, has broken up the rocks and then lubricated the surface to enable the eroded rock to slide down the slope and be removed from the hillside.

(3) The Icknield Way and Bunyan Trail lead into the Sundon Hills Country Park where there are several delightful walks as well as a picnic area near the car park at grid ref 047287. Sundon Country Park covers an area of 38 hectares (93 acres) of woodland, chalk scarp and grassland. The Bunyan Trail begins at Sundon Hills Country Park (grid ref 048287) and follows a circular route past Ampthill and Elstow, and south again. John Bunyan was born in Elstow, south of Bedford, in 1628 and became a poor tinker who travelled around his local area. By 1656 he was beginning to preach, and although this became a crime against the established church, he would not or could not stop it. He was imprisoned for a time for his non-conformist views and illegal preaching, and spent eleven years in Bedford Jail, and later a second spell from 1676–7. He wrote much of *Pilgrim's Progress* whilst in prison, and it was published in 1678, the second part following in 1684. He died in 1688.

(4) Norman Cairns Robertson was a Captain in the 2nd Battalion Hampshire Regiment who died on 20th June 1917 at Hanover in Germany, and Lawrance Grant Robertson was a 2nd Lieut. in the 2nd Battalion King's Own Scottish Borderers who was killed in or near Delville Wood in the Battle of the Somme on 30th July 1916.

(5) The village is situated at the foot of the Barton Hills which are possibly the basis for the Delectable Mountain seen by Christian in *The Pilgrim's Progress*. The Manor House was the home of Thomas Norton (died 1584) one of England's earliest playwrights, and the co-author of the tragedy *Gorboduc*. He has sometimes been described as the founder of English drama, and is buried in the nearby village of Streatley. Another resident in the manor for a time was Edmund Wingate who was an expert arithmetician in the time of Shakespeare. He wrote the famous mathematical book, *The Rule of Three*.

(6) The information board mentions that this land was given to the National Trust in 1939 by the W. A. Robertson Memorial Fund. The Clappers is a spur of chalk, crowned by beech trees planted in the mid-nineteenth century. Sycamore are now invading the beech trees, and hawthorn and elder scrub grow on the slopes. The downland area of the south-eastern sides has a wealth of flowers, such as yellow wort, fragrant orchid, violets, rock roses, horseshoe vetch and dwarf thistle. Much of the area is an SSSI and is very rich in wild life. Butterflies include the chalk hill blue, marbled white and orange tip. Birds include greater spotted woodpecker, which may be heard drumming in the spring. Numerous woodpecker holes can be seen in the dead trees.

Sheep occasionally graze the grassland areas as part of the management planning. Part of the western steep slope of Sharpenhoe has been grazed by Hebridean sheep. They are a primitive breed used to control scrub on steep slopes, as they are specialists at eating rough scrub and brambles. Therefore they are excellent for conservation of the site.

The hill with its beech capping is a scheduled Ancient Monument and is managed in consultation with English Heritage. The trees were planted between 1840–50 on what is thought to have been an Iron Age fort. There is just one large rampart which crosses the ridge at the southern end, and a wide but shallow ditch. A wooden structure was probably used to cut off the northern part of the spur from the main mass of the hill during the Iron Age. The western slopes of the hill seem to have had earth piled up on them, possibly to help create the rabbit warren which definitely existed in medieval times. The name clapper is thought to have been derived from the French word *clapier*, meaning a rabbit hole.

Walk 2 – Dunstable Downs and Whipsnade

Located on OS Landranger 1:50 000 sheet 166 and OS
Pathfinder 1:25 000 sheet 1095.

Length of walk is 9 miles, plus 4 miles (2 miles each
way) if you walk from the centre of Dunstable.

Time required is 4–5 hours.

Terrain – gently undulating with no steep hills, but the
possibility of muddy patches in wet weather. Walking
from Dunstable will also add a steady climb up from the
town.

Start at the Countryside Centre on Dunstable Downs
(grid ref 007197), situated 2 miles out of Dunstable along
the B4541 Whipsnade road, a turning off the B489
Dunstable to Tring road. It is accessible by bus and there
is ample car parking.

We begin this walk on chalk downlands, pass through woods
and farmland, look into a wild life park, and visit two small
villages one of which has a tree cathedral. There are magnificent views, especially near the beginning and the end of the
walk, looking out across the lowlands towards Leighton Buzzard and Aylesbury, with excellent views along the line of the
Chiltern scarp towards Beacon Hill at Ivinghoe.

The grassy slopes of Dunstable Downs are often windy,
popular for kite-flying, and at the foot of the scarp slope is the
London Gliding Club. The sight of gliders floating overhead
will be a regular feature of this walk, and near to our starting
point gliders will be landing and taking off. Some are launched
by winch and strong elastic, and others are towed up by a
small power-driven aeroplane. The Gliding Club offers flights
for beginners, up to 305 or 610 m (1000 or 2000 ft), as well as

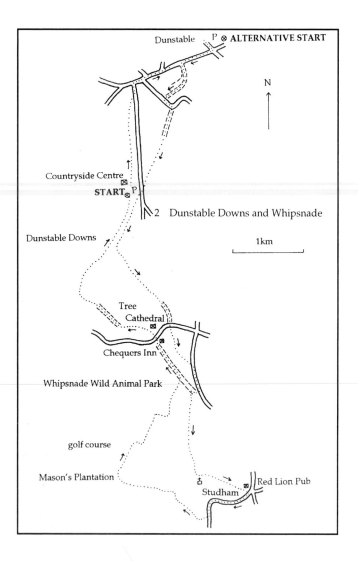

Dunstable P ⊗ **ALTERNATIVE START**

N

Countryside Centre

START ⊗ P

2 Dunstable Downs and Whipsnade

Dunstable Downs

1km

Tree
Cathedral

Chequers Inn

Whipsnade Wild Animal Park

golf course

Mason's Plantation

Studham

Red Lion Pub

courses of instruction and gliding holidays with full board. Club membership enables members to fly whenever they wish, on 364 days a year.

The Dunstable Downs are also the site of the custom of rolling oranges on Easter Monday. As the oranges were rolled down the steep scarp slope, the children would scramble to catch them. It was a traditional fun activity, but has not taken place for a few years.

Straw-plaiting was well established in Dunstable before the end of the seventeenth century when competition from woollen hats produced an outcry from the workforce. A century later the French wars (1793–1815) reduced foreign competition and boosted the industry, but a major period of decline came after 1870 because of cheaper foreign goods, notably from China. This problem of foreign competition is not new!

If starting from the centre of Dunstable, in order to reach the Countryside Centre on the Downs, walk west along the B489 towards Ivinghoe, and after about 400 m turn left along Kirby Road, signposted to the Christadelphian church. At the end of this road, when the Recreation Ground is opposite, turn right on the stony cindery track between gardens and houses. Pass allotments on the right and then the cemetery, and at the road turn left, following an Icknield Way arrow. At the T-junction turn right along Canesworde Road, and after 30 m, as the road bends left, go straight on along a surfaced track, and begin to climb. When the track bends left, our path goes straight ahead.

The narrow path between bushes and trees climbs steadily and soon the Dunstable Downs Golf Course is seen through the hedge to the left. The path emerges on to the course by a 'Danger beware of golf balls' notice and leads straight ahead to pass just to the left of the club house. Go between two marker posts in front of the club house, and on through the car park. Beyond the car park a broad green path leads between small trees, and then through a small clump of hawthorn and out to the road. Across the road is the car park and the Countryside

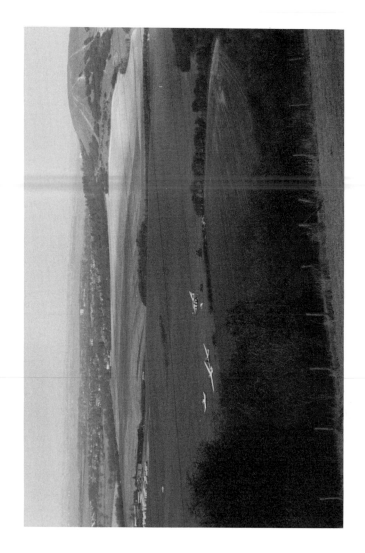

Centre. Just a few metres up to the left is Robertson Corner, with a memorial to the two brothers of W. A. Robertson (see Walk 1). Further along the road is the triangulation point of 243 m (797 ft) on Kensworth Hill, the highest point in Bedfordshire.

At the end of the walk, for the return into Dunstable, once past the Countryside Centre, take the broad clear path running parallel to the road which is just to the right. Join a path slightly to the left, and walk alongside the wire fence at the top of the very steep slope. All the way along this route there are magnificent views out across the plain, over the gliding club field. This is the Icknield Way (see Walk 1), and passes along the top of the very deep coombe (see Walk 6) dropping down to the left. In the coombe, as well as on the level top, there are numerous worn patches, a sign of the popularity of this area as a playground for visitors. To the right of the path is a hummocky area with mounds and hollows and a National Trust notice tells that this is Five Knolls, a group of round barrows (5). Once past the mounds the path begins to descend quite steeply into the trees and then out on to the road. Go down to the island and the main road, turn right and walk back in to the centre of Dunstable.

MAIN WALK

Start from the car park by the Countryside Centre on Dunstable Downs, a large grassy area, useful as an open space and an excellent chalk habitat. As on the other chalk grasslands in the Chilterns a wide range of plants can be found, often as many as forty species in a square metre. The plants encourage a variety of butterflies too.

View down on to glider field, Dunstable Downs

Follow a horizontal route southwards, passing the emergency landing place for gliders and heading towards the wood visible straight ahead. Take the path through a small shrubby area, and then at the end of the small wood, pass through a gate and on to an open grassy field, with the scarp sloping down to the right, and a cultivated field on the left.

Walk straight ahead to the wood, and turn left through the small gate to walk along the edge of this wood. Cross straight over a concrete driveway, and when the path splits by a pylon, take the left fork following the edge of the wood, with an open field on the left. Now heading towards another patch of woodland, follow the well-worn path straight on through the small wood, then along a field margin and on to a track with some chalet houses behind the hedge to the right. These are the Whipsnade Park Residential Homes. The track becomes sunken for a short distance, before emerging to the open grassy common in Whipsnade village.

Turn right, and cross the road and the common to Whipsnade church of St Mary Magdalene. (1) Walk on from the far side of the churchyard, over a stile and along the left margin of the field. At the end of the field go over another stile, and straight on with a hedge to the right now, to another stile and out on to the road. Turn right and follow this for about 400 m, passing the 40 mph sign and using the pavement on the left side. Turn right at the first turning, a narrow road with a No through road sign, and after about 40 m turn left through a small asymmetric gateway and follow the left margin of the field. The footpath has a slight left turn where the hedge turns left for 20 m, and the path turns right to keep straight ahead across the middle of a field, through a gap in the hedge and along the next two fields to the church in a clump of trees straight ahead.

Our route ahead involves turning left just before the church, but make a little detour to visit the remarkable church of Studham. (2) Walk on beyond the church, passing the large

Manor Farm on the right and continue along two field margins to emerge via a small stile out on to the road adjacent to the village green, with a Methodist church, the village hall, a shop, the Red Lion and a First World War memorial, with a clock.

Studham is the most southerly parish in Bedfordshire and is also the highest village in the county. It can be reached by bus, even on Sundays.

Walk away from the memorial, with the green on the left and Red Lion on the right, and follow the road through the village, passing the school on the left, where the road bends right. Pass the road which leads right to the church and, shortly after leaving the village, and passing the speed derestriction sign, turn right at the bottom of the hollow. There are two footpaths here, but take the right fork and follow the field margin. Go over a stile and continue straight ahead along the field margin, with the magnificent building of Studhamhall Farm away to the left. After another field and stile, the path moves slightly right and into the edge of the wood. This is Mason's Plantation and a notice tells that this a wild life area. At the junction of paths turn right, and walk on to a corrugated iron hut. Turn left here and then straight ahead on a broad path, to emerge from the wood with an open field to the right. Follow this field margin with the wood on the left for about 100 m. At the end of this field go diagonally right across the next field to a line of small trees and bushes which mark the edge of the golf course.

On the golf course go straight ahead and along the fairway for 150 m to a marker post with a choice of routes, straight ahead or turn right. Turn right here following the pale blue Icknield Way arrow, as well as darker blue arrows, to cross fairways to the edge of the golf course and the boundary fence of Whipsnade Wild Animal Park. Follow the path alongside the boundary fence, with a left turn, and then a right turn. Where the fence next turns left, we go straight ahead through a small wood, but then turn left along a flinty path to rejoin the fence. There are likely to be many varieties of deer visible in the Park and perhaps camels, wallabies and other animals. Notice the boundary fence has its overhang on the outside, to prevent predatory animals getting in rather than to stop anything from escaping. (3)

The path reaches a surfaced track, Studham Lane, and here we turn left and follow this, still parallel to the boundary fence. When the track splits, take the right fork to emerge on the green adjacent to the Chequers Inn. Cross the green by going up to the far right corner and sign to the Tree Cathedral, where a little detour is worth while. (4)

We proceed by following the Icknield Way, now with a yellow arrow, along the left side of the cathedral. Once past the cathedral go over a stile, and along the left margin of the field to another stile, and a few yards beyond this turn right just before the wooden fence. The Icknield Way sign is blue again here, and we walk along a track which widens out and becomes sunken between large hedges. This is a very good location for wild flowers, but can be quite muddy.

Emerge into an opening just above a car park (the National Trust car park alongside the B4540 quite close to the main entrance to Whipsnade Park), and enjoy the wonderful views out across the plain, with Beacon Hill at Ivinghoe slightly to the left. There are likely to be gliders in sight now, for the remainder of this walk.

Turn left to follow the pale blue Icknield Way arrow, and the car park is now to the left. At a junction of several paths, turn right and still follow the pale blue arrow to emerge out from an area of shrubs and small trees, on to the grassy downland. Follow a fairly horizontal path along the grassy area, with trees up to the right and the scarp slope going down to the right. We are now back on Dunstable Downs.

At the end of the grassy area head for the small gate in the middle of the wood ahead, and up to the right you will see the line of the path used at the beginning of this walk. Pass through the gate with a pale blue arrow and go straight ahead through another area of scrub and then out on to more grass and continue to the car park and the Countryside Centre, with a small refreshment kiosk and Information Centre.

(1) This brick-built church with a sixteenth-century tower and eighteenth-century nave has an interesting set of bells. A peal of 5040 changes was rung with new bells here on Saturday 23rd May 1981 in 2 hours 27 minutes, both to celebrate the new bells and also for the 50th anniversary of the opening of Whipsnade Wild Animal Park on 23rd May 1931. The church has an unprepossessing exterior but the interior is cared for and has a lovely set of kneelers, as well as interesting old tiles on the floor.

(2) The dull exterior of Studham church is covered by a layer of rough cast, necessary because the original church walls of Totternhoe stone, flint and clunch are quite soft and would crumble. The church dates from the thirteenth century, or possibly late in the twelfth, and the interior reveals some of the ancient walls behind the font. It originally had altars in the aisles and was known as a five-altar church. The columns date from the thirteenth century and have hand-carved foliate capitals which is why they are all slightly different. There are four bells dating from 1599. The church kneelers were made by village craft workers, and in the past Studham was noted for another craft, that of straw-plaiting. The tradition for making straw plaits for hats dates back to at least 1684, when the villagers signed a petition sent to the government, protesting against the encouragement given to woollen hat-makers.

(3) Whipsnade is the country location of the Zoological Society of London, and the Wild Animal Park was opened in 1931 by Sir Peter Chalmers Mitchel who was the Secretary of the Zoological Society in London. Animals came out from London Zoo to enjoy the freedom to roam around. The Zoological Society of London is a registered charity, and research and

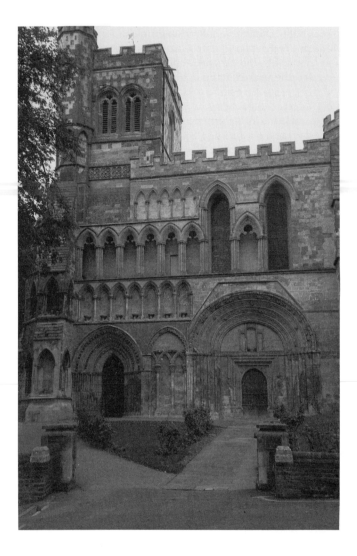

breeding are part of the Whipsnade plan. Amongst the 1996 births here were pigmy hippo, giraffe, camel, chimpanzee and dwarf crocodile. Whipsnade is open daily, except for Christmas Day, and the park contains a small railway, a children's farm and playground as well as a large range of animals. There are more than 2,500 animals in the Park's 240 hectares (600 acres). It is possible to drive around on the two miles of perimeter roads, or travel on the open-top Safari tour bus, or merely walk around. The Whipsnade Wild Animal Park attracts about 900,000 visitors per annum, comparable in popularity with our National Parks.

(4) The Tree Cathedral was created by Edmund Kell Blyth, a local landowner, who was inspired with the idea of creating a cathedral after a visit to the new Anglican Cathedral in Liverpool in 1930. Planting the trees in the shape of a cathedral took place between 1930–9. There are twenty-five species of trees. The chancel contains silver birch, and the transepts have twin avenues of chestnut. There is a Christmas chapel of Norway spruce and the summer chapel has whitebeam. The centre of the cloisters has a selection of flowering shrubs, with a dew pond (generally dry) in the middle. Yew, rowan, beech, cherry, oak and cedar are amongst other varieties of tree. Although the cathedral has never been consecrated, several services are held here each year. Some changes in trees planted have been made, to replace unhealthy or dead trees, with limes replacing poplars in the nave, and whitebeam replacing elm in the summer chapel. The avenue of hornbeam leading from the car park was planted as a memorial to Tom Blyth (1937–78) who cared for the cathedral after his father died in 1969. The cathedral is now managed by the National Trust.

(5) Five Knolls is a group of round barrows used for burial of the dead 4000 years ago, in the Late Neolithic or Early Bronze

The front of Dunstable church

Age. A second identical notice is located at the far end of these mounds. One of the mounds was excavated in 1929, and in the 1960s there were further excavations by Sir Mortimer Wheeler and Gerald Dunning which revealed forty bodies with their hands tied behind their backs. They are presumed to have been executed in the sixteenth or seventeenth century, possibly in connection with witchcraft. It is likely that during medieval times, a gallows was located in this area.

Hertfordshire and Buckinghamshire – near Tring

Walks 3, 4 and 5 are all situated near Tring, which is accessible by bus and train.

Meltwater during the Ice Age contributed to the creation of the gap in which Tring is situated, and this gap has always been an important routeway to and from London. The prehistoric Icknield Way crosses the Roman road called Akeman Street (followed by the present day High Street in Tring) here. The name of Tring is derived from a word meaning hanging trees on a slope. There were two windmills in the town, which were used for gristing, and Tring has long been a well-established market town. The Rothschild zoological collection is housed in the museum here. Tring Park was bought by the Rothschild family in 1872 and they lived there until the 1940s, in the house designed by Sir Christopher Wren. The Park was bought by Hertfordshire County Council in 1938 for use by the general public. The Rothschilds used to have kangaroos, emus and rheas running wild in the park, and the 2nd Lord Rothschild had a cart which was pulled by a pair of zebras.

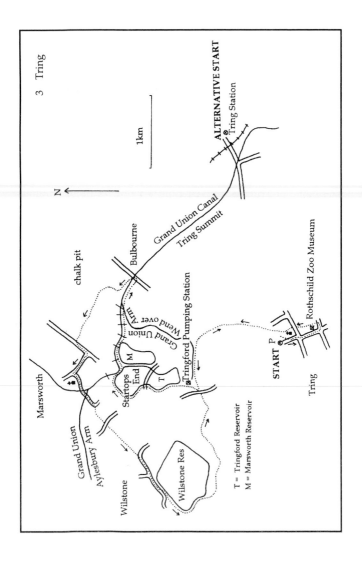

3 Tring

1km

ALTERNATIVE START
⊗ Tring Station

N ←

Grand Union Canal
Tring Summit

Bulbourne

chalk pit

Grand Union
Wendover Arm

Tringford Pumping Station

Marsworth

M

Startops End

T

Tringford Pumping Station

Rothschild Zoo Museum

START P

Grand Union
Aylesbury Arm

Wilstone

Wilstone Res

Tring

T = Tringford Reservoir
M = Marsworth Reservoir

Walk 3 – Tring Reservoirs

Located on OS Landranger 1:50 000 sheet 165 (grid ref 925116)
Length of walk is 10 miles.
Time required is about 4 hours of steady walking, but many more hours with frequent stops if looking at the birds.
Terrain – flat but with several muddy patches in winter.
Starting point in Tring town centre car park, which is reached by leaving the A41 between Aylesbury and Berkhamsted and following Tring town centre signs.
An alternative starting point can be from Tring station (see p 69), grid reference 951123.

This is a generally flat and gentle walk round the Tring reservoirs and along the Grand Union Canal. The canal's route is from London to Hemel Hempstead when it turns west to cut through the Chilterns via Berkhamsted to Tring and thence to Leighton Buzzard. The interesting bird life on the reservoirs could make this a very slow walk. Be sure to take your binoculars. The route also passes through the village of Marsworth, and there are good views of the Chiltern scarp from many points on the walk.

Tring Reservoirs became a National Nature Reserve in 1955, and a Site of Special Scientific Interest in 1987. They are particularly famous for their birds, for instance the first record of British nesting black-necked grebes in 1918, and the first British nesting little ringed plover in 1938. It was on the Tring Reservoirs in the 1930s that Sir Julian Huxley made his famous studies of the courtship display of the great crested grebe, which can be seen between December and May. The reservoirs are also good for fishing, being well stocked with tench, bream, roach and perch, as well as carp and pike. The reservoirs were created between 1802–17 in a formerly marshy area, fed by natural springs. The lakes are lined with marl and puddled clay, similar to the lining used in canals. The water is used to replenish the Grand Union Canal, especially where there is the great water loss from the locks which enable the canal to cross the Chilterns.

Leave the car park by walking back on to Frogmore Street and turn left. Just before reaching the cross roads in the town centre, look to the right at Tringfellows and Parsonage Place, and up this narrow road can be seen the sixteenth-century tithe barn. Keep straight ahead at the cross roads and on the right is the impressive old Market House, built to commemorate Queen Victoria's Diamond Jubilee. It was formerly used for trading in straw plait. On the left is Victoria Hall, once a theatre, then a pickle factory, and presented to the town by the 3rd Baron Rothschild. On the right is the Baptist chapel, erected in 1808 and rebuilt in 1832, then on the left is Rodwells, makers of soft drinks, and at the end on the left is the Walter Rothschild Zoological Museum. (1)

After visiting the museum, turn left from the entrance and there is Park Street, running alongside the museum. Before turning left along Park Street, look to the right, to see the Louisa Cottages, built in 1893 and 1901, as almshouses for pensioners who had worked on the Rothschild estate. About 100 m along Park Street, which used to be the main road through the park, note a footpath going right to Tring Park and Wigginton, and alongside it is the interesting Lodge House. Our route is back into the town, so we turn left on the footpath to the town centre. This reaches High Street between two banks, the National Westminster and the Midland, the latter having been based on a design by Sir Edward Lutyens. Turn right here and walk as far as the Rose and Crown inn, built in 1905 to accommodate visitors to the Mansion in the park. As with the Market House, the Lodge House and many other buildings, it was built by the local architect William Huckvale for Lord Rothschild. Just beyond the Rose and Crown is the Mansion Way which leads up to the Mansion which was designed by Sir Christopher Wren, though altered considerably in the 1870s. However we cross the road here to go to the church. (2)

Our onward route is past the right side of the church, and at the archway leading into Sutton Court, formerly the Vicarage, turn right for a few yards, and then left following the signpost to the Hall. This path leads on to an open grassy area with a small children's playground. To the left is the car park, but bend right along the level path, not going uphill towards the Hall. The surfaced path leads alongside a flint stone wall to the right, and at the end of the grassy area there are houses on the left. Beyond the wall, a small stream and a road are to the right, and where the path splits, fork right to go down to the road. Cross straight over and along the path on the other side, with houses to the left, and some undergrowth and a few trees to the right, with houses just beyond. The path emerges out on to a small cross roads, but go across the end of Morefields, and straight ahead, passing the New Mill Baptist church (1689, rebuilt 1818) on the left, and follow New Road until it reaches a T-junction with a major road (B488).

Turn right for 30 m, and then left following the public footpath sign, to walk along the right margin of the field, with houses just to the right. This leads through to a canal, the Wendover arm of the Grand Union Canal. Proceed alongside this canal and notice that when the canal bends left, a pumping station can be seen on the other bank. This is the Tringford Pumping Station. (3)

Climb up a few steps on to a narrow road, and turn right. Just beyond the houses of the small hamlet of Little Tring, turn right along the drive to Tringford Pumping Station and pass the Manor House to the right. Where the track bends right to the pumping station, go straight ahead over the stile. The path soon splits, but take the left fork to walk along the left side of Tringford Reservoir. (4)

The path leads on through the trees, with open fields just to the left, and when the path splits, take the right fork to stay close to the lake. Cross an overflow channel and walk along the embankment, with the lake to the right. Birds, as well as fishermen, may be seen on the water. Near the end of the reservoir is a wooden seat, and then we reach the road.

Cross straight over and turn left to walk alongside the next reservoir, Startop's End (pronounced Starrups End). This is more open than Tringford and the straight path goes along the top of the embankment. The impressive church tower in Marsworth can be seen over to the right, and also, the less impressive chimneys of Pitstone cement works, which has been here since the 1940s, but is now closed; its future use is as yet uncertain. A planning decision in February 1997 rejected the request to use it as a dump. There is a heronry alongside this lake. At the corner turn right and continue along the embankment, to the end of the reservoir. Turn right again here, to follow the margin of the reservoir and to the left will be seen a car parking area which could be used as an alternative starting point. A notice board gives information about fishing permits, but adds that no swimming, no boats, no camping and no fires are allowed. The path alongside the reservoir joins the tow path of the Grand Union Canal which is just to the left here. (5)

Follow this path, with Startop's End Reservoir to the right at first, and then after passing an embankment we see the Marsworth Reservoir on the right. Great crested grebes are particularly numerous here, and the extensive reed beds are used by many sedge and reed warblers in summer. Large numbers of ducks will be here during the winter months.

Yellow, green and red coloured arrows will be seen in many places. They indicate the routes of the waymarked walks around the reservoirs. The red route is 2½ miles, around

Startop's End and Tringford Reservoirs; the green is 3 miles around Tringford and Marsworth; and the yellow is 5¾ around Marsworth, Tringford and Wilstone.

On our left is the main channel of the Grand Union, and this is likely to be busy with boats. These locks we pass raise the canal by nearly 13 m (42 ft), and on the right of the path are the regulatory side ponds for the locks. Marsworth Reservoir is still to the right, fringed with large reed beds, and we continue the gentle ascent, to reach a house on the right and a sign saying Lock 42.

Notice a house on the left, dated 1809, at the fifth lock, and the next lock after that is Marsworth Top Lock. On the right is a house called Toll House, and the signpost says that it is 55 miles to Braunston, 38½ to Brentford, with Wendover 6¾ to the right. Then we have to climb over a bridge to cross the Wendover arm (6), and continue the walk straight ahead.

Pass the houses on the right and then a picnic and barbecue area. The Bumble or Chiltern Chugger may be moored near here, a small self-drive hire boat for half-day or full day trips along the canal. A little further along the canal we reach Bulbourne with its magnificent Victorian workshops in which a small team of craftsmen still make lock gates for use all over England.

ALTERNATIVE STARTING POINT The bridge at Bulbourne is the point where the walk can be joined from Tring station. Motorists may wish to start from here, too, as there is a large car park, which is free after 10 a.m. It is about 1½ miles each way, to and from the station, but it is very flat and gentle as the canal crosses the Tring Summit. (7)

If starting from the station, walk up to the road at the Royal Hotel, cross over and turn left. After nearly 300 m, go down the steps on to the canal tow path and turn right to walk west and then north-west. After about a kilometre the path goes up on to a bridge on Marshcroft Lane, a narrow road leading to a

farm, and crosses to the other side of the canal to pass a milestone saying Braunston 56 miles and continues towards Bulbourne and the pub. The canal is bordered by trees as well as wild flowers and blackberries in season, and there may be birds, butterflies and damsel flies to be seen on this stretch of the walk. As with most stretches of canal, there is a wealth of wild life. Canals are all like nature trails.

At the Grand Junction Arms go onto the road and turn right, pass the workshops and you have now joined the main route.

For the return to TRING STATION just retrace your steps along the canal bank from Bulbourne when we reach this point on the walk alongside the canal from Startop's End.

MAIN WALK

The bridge is the point where anyone starting from the station at Tring will join the route, and also where the return walk back to Tring station will leave the main route.

The Grand Junction Arms is on the right, and we go up on to the road here, turn left over the bridge and about 30 m beyond the entrance into the workshop area, turn left along the public footpath and bridleway.

Before turning along this bridleway, you may be interested to visit the College Lake Wild Life Centre which is nearly 400 m along this road. (8) There is no footpath, so hug the narrow verge, as this road is quite busy.

The path from the road can become muddy and chewed up in wet weather. The canal is to the left, and a large chalk quarry is to the right. After about 300 m the path turns right, away from the canal, and soon has another right-angled bend this time to the left. The chalk quarry is to the right all the time, with a lake in the large hollow, and chimneys and a factory beyond. Open fields are to the left of the track, and a fairly

Long boats on the canal near Tring

straight half mile (800 m) along here, leads through to the road and to Marsworth (always known as Maffers to the old canal boatmen).

Turn left at the road, and take the second turn right by the post box and village hall to walk along Vicarage Road to the church. Turn left along Church Lane and pause to visit All Saints church (9).

Walk on down Church Lane, passing Horseshoe Cottage and Manor House with its huge seventeenth-century barn, and over the main branch of the canal, with the works of Fencrete Products next to the British Waterways Office. Fencrete makes paving stones, block paving, concrete posts etc. and some of its products were used as piles for the canal bank towards Aylesbury. Pass the works yard to the left and a house and garden to the right, and continue along the narrow Watery Lane to another canal bridge, this passing over the Aylesbury arm. (10) To the left of the bridge is a staircase lock, where the top gate for one lock is the bottom gate for the next lock.

Pass a playing field on the left, and when the road bends left, go straight ahead through an old iron gate, between hedges and over a footbridge and a stile, into a field. Head diagonally to the far right corner, to a stile and then straight ahead along the right margin of the next field. Skylarks and yellow hammers may be heard singing here. At the end of this field, walk out on to the road and turn right. After 30 m turn left at the public footpath sign, and follow the right margin of this large field, admiring the good view of the Chiltern scarp ahead. At the end of this field pass through a gate and continue along the right margin of the next field. Go over a stile at the end of this field and out on to the road. Turn right and use the verge on the left side of the road, walk past the farm shop and keep going along this road, ignoring the right turn to Wilstone.

When we reach the small car parking area, climb up the steps on to the embankment and turn right to walk along the edge of the Wilstone reservoir. (11)

At the end of the embankment, pass a seat and then turn left, following the path along the side of the reservoir, but now in trees, with open fields to the right. These woods are noisy with small birds in the summer, not only the resident tits and finches, but also large numbers of warblers. Soon reach an information board and from here is a narrow path going left to a hide which provides wonderful views of some of the rich bird life to be seen on this reservoir. Be sure to allow time for a visit to the hide, you never know what you may see. I saw the flashing blue of a kingfisher in the reeds on my last visit. The path to the hide passes through a wetland environment with reeds and yellow flag irises. (12)

After visiting the hide, return to the main path and the notice board, and turn left for 20 m to reach a stile leading straight ahead. Once over this, the path splits and either route will lead to the same place. The clearer path is the right fork and this takes us alongside a hedge to the left of the path. After being joined by the path which stays near the lake margin to the left of this hedge, go on over a stile, cross a footbridge and up a few steps and follow the field margin. The hedge and a small stream are to the left and an open field to the right, with farm buildings just visible across this field. At the end of this field, climb a small stile, and follow the left margin of the field, passing a telegraph pole, one of a line which can be seen going straight away to the right and over the top of the small hill. We follow the field margin as it bends sharp right, and at the end of the hedge, turn left, to follow another hedge. At the end of this field, turn right to walk slightly uphill, passing left of an isolated tree to the right of the path, and arrive at a stile with a doggy flap.

Once over the stile, go up a few steps and turn left along the broad path which was the towpath of the Wendover Arm of the canal. Across to the right of the path is the old canal trench, now full of dense vegetation and very good for rabbits and small birds such as warblers, finches and tits. An open field is to the left of this path and the Wilstone reservoir is visible 300 m away.

At a cross paths, reach a gate, and go over the stile to the left of the gate, and keep straight ahead, to another gate and straight on to the road. Turn right and soon pass the entrance to Tringford Pumping Station, seen earlier, and anyone who is walking from Tring station and does not wish to go into the town, should turn left here and follow the directions of the walk 3 lines from the bottom of page 67.

For the return into Tring town, climb a slight hill, a rarity on this walk. Turn left following the sign to New Mill (¾ mile–1 km) and retrace your steps alongside the canal. Cross the road and walk along New Street and back into Tring.

(1) Opening hours at the Zoological Museum are 10.00–17.00 on Mondays to Saturdays, and 14.00–17.00 on Sundays. It was opened in 1892, and contains one of the finest collections of mammals, birds, reptiles and insects in Britain. The museum originated as the private collection of the 2nd Baron Rothschild, and was given to the British Museum on condition that it became an annexe of the Natural History Museum, and continued to be a centre for research. It has become especially important for birds, with the national bird collections having been transferred here from London in 1971.

(2) On the pavement in front of the church is a Victorian-style pillar box, and adjacent to this is a pavement maze, with the shape of a zebra's head, created as a memorial to Walter Rothschild. The church of St Peter and St Paul dates from the thirteenth century but was restored in the eighteenth century. It is built of the local Totternhoe stone and flint and contains many interesting features. There is a family tree for George Washington whose ancestors lived in a house on Frogmore Street. The great grandparents of George Washington migrated to Virginia in 1657. The font of Streetly stone has some unusual decoration of coloured marble inlay. The slender stone pillars in the nave

have surprising and rather ugly carved figures at the top, and higher up near the roof are wooden carvings of the Apostles. There are two church wardens' pews at the rear of the nave, and in the north aisle is the memorial to the Gore family. This memorial dates from 1707 and has been attributed to Grinling Gibbons, but is probably the work of one of his pupils.

(3) Tringford Pumping Station is vital to the Grand Union Canal as it feeds water from the reservoirs via underground channels into the main Grand Union along this Wendover arm, and thence up to summit level. The old beam engines in this pumping station have been replaced by modern diesels, which lift 4 million gallons of water per day. The canal ends just round this bend, and our path is joined by the path coming along the other bank.

(4) A hide alongside the path will provide a good opportunity to see what birds are on the lake. Regulars include swans, ducks and coots, but other birds are present here for part of the year. The autumn migration brings sandpipers, redshank and many other waders. There are woods alongside this margin of the lake, containing many small birds, notably warblers in the summer months.

(5) The Grand Union Canal was originally the Grand Junction Canal linking Oxford with London, and it rises almost 122 m (400 ft) from the Thames to its highest point in the Chilterns through 57 locks. Three miles of the canal cut through the Chilterns. The canal was opened in sections from 1793–1805, and the higher parts are fed with water from the reservoirs. Tring Summit is situated east of Bulbourne, near Tring station, and every time boats pass through the locks at either end of the summit, approximately 56,000 gallons are required. From the high point east of Bulbourne, the 9 Marsworth and 3 Seabrook locks take the canal down to the plain. There will be highly decorated long boats passing through these locks, but the traffic is for pleasure now, and not commercial.

(6) At the canal junction on the side of the bridge is a map of

the Wendover arm, and an information board. The Wendover arm is navigable for 1½ miles of its former length of 6¾. It was opened in 1797 as a navigable feeder supplying the summit level of the Grand Junction Canal with water from the Chiltern Hills. The supply was augmented by water from the Tringford, Marsworth, Startop's End and Wilstone Reservoirs. Problems with leakage necessitated the building of a stop lock at Tringford. The Wendover arm was situated at about the 119 m (390 ft) contour, and partially on chalk, and was using up water from the Grand Union Canal, which it was supposed to be supplying.

(7) Tring station is modern but the Royal Hotel dates from the opening of the railway. It was a posting house with courtyard and stables. The railway goes through a cutting dug in 1838 to cross the Chiltern Ridge, which is 2½ miles in length. The canal cutting was completed in 1797 and is 1½ miles long.

(8) The College Lake Wild Life Centre is a lake and wetland reserve, managed by the BBONT, and is noted for its bird life, including great crested grebe, herons, little ringed plover, redshank, snipe, ducks and terns. There is also a wealth of flowers, and numerous butterflies in summer.

(9) All Saints church is another flint-faced church, and the lych gate also contains flint, as well as a plaque to record that this was mentioned in the Domesday Book of 1086. There is a small group of Polish graves in the churchyard, burial place of men who worked on the nearby American airforce base in World War II. The church was renovated in 1880 by the vicar, Rev. F. W. Ragg, who did much of the work himself, with some workers he trained. The east window is dedicated to his memory. There was a twelfth-century church on this site, though nothing remains from that time. The chancel, nave and south chapel of the present church date from the fourteenth century, and the tower is fifteenth century. There are several memorials to the West family, including a table tomb and brasses on the floor of the south chapel.

(10) The Aylesbury arm is a 6¼ mile long canal, which was opened in 1815. Sixteen locks, which are narrow in order to save water, take the change of level down by nearly 29 m (94 ft) between Marsworth and Aylesbury. Because it created a need for extra water, the Tringford and Startops End Reservoirs were built.

(11) Wilstone Reservoir was built in 1802 on the clay soils of the plain to supply the Wendover arm with water. It is now a paradise for birds, and amongst those to be seen are ducks, geese, coots, moorhens, great crested grebes, herons, swallows, martins, terns, gulls and cormorants. Hobbies, swallows and martins will be here in the summer, as well as dragon flies in profusion. Hobbies feed mainly on insects, but in late summer can be seen taking young swallows or house martins, a very impressive sight. Large numbers of wildfowl will be here in the winter.

(12) The reed beds on Wilstone Reservoir, as well as on Marsworth, provide good territory for reed and sedge warblers, and are the largest reed beds in Hertfordshire. Studies have shown that these tiny birds can fly to Africa for the winter and then return to the same reed bed again the following summer.

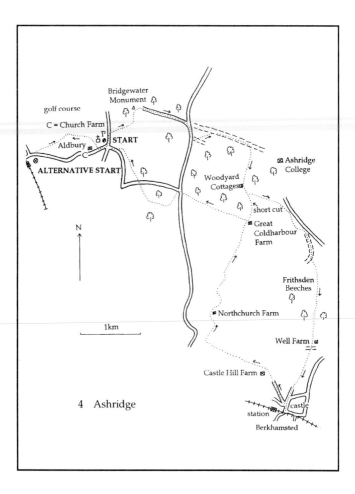

golf course

C = Church Farm

Bridgewater
Monument

Aldbury

START

ALTERNATIVE START

Ashridge
College

Woodyard
Cottages

short cut

Great
Coldharbour
Farm

N

Frithsden
Beeches

1km

Northchurch Farm

Well Farm

Castle Hill Farm

4   Ashridge

station

castle

Berkhamsted

Walk 4 – Ashridge

> Located on OS Landranger 1:50 000 sheet 165 and OS Explorer 1:25 000 map 2.
>
> Length of walk is 10 miles with a short cut possible to reduce the distance to 5 miles. If starting from Tring station, the total walk will be 12 miles.
>
> Time required is 5 hours comfortable walking.
>
> Terrain – mostly gentle, with one steep climb up the escarpment.
>
> Starting point in Aldbury (grid ref 965125) can be reached from the A41 near Tring. Park near the duck pond in the centre of Aldbury, outside the Greyhound Inn, or a few hundred metres along the Ivinghoe road.

The village of Aldbury is full of interesting buildings and, in the best tradition of villages, has the school next-door to the flint and chalk church of St John the Baptist. Parts of the church are from the thirteenth century and the tower dates from the fourteenth. Behind the magnificent stone screen is the Pendley Chapel, containing remains of several members of the Verney and Whittingham families who occupied Pendley Manor House for 200 years. An unusual brass memorial to Sir Ralph Verney with his wife and nine children is on the marble tomb in the north-east corner of the church. There is a priest's chamber over the porch.

The stocks, last used in 1835, are situated alongside the village duck pond and the green, and there is also a whipping post. At the side of the green is the old manor house, one of several half-timbered houses to be seen here. It dates from the seventeenth century and helps to complete the picture of the traditional English village. There are even a few old houses which have thatched roofs, not very numerous in western Hertfordshire.

Much of this walk is in woodland, part of the Ashridge Estate, but it also passes the tall Bridgewater Monument and reaches the old castle on the edge of Berkhamsted. It is mostly a gentle walk, though it does include one very steep climb up the escarpment from Aldbury. It can be muddy on woodland paths. The walk is situated in Hertfordshire, in the long finger of the county which extends into the heart of Buckinghamshire.

If starting from Tring station, walk out on to the road by the Royal Hotel and turn right. Pass the car park entrance and the left turn of Northfield Road signposted to Pitstone and Ivinghoe. Go straight on towards Aldbury and Ringshall, using the verge on the right of the road and after about 100 m take the footpath on the left side of the road. Walk along the concrete driveway, signposted the Ridgeway bridleway, and when the concrete bends left go straight ahead on the grassy path to the Ridgeway notice board. Go through an iron gate, cross a track, the Ridgeway bridleway, and on through an old wooden gate to a broad path between fences with open fields on both sides. The woods of the scarp and the top of the Bridgewater Monument can be seen ahead. Go through another gate and keep straight ahead, with the golf course to the left and views of Aldbury church tower coming into sight on the right. At the cross paths, turn right through a kissing gate to walk to Aldbury along a narrow path between open fields. Go over two stiles in quick succession, each with a movable top board, and the path leads to the left of a large barn in Church Farm, which has several magnificent and recently modernised buildings. The path goes on through a wooden kissing gate and along the right margin of a small field, then over a stile and across a small field to another stile and the road. Turn left here to walk into the village centre. For the return to Tring station at the end of the walk, just retrace steps along the same route.

THE MAIN WALK – START

Set off along the road towards Ivinghoe, passing the signpost to a track on the right (Northchurch 3), then a path to Tring station on the left. Across the road from the games field and some more parking space, is a footpath on the right of the road. Turn here, go over a high stile and follow the field margin uphill towards the scarp. At the top corner of the field is a fairly new stile, with a movable top rung, which makes it much easier for small people to get through. Go straight up through the woods, passing signs of badger digging, and with a wealth of wild flowers and birds. Nearly at the top a broad track is reached, turn left along here and where the path splits, fork right and climb slightly along the Ashridge Estate Boundary Trail, which leads to the top of Moneybury Hill and the Bridgewater Monument, with a large car park, and a National Trust Information Centre and shop. (1)

Walk along the long straight tree-lined avenue, towards Ashridge House 1½ miles away in the distance. Follow the surfaced driveway, with numerous picnic places alongside. At the road, turn right and just after passing the Ashridge Estate yard, turn left at the lodge house, built of flint and chalk, two popular local building materials. The drive is surfaced and is accessible for riding and cycling, but after 50 m fork left into the woods, along a footpath marked by a yellow arrow. This path leads through to the grassy ride seen earlier when looking towards Ashridge House. When I last walked along this path I disturbed a woodcock which flew away with characteristic swerving flight, and naturally with a name like mine I was delighted to see this wonderful bird. The woods are rich in bird life, with a variety of warblers in the summer and a few pairs of redstarts. All year there are nuthatches, woodpeckers, goldcrests and several types of tits. In the winter months, flocks of redwings and fieldfares appear. Deer may be seen throughout the year, generally the small muntjac or the larger fallow. Wild flowers are particularly

abundant in the spring, with bluebells, primroses and wood anemones.

At the grassy ride, turn right and walk towards Ashridge House, with trees on both sides, and just a few metres to the left is a golf course. Keep straight ahead along the grassy ride to a fence where the golf course extends across to the right. Turn right here and follow the path into the woods, cross over a bridleway, likely to be chewed up and muddy. Go on between the posts with a yellow arrow and a 'No Horses' sign, and keep going across a track, and straight on to a stile at the edge of a field. Cross this field and over another stile in the bottom corner to reach Woodyard Cottages. Ashridge House is to the left of this last section of the walk, and is occasionally open to visitors. (2)

From here continue on the broad drive bending round to the left by a wooden fence and a small paddock to the left of the path. Ignore the path going diagonally back to the right, but the drive continues straight ahead, and this is the route to follow if taking the short cut to Coldharbour Farm and back to Aldbury for the 5-mile walk. Just keep on this main track to a major cross tracks a few metres before reaching Coldharbour. Turn right here for the onward route.

For the full length walk, fork left off the main track, on the narrow path going slightly downhill, near to the post numbered 41. The path leads into the woods, and is well worn, though it can be muddy, but with a grassy border. Pass through stands of silver birch at first, but then other trees as well – hawthorn, oak, beech, holly. There is a valley down to the left. The path bends round to the right and passes to the left of an open patch, with few trees but tall bracken in summer. The fairly level path heads southwards, and is joined by a thin path

Wintry tree trunks in Ashridge Woods

from the right, but just keep straight on along the worn path, to pass through a glade of huge beech trees. Emerge to an open grassy patch where there is a cap of trees at the top of the field. Turn left here, with the open area on the right and the woods to the left. The grassland is an area which has been reseeded with native grasses and it is hoped that a variety of flowers as well as grasses will thrive here.

At the end of the field, just 20–30 m before reaching a road, turn right along the margin, following the bridleway sign. When this path reaches a surfaced track, keep straight ahead along this. The track soon becomes stony and, when it begins to bend to the right, following the edge of the woods, go straight on along the path into the woods. This is the area called Frithsden Beeches and a notice mentions that this is an ancient area with historic interest because of its old pollarded trees, some of which are likely to shed their branches – so beware. There has been much recent planting and many young trees are growing in this area, too.

Descend to a hollow where footpaths cross, but keep straight ahead and up the other side. Pass a faint cross paths and then on an open patch reach a major cross paths, but still keep straight ahead. There are numerous paths in this area which could be confusing, but just keep walking in a southerly direction. The next major cross paths is on the edge of an open area where heathland restoration has been taking place, removing bracken and birch scrub to provide opportunities for heathland plants to colonise. The major path here is a track coming in from the right and going diagonally ahead to the left, but our route is the narrower path straight ahead, and is signposted Grand Union Circular Walk. This path descends across the open area and then steeply through trees, to reach a stile at the bottom of the woods. Go over the stile and turn left along the field margin. The path leads to a stile and then on to a stony driveway between fields, heading southwards along the bottom of a dry valley.

Pass some barns on the left and then go straight ahead over a stile and along the right margin of a field. Go on over two more stiles and along field margins to reach Berkhamsted Cricket Club, with pitches on both sides of the path, and tennis and bowls to the left. The path becomes a track and then leads on to the road and go straight ahead to reach the castle (3), and the railway station.

Berkhamsted castle is very close to the station in Berkhamsted and could be used as a starting point for this walk.

From the castle or station, walk a few yards along Brownlow Road, then turn left along Bridgewater Road. After about 150 m turn right along Castle Hill Avenue and soon the road begins to climb. Where it bends left we follow the footpath sign for a Canal Circular Walk pointing straight ahead along a gravel path in a grassy stretch between hedges. (The canal circular walks are a joint project by British Waterways, the Countryside Management Service and North London Railways.) At the top of a short rise, reach a road and cross over, to go straight ahead along the right-hand stony track, between houses. Pass to the right of Castle Hill Farm and its large old barn. Ignore the path going off to the right, but then soon go over a stile with a movable top rung, and proceed more or less straight ahead. These movable top rungs are a very thoughtful and useful idea, and they weaken the well known argument that all stiles are designed by and built for tall men. The hedge is just on our left, and as we follow the stony remnants of an old track, the path levels off after the climb out of Berkhamsted. At the end of the field go over another stile with a movable top rung, and keep straight ahead along a track between a hedge and a fence, with playing fields to the left. Beyond the playing fields can be seen part of Berkhamsted, down in the valley and also climbing up the other side of the Bulbourne valley. At a cross paths go straight on, to a stony track with houses on the right. At the end of the houses reach a narrow surfaced road, and turn right along a stony track. Houses are on the right and woods to the left, and where the drive bends right to the last house, keep straight on and the stony track becomes grassy with occasional flints and often muddy patches. The path leads through woods, with a field not far away to the right, and soon emerges at the magnificent buildings of Northchurch Farm.

Turn right along the driveway and pass to the left of the main buildings, going over a stile signposted the Ashridge Estate Boundary Trail. Near the large metal barn are two stiles, one to the left and one to the right, both of which lead across to the same place. Take the one to the right, and pass over the large stile and along a grassy track between fences. At the end of the field, turn left to follow the hedge, and at the end of this field, turn right and descend to the valley with a hedge on the left. At the bottom of the field, go over a stile and into a small wood. Follow the stony track as it bends left and then emerges from the wood. Bend right here and go along a stony track between two open fields. Keep straight ahead here, and at the end of the field go over a stile with a lift-up top pole, and head diagonally left to pass to the left of the pond. Go over the next stile and walk along the drive, with the farm buildings of Great Coldharbour Farm to the left. At the major cross tracks we meet the short cut route which has come up from Woodyard.

Turn left at the cross tracks, and pass one house and then a second house, called Little Coldharbour Farm. Keep straight on, following a blue arrow, close to the edge of the woods, with open fields just a few yards to the left. When the woodland extends further away to the left, keep straight ahead along a broad grassy path. There is a footpath just to the right of this bridleway, and the path might be less muddy. Reach a cross tracks, but keep straight ahead with a blue arrow and horseshoe along route 45. The edge of the woods is now about 100 m to the left. Reach a grassy glade and then arrive at the road, where there is a T junction. Go straight across following the road sign to Aldbury and Tring.

After 100 m turn left at the bridleway sign and go back into the woods. Follow a blue arrow and a line of old beech trees which are growing up from an old boundary line shown by a slight embankment. An open field can be seen about 50 m to the left and continue parallel to this.

At a cross paths where a field becomes visible to the right of the path, turn right so that this field is then on your left. This path will have a blue arrow as well as the marker for the Ashridge Estate Boundary Trail. Just keep straight ahead along this broad path, even when the edge of the wood bends away to the left so that the open fields are no longer visible.

Reach a minor road in Gryme's Dell and go straight across and then cross a track where a house will be visible about 50 m up to the right. Soon arrive at a complex junction of paths. We do not turn left here to go downhill, but take the route diagonally left, passing two wooden benches, where there are views out over the village and the church down below. This path, which is located just above and to the left of a sunken, eroded and often muddy path, gradually leads steadily downhill, with a fence on the left.

Reach a sunken track and turn left, still going downhill. At the road turn right and walk into the village at the duck pond and back to the starting point.

(1) Carved into the base of the 33 m (108 ft) monument it states 'In honour of Sir Francis, 3rd Duke of Bridgewater, Father of inland navigation 1832'. His first major project was the Bridgewater Canal, built in 1761 by James Brindley, to carry coal from the Duke's coal mines at Worsley in Lancashire to Manchester. The canal was subsequently extended to the Mersey.

There is a small admission charge to climb to the top of the granite monument, but it is well worth the effort and the money to climb the 172 steps on a clear day, for the views are extensive. It was erected in 1832 and was repaired for the first time in 1996, when the joints between the granite blocks were grouted and the staircase was fitted with electric lighting to provide safer access.

Ashridge Estate Visitor Centre shop opening times:

From Easter–end October: Monday to Thursday 2–5 p.m.

Saturday and Sunday 2–5.30 p.m.

1st November–17th December

    Saturday and Sunday only, 12 noon–4 p.m.

Shop is closed on Fridays except for Good Friday. Telephone number: 01442 851227.

(2) Ashridge House and garden are occasionally open to visitors. Opening times for the gardens are 2–6 p.m. on Saturdays, Sundays and Bank Holidays from 1st April–31st October. There is a charge for entry. The House is only open at Easter and Spring Bank Holiday weekends, and for five days in August.

In 1283, Edmund Earl of Cornwall, grandson of King John, founded Ashridge House as a monastery, the College of Bonhommes, which remained here for 250 years, until the time of King Henry VIII. Located in the monastery was a Holy Phial supposedly containing the blood of Christ, given to Edmund by the Patriarch of Jerusalem. After Henry VIII dissolved the monasteries he used the converted house as a home for his children. Prince Edward (Edward VI), Mary Tudor and Elizabeth I all lived here for a time. In the early seventeenth century Sir Thomas Egerton, who became Lord Ellesmere, took over the estate, and began to make improvements. Lord Ellesmere's son was made Earl of Bridgewater by James I, and he continued to look after the estate, as did his immediate descendants. It was when the 3rd Duke of Bridgewater became more interested in his lands in the north and in canal-building that this estate and the building fell into a poor state of repair during the eighteenth century. After his death the estates went to a cousin who took the title of Lord Bridgewater, and he commissioned

James Wyatt to rebuild the house. Only a barn and the thirteenth-century crypt remain from the Tudor building.

Work began in 1808, using Totternhoe stone, and a huge neo-Gothic mansion was created, with turrets and battlements. The scale of the building was very grand, and included a hall 30 m in height and a chapel designed like a miniature church. The interior was redecorated in Italian style by Matthew Digby Wyatt, a relative.

The mansion and garden were sold separately from the estate, and in 1928 the house was presented to the Conservative party as a memorial to Bonar Law, and was used as a College of Citizenship. Since 1959 it has been a management training centre, with a private charitable status and no political links. In 1969 the spire of the chapel became unsafe, and a new fibre-glass replica was lowered by helicopter.

The gardens and part of the park were laid out by Humphry Repton and Capability Brown, and a major feature is the long drive from the house straight to the Bridgewater Monument. The area was well wooded when Brown arrived and so he felled trees and opened up the views, rather than planting trees to create new landscapes. Repton's work was mainly in the gardens, which he completely redesigned. The gardens are still magnificent.

The house is surrounded by woodland and commonland, now part of the Ashridge Estate which has been in existence for over 700 years. It covers an area of 1600 hectares (4000 acres) of woodland, common land, downland and farms, managed by the National Trust. For centuries some of this land has been used by local people as common land, not that it was the open scrub associated with the name, but much of it was true woodland. In 1866 a major dispute developed over the common rights, when Lord Brownlow, the owner at that time, erected fences. They were torn down overnight by local people, backed by a group of London navvies, hired for the occasion.

(3) The castle site is now a well cared for grassy area with

remnants of walls standing up around the periphery and a pleasant place for a picnic or for a stroll. A small Victorian cottage is situated inside the castle grounds. Berkhamsted is a motte and bailey castle, and the earth mound of the motte can be clearly seen today. On top of the motte would have been a tower. The bailey was the original courtyard and is now seen as a large grassy area within the walls. The castle was well defended, with two moats and three sets of earthworks.

The importance of the castle in former centuries was considerably greater than its present day remains would suggest, and Berkhamsted has been a fortress town for a long time. It had strategic importance on one of the major coaching routes north from London to Birmingham, still followed by road, rail and canal today, though thankfully the A41 now bypasses the town centre. It was at Berkhamsted that William the Conqueror met the English noblemen after the Battle of Hastings, and took over the throne of England. It is likely that Robert, Count of Mortain, a half-brother of the Conqueror, took over the castle which was then a timber building. A stone castle was probably first built in the twelfth century, and was put to the test in 1216 when it was besieged by Prince Louis of France.

During the Middle Ages members of the royal families often came here, and being the Warden of Berkhamsted Castle was an important appointment. Thomas à Becket was one such holder of the post, when he was Chancellor and Archbishop of Canterbury. The castle was never occupied after 1495 and, as it fell into ruins, some of the stone was used to build the Tudor house, Berkhamsted Place. As the stone was removed, the eleventh-century earthworks were revealed, the only remnants from that time.

Two fragments and the Keep Mound of Berkhamsted Castle

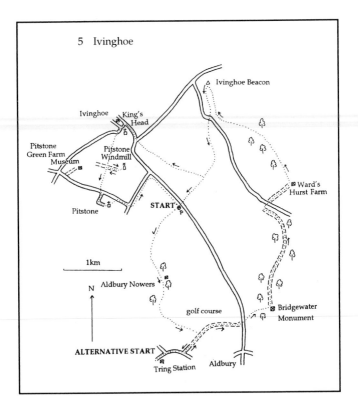

5 Ivinghoe

Ivinghoe Beacon

Ivinghoe   King's
            Head

Pitstone
Green Farm   Pitstone
Museum   Windmill

                                    Ward's
                                    Hurst Farm

Pitstone

              START

                                    Bridgewater
                                    Monument

1km

N   Aldbury Nowers

                    golf course

ALTERNATIVE START

Tring Station   Aldbury

Walk 5 – Ivinghoe

Located on OS Landranger 1:50 000 sheet 165 and OS Explorer 1:25 000 map 2.

Length of walk is 8 miles, with an additional 2 miles if the extension to the windmill is included. Anyone walking from Tring station will add a further mile to the total distance.

Time required is 4–5 hours.

Terrain – clear paths but including several steep climbs and descents.

Starting point is the small car park at grid ref 955148, on a minor road in the midst of chalk scenery. In order to reach this point, take the B489 southwards from Dunstable, and at the T-junction where the village of Ivinghoe and Leighton Buzzard are signposted to the right, take the B488 going left towards Tring. Pass the small parking space for the windmill, where the road bends left, and after a further 400 m the road bends right, but go straight on here, along the narrow unsignposted road. This climbs steadily and after half a mile reaches a small car park on the right-hand side. If approaching from the A41 near Tring, follow the B488 signposted to Dunstable and at a sharp left bend, turn right along the narrow unsignposted road about half a mile before reaching Ivinghoe village. If travelling by train, use Tring station and walk from the station to Aldbury, to join the route of this walk.

Ivinghoe means the *ho* of Ifa's people, with *ho* being the Saxon word for a spur or hill. The village grew up near the foot of the steep Chiltern scarp close to Ivinghoe or Beacon Hill, and is situated on the minor road between Dunstable and Tring. Evidence of ancient settlement in this area is the old Pitstone flint mines, one mile south of Ivinghoe, and the line of a section of Grim's Ditch which curves round them. In the centre of the village, close to the church and opposite the green, is the old town hall, probably sixteenth-century though now modernised but with some old timbers retained, and evidence that Ivinghoe was much larger and more important in former centuries. The King's Head, which also looks out over the green, was rebuilt in the seventeenth century, but has still retained some of the fifteenth-century beams and the open fireplace. In spite of the different spelling, it is thought that the village was the origin of the title of Sir Walter Scott's novel, *Ivanhoe*.

Close to Ivinghoe is Pitstone, with its contrasting large buildings, a church and a cement works. The cement works was one of the largest in Europe, but has recently been closed. The company (Castle) had hoped to use some of the space as a tip but there was opposition from the local council and Herts and Bucks County Councils, as well as Anglia Water and the National Rivers Authority. The future of the site is uncertain, and there have been proposals for housing development as well as a tip, but there are possibilities that some buildings or chimneys may be retained as an industrial museum, or the quarried out hollows could be turned into boating lakes and tourist amenities. One lake is already an important nature reserve, College Lake Wildlife Centre, managed by the BBONT (see Walk 3).

The walk starts and ends on chalk grassland, but in between passes the village of Aldbury and through the large woodland area of Ashridge. Several steep slopes are encountered on the way, going up and down the escarpment, with extra steep slopes if the detour to the windmill is included in the circuit. Beacon Hill is the most northerly part of an area of chalk grassland and scrub, and has commanding views in all directions. To the east can be seen the Whipsnade lion cut into the chalk (1), and to the west are even better views over Ivinghoe and Pitstone villages, with the windmill clearly seen down on the plain. The prominence of the summit was the reason for a beacon being set up on this hill in the time of Elizabeth I to summon men quickly in case of a Spanish invasion.

Leave the car park on Pitstone Hill (2) by going over the stile and heading across the open field towards the hill top. Half way up, bend to the left near a small hawthorn tree. Note that beneath this tree, and many others on the hill, there are different grasses growing in the shade of the tree compared with those out on the open hillside. Follow the fence on the left of the field. Pass a stile and path going over to the left, but just keep straight ahead on the Ridgeway path. Views down to the right are mixed, but dominating is the cement works in Pitstone, and just alongside is the tiny village church with quite a large tower which is dwarfed by the quarry works. To the left of the church is the windmill, and further over can be seen the water of the Tring Reservoirs – looking a different colour from the blue pool in the quarry works.

The chalk grasslands have their own distinctive flora and fauna which are increasingly rare, and only surviving in areas where there is special care and protection. The National Trust, English Nature and BBONT are amongst the organisations looking after areas of chalk in the Chilterns. (3)

The fence bends left but we stay close to it until reaching the end of the field. Turn right here and descend the slope as far as the wooden kissing gate, then turn left to walk into the woods. This is the Ridgeway, and relics of Grim's Ditch can be seen along this stretch of the path (see Walk 9).

Walk on through the woods, along a fairly level path on the side of a scarp, with the hill top of Aldbury Nowers up to the left. Flowers include small potentilla, and large clusters of rose bay willow herb in the summer. Occasional views open out to the right, through the trees. Several uprooted trees will be noticed around here, relics of strong winds in recent years, but merely part of the ongoing cycle in woodland, as trees fall, young ones grow and a variety of habitats for different plants and animals can be maintained.

Pass a few wooden steps and then reach a more open patch, with a wire fence to the right of the path. Go down a few more wooden steps into a hollow, ignoring the path going down to the right, and after a further 15 m reach a major track and a cross paths. We turn left here, but before doing so, it is worth going a few metres to the right where there is a useful information board for Aldbury Nowers. (4)

Now turn left from our original path, and go slightly uphill. When this path splits after about 30 m at a wooden marker post, take the right fork which goes on near the edge of the woods, where the golf course can be seen to the left. The path leads to the edge of the wood at a kissing gate. Go straight on here, across the track and over a stile on to the golf course. Follow the hedge on the left and then a few marker posts. Aldbury can be seen ahead, at the foot of the tree-lined scarp, with the Bridgewater Monument just showing above the tree tops. Our route leads straight on over the golf course, not crossing any fairways, so no real worries about flying golf balls, and joins a surfaced path for nearly 100 m before reaching a stile, and a cross paths. Go over the stile and turn left, to follow the sign for Grand Union Canal Circular Walk, Berkhamsted-Tring. This circular walk extends for nearly 10 miles from Berkhamsted to Tring, and back via Aldbury and Northchurch. It was created by British Waterways, the Countryside Management Service and North London Railways as a joint project, to provide a good day's walk using the train as the means of transport to and from the area.

IF STARTING THE WALK FROM TRING STATION, this is the point at which you will join the main walk, and also the point at which you leave the walk to return to the station.

From the station walk out to the road at the Royal Hotel, and turn right. Pass the entrance to the car park and Northfield Road, which is the left turn to Pitstone and Ivinghoe. Keep straight ahead along the right verge and, after about 100 m, take the footpath on the left, along a concrete driveway. When the drive bends left, go straight ahead on the grassy path to the Ridgeway notice board. Go through an iron gate, cross a track (the Ridgeway bridleway) and straight on through an old wooden gate to a broad path between fences, with open fields on both sides. Keep straight on through the next gate, and then reach a cross paths. To the left is a gravelled path on the golf course and this is the route which is followed by our walk, coming to the stile and turning left. So Tring station walkers just keep straight at this point and follow the path as it leads into a tunnel between high hedges and on towards Aldbury.

For the return journey to Tring station you will cross the golf course and reach the stretch of gravelled path, then go over the stile and turn right to retrace steps to the station, when the main walkers will turn left.

CONTINUING THE MAIN WALK

We follow this route for just a quarter of a mile, along the edge of the golf course and then between buildings on the left and a playing field on the right, until reaching the narrow road in Aldbury. Here we leave the Grand Union Canal Circular Walk as it turns right into the village, whilst we turn left along the road for about 100 m to a stile in the hedge on the right. Straight ahead along the road is Stocks Farm and just beyond is Stocks Manor, now a hotel and country club. The Stocks Estate formerly covered over 200 hectares (500 acres), and a manor house was built in 1773 by the Duncombe family who have been associated with Stocks for over 300 years.

Turn right over the stile, and follow the field margin. After about 50 m, at a stile in the hedge to the left, cross into the next field and head diagonally right, to a stile in the middle of the fence at the top edge of the field. Once over this stile there is a steep climb through the woods and up the scarp slope, and the path might be slippery in wet weather. Near the top of the slope, a path comes in from the left, and a house can be seen a few yards to the left. Where the path divides, take the left fork which is clearer, and soon reach a cross track. Turn left along this and the house is now below us to the left, and on reaching a stony track, turn right to go slightly uphill, directly to the Bridgewater Monument (see Walk 4). The column can be seen from many miles away and the views from the top are magnificent.

From the tower, head northwards along the broad stony track marked by a blue arrow, and after 20 m is another marker post with the Ashridge Estate Boundary Trail sign. The track soon splits but we go straight on, passing beneath some very tall and straight oak trees, with few lower branches. Pass over a small bridge, often with no water beneath it, and just follow the main broad gravelled path. To the left of the path is a log cabin. Keep going along the Ashridge Estate Boundary Trail, ignoring other routes which go off to the right, and keep heading more or less northwards, on a bearing of 10°–20° at first, then becoming 350°–340°, walking along the Duncombe Terrace. The land slopes down steeply to the left, a view opens out, and there is a brief glimpse of the top of the chimney at the cement works, peeping over the top of the next hill. Begin to bend round to the left, on to a bearing of 320° and then 280° as the path begins to climb slightly.

At a cross paths, where the left path is small but the right path is broader and clearer, turn right to head northwards and climb slightly uphill. Just before reaching the road the path splits, and we take the right fork out to the road opposite the driveway into the Ward's Hurst Farm. Walk along the driveway, between fields likely to contain some of the herd of Holstein Friesian cattle, and at the farm yard go slightly left to pass between the buildings to emerge near an open field, with views of the chalk scarp and the Whipsnade lion straight ahead.

Just before the iron gate into the field, turn left along a path by the wire fence, go over the stile, and on to the path through the woods. The path is close to the edge of the woods at first, but then drops down steeply to a valley, called the Coombe (see Walk 6). Wind on through the ancient beech woods, then pass an area of conifers before emerging at a wooden kissing gate, with evidence that this is on both the Icknield Way (see Walk 1) and the Ashridge Estate Boundary Trail. In the woods near here, the filming of a costume drama called *Plotlands* was taking place when I last walked this path.

Carry straight on near the right margin of the field into a magnificent area of chalk grassland. At the end of the field, one path bears round to the right, but here we go slightly left, through a wooden kissing gate and along the right margin of the field. This field slopes steeply up a grassy chalk slope, but we remain along the bottom edge. Head towards the Ivinghoe ridge which stretches from directly ahead around to the right in a semi-circle, with three summits. In the middle is Beacon Hill (Ivinghoe Beacon), and over to the right is Gallows Hill at the end of the ridge, but we go straight on, to the unnamed left-hand summit of the ridge. Model planes are often being flown from the top edge of this field, as there is easy access from a large car park up to the left. Near the end of this field go through a gate, and the main path goes straight ahead now with the fence to the left, but we turn right here and head along the right side of the field directly towards Gallows Hill. Once through the gate at the end of this field, bend left to head straight towards Beacon Hill, one of the highest and best viewpoints of the Chilterns. The triangulation point is at 233 m (764 ft) and adjacent to it is a map of the Ridgeway (5). As well as the Ridgeway, the Two Ridges Link Path also starts from here, going via Ivinghoe Aston to join the Greensand Ridge

Walk at Leighton Buzzard. The top of Ivinghoe hill was the site for an Iron Age fort. (6)

Near the summit are many wild flowers in summer, and a variety of bird song including yellow hammers and skylarks. One of the most colourful flowers is the great knapweed with its purple heads, looking quite similar to thistles. Other flowers seen here include kidney and horseshoe vetch, yellow rattle and stemless thistle, and on sunny days the small blue and chalk hill blue butterflies can be seen. Scrub has been cleared from parts of Ivinghoe Beacon by the National Trust, in order to allow grasses and flowers to grow, and occasionally some grazing takes place to help control the growth of the shrubs and bushes which kill off the interesting small flowers.

The final section of this walk is along the ridge top, commanding glorious views to Aylesbury or to Whipsnade and Dunstable. Do not go on northwards to Gallows Hill, but turn southwards and follow a clear path towards a narrow road. Just before reaching the road is a concrete marker post by a stile which leads left back to the field we walked alongside earlier. A concrete post shows the old axe symbol for Icknield Way.

Cross straight over the road, and follow the Ridgeway signs slightly uphill, through wild flowers and insects in summer, though this can be very windy and exposed in winter. Amongst the most delightful summer flowers are the harebells, known aptly as fairy thimbles. The Latin name is *campanula rotundifolia*, meaning a little bell with rounded leaves.

At the end of the first field go over a stile and turn left, to go uphill slightly, alongside the fence, and then into a small wood of hawthorn and some gorse. Emerge from the wood into more grassland with the wonderful deep coombe of Incombe Hole down to the right, with some terracettes (7) on the steep slopes. Walk around the top edge of this coombe, with woods on the left of the path, and at the field boundary on the far side the Ashridge Estate Boundary Trail goes left, but we either go straight on through the kissing gate and across the next field back to the starting point on Pitstone Hill, or turn right.

Straight ahead is A SHORT CUT back to the parking place, but an interesting detour takes in Ivinghoe and Pitstone villages, and adds two miles to the distance.

For the visit to the villages turn right just before the fence, and follow it downhill. After about 200 m take the stile on the left and go diagonally right across the field. The windmill is straight ahead but rather dwarfed by the towers of the cement works. At the bottom of the field go through a gap in the hedge and continue straight on across the next field. The path leads across to a hedge and follow this to the end of the field and a low stile. The path goes on between fences, with an orchard to the left and a field to the right. The path ends at another low stile and we have now reached the road, where we turn right to walk into Ivinghoe village.

Just before reaching the church (8) notice the lovely old houses on Vicarage Way on the right. Opposite the church is the King's Head restaurant and then the green. The YHA on the left is in the Old Brewery House, and next is the Ivinghoe Town Hall. Along the road to the right, passing in front of the King's Head is Ford End Farm and old watermill which dates from 1781 or earlier, and is normally open on Sundays and Bank Holidays from May to September. It has been restored by the Pitstone Local History Society.

Beyond the school and the post office, as the road bends to the right, turn left along the narrow Green Lane, between houses. The track soon becomes a path and leads through a wooden kissing gate to emerge into a large field. The windmill is in the middle of this field, and beyond are quite magnificent views of the Chiltern scarp. The view to the right is less attractive. The path does not lead direct to the windmill but to the far side of the field. Just before reaching the end of the field the path meets a track, and to the right this leads to the Pitstone Green Farm Museum (10), but we turn left and soon go left again to reach Pitstone Windmill.(9)

From the windmill retrace your steps and continue along the path to the end of the field, pass through a gap in the hedge and go straight ahead across the next field to the village of Pitstone. Go through the iron kissing gate on to the road and turn left. After about 50 m turn right along Church Road, which leads round to the old church. (10) The churchyard is a real haven of peace and has some seats which could be useful for eating packed lunches. Go over the iron fence at the far end of the churchyard and walk along the right margin of the field, with an iron fence to the right. At the end of the field is a stile and beyond that is a road. Turn right and walk up to a major road, the B488. Cross over to the wide verge and turn left along a grassy track. Evidence of old chalk workings can be seen to the right. When the track reaches a narrow field, go right over an old wooden stile, but keep more or less straight ahead, with a fence and the small field to the left of the path, and a narrow strip of woodland to the right. Masses of sloe berries line the path in late summer. Over to the left the Silver Birch Cafe may be seen and then the road draws very close to the path for a few metres. Reach a stile and cross a track but keep straight ahead, still with a narrow strip of woodland to the right. When the path bends right, and a stile is on the left, follow the path which is now parallel to the narrow road leading up to the car park at the end of the walk. The path is between a variety of small trees and undergrowth, a haven and a real nature reserve for small birds and butterflies in summer. Hawthorn and wild roses are most numerous, with more wayfaring trees, rich in berries, higher up, as well as many other small and young trees.

Emerge from the trees at a wooden gate, and keep straight ahead up the hill, alongside a small rectangular area fenced off by Anglia Water, and soon over to the left will be seen the car parking area and the end of the walk, except for anyone who started from Tring station.

(1) The Whipsnade lion was cut between 1931–3 as an advert for the Wild Animal Park. It took eighteen months to complete and covers 0.6 hectare (1.5 acres) of chalkland. It was concealed by bracken during World War II.

(2) Pitstone Hill is managed by Buckinghamshire County Council and an information board in the car park tells us about this area of 54 acres of chalkland, which has been designated an SSSI. Amongst the many interesting plants and animals to be seen here is the chalk hill blue butterfly, feeding on the horseshoe vetch which flowers in June and July. Note the small anthills, formed by the yellow meadow ant, on which flowers such as rock rose, squinancy-wort and thyme often thrive. The delicate violet colour of the Pasque flowers, members of the anemone family, can be seen here in April or May. There are picnic tables in the car park and magnificent views all round. A notice at the entrance to the car park states 'No Hang Gliding and No Parasending' (with the incorrect spelling). Hawthorn scrub was removed from part of Pitstone Hill by a group of volunteers in 1980, in order to help the growth of small flowers and grasses. Hollows on Pitstone Hill are old flint diggings, many of which have hawthorn bushes growing in them nowadays.

(3) Chalk grassland. Much of this has been ploughed up but several hectares at Pitstone and Ivinghoe have escaped the plough, enabling large numbers of chalkland plants to survive. Specialities in Pitstone and Ivinghoe include the violets and primroses on Pitstone, and chalk gentian at Ivinghoe; and many butterflies are to be seen in the summer.

(4) Aldbury Nowers is Queen Elizabeth the Queen Mother's Nature Reserve of Duchie's Piece and an SSSI. In 1991 this area became a protected nature reserve and was presented to the Queen Mother to honour her ninetieth birthday. Noted

especially for its butterflies, this is one of the last places where the Duke of Burgundy fritillary still survives. It looks like many other fritillaries but is not a member of the same family, the *Nymphalidae*. The Duke of Burgundy is the only British member of the *Riodinidae*, called *Hamearis lucina*, and generally emerges in late May or June, and lives for about twenty days. It is a woodland butterfly and requires primroses and cowslips as food for its caterpillars. There are also lots of marbled whites, especially in July and August.

(5) Ivinghoe Beacon is the beginning, or the end, of the Ridgeway long distance path which extends for 85 miles (137 km) to Overton Hill near Avebury, much of this distance being on the top of chalk ridges. It was designated a National Trail by the Countryside Commission in 1972 and follows the old Icknield Way in places. Parts of the Ridgeway may be used by horse riders, cyclists and four-wheel vehicles, and many parts can become rutted and very muddy in wet weather. Only walkers can follow the entire length of this National Trail. The Ridgeway is cared for by the Countryside Commission in partnership with the five County Councils of Wiltshire, Oxford-shire, Berkshire, Buckinghamshire and Hertfordshire. A small staff manages the Ridgeway from Oxford County Council offices, helped by a large group of volunteers.

(6) The Ridgeway may be the oldest road in Britain or even in Europe, and is likely to have been used for at least 5000 years. There are many ancient remains and burial sites along its route, including an Iron Age fort on Ivinghoe, which was excavated in 1963. The hill fort on Ivinghoe Beacon probably had a wooden rampart, covers an area of 2.2 hectares (5.5 acres), and has banks dating from the seventh century BC. The defences are not very impressive, merely a single rampart of chalk rubble and a ditch, but with an extra ditch on the south side.

Icknield Way stone, with Whipsnade Lion in the background

The entrance was from the east, and several round and rectangular huts existed in the camp. It was a very early hill fort, and possibly only occupied for a short period, perhaps as little as forty to fifty years. Some late Bronze Age metal work has been found on this site as well as pottery thought to be from the early Iron Age.

In addition to the hill fort, there are two barrows on the west side of the track leading up to the fort from the car park, and another barrow on the summit.

A problem faced when trying to date here and elsewhere in chalk areas is that pollen does not survive well in the dry alkaline soils.

(7) Terracettes are small terraces just a few centimetres in width and height which extend horizontally along steep slopes. They are often referred to as sheep tracks, and although they may be used by sheep, they are unlikely to have been formed by them. They are normally the result of soil and small stones slipping down the slope by a process known as solifluction or soil creep. This occurs when the land is wet and then freezes and the ice enables the soil to slide downhill more easily. Continued freezing and thawing over a period of thousands of years is likely to move large quantities of earth.

(8) Dominating the centre of Ivinghoe, the church of St Mary the Virgin is situated alongside the green. The cruciform-shaped church dates from about 1230, but was changed in the fourteenth and fifteenth centuries. Amongst its interesting features are the thirty-eight bench ends (poppyheads) which date from the fifteenth century. Several of the carvings are of distorted and leering faces, but the more pleasant sight of a mermaid is on one of the pews opposite the south door. The pulpit is Jacobean, and the roof has heads of animals and humans carved in stone corbels, as well as the large wooden carvings of angels. On the churchyard wall is a plaque commemorating the coronation of King Edward VII in August 1902, as well as two relics of life in former centuries. One is a

man trap 'to discourage intruders', and the other is a remarkable implement, a long pole with a hooked end, used to pull burning straw off thatched houses to prevent the fire from spreading.

(9) Pitstone windmill dates from 1627, and may be the oldest post mill in England (post mill means that the complete windmill rotates round on the post). The field in which the mill stands was still being farmed on the strip system until 1854. Repair work to old mills would take place every few years, and this mill had some major repairs in 1895. Unfortunately, in 1902 a powerful storm with strong gusts hit the sails from behind, before the mill could turn round, and caused serious damage. The mill was never repaired and did not work commercially again, so the gradual deterioration of the building began. In 1937 the owner of the land, Leonard J. Hawkins of Pitstone Green Farm, realising that he could not afford to repair it, gave the mill and an access route to the National Trust in the hope that they might restore it. A few urgent repairs were undertaken immediately, but the real restoration work came with the formation of the Pitstone Windmill Restoration Committee in 1963. An appeal raised money for materials, and volunteers have managed to restore the mill to its original magnificence, and in 1970 some corn was ground, sixty-eight years after it had last been working. It is open from 2.30–6 p.m. on Sundays from June to the end of August, and on May Bank Holiday.

(10) The church at Pitstone is thirteenth century and contains a Norman font and some sixteenth-century pews, as well as the oldest brass in Buckinghamshire, and a chest reputed to be 700 years old. Whilst the church was attached to the monastery at Ashridge College, the chancel was lengthened in about 1420. The tower was built and the nave rebuilt later in the fifteenth century. Important repair work took place in the nineteenth century, and Pitstone was affected by the religious revival associated with the Oxford Movement. More recent decline led

to the church being declared redundant in 1973. It is now looked after by the Redundant Churches Society, and is open 2.30–6 p.m. on Sundays and Bank Holidays from May to the end of September. At the other end of the village, at Pitstone Green Farm, the local Historical Society have a small museum of old agricultural implements, which are displayed in nineteenth-century farm buildings, open to the public on the last Sundays and on Bank Holidays in each month from May to September, as well as the second Sundays of the month in June, July and September.

Buckinghamshire – near Wendover

Wendover is a small town and often described by locals as a village, with a population of only 7000. The name is derived from *wend* (winding) and *ofer* or *oves* (bank or shore), making up the name of a settlement on the banks of the winding stream. There is a small stream, and many other features to interest the visitor include old inns, old timbered cottages and fine Georgian houses along the broad streets. It is an ancient settlement, and part of the old Icknield Way runs along the High Street, and turns right on Heron Way near to the Clock Tower. The hill forts nearby, on Wendover Hill, on Bacombe and near Kimble, were placed where they could overlook this old route.

Along Aylesbury Road, interesting old buildings include Sturrick House, once a Temperance House, and the seventeenth-century Chiltern House, once a Boys' Academy. The windmill on the left, now a private dwelling, has a date of 1790, with the tiny flint miller's cottage next door. The mill had its sails removed in 1906 when steam-power was introduced.

At the end of Back Street, nearly opposite the Tourist Information Centre is a puddingstone (see Introduction page 15) just below the street name. Walking beyond the Tourist Information Centre on the Tring Road, pass the end of Hale Road and on the right is Bank Farm, a very old building, parts of which date from the fifteenth century, though it was altered in later centuries. On the other side of the road are the sixteenth-century thatched cottages known as Coldharbour Cottages, which were formerly called the Anne Boleyn Cottages, having been given to her by Henry VIII. Further up the hill on the left side is the old pub, formerly the Rising Sun, with murals of the four seasons on the front wall. It is now a fish restaurant, but still has the murals. At the opposite edge of the town is St Mary's church, nearly half a mile from the centre, out on the London road. This large flint church dates from the thirteenth century with some fourteenth-century additions. There are magnificent limes, chestnuts and sycamores in the churchyard, as well as many yews. If the church is open look at the carvings of fruits, flowers and animals on the capitals of the pillars. The mill pond is on the other side of Church Lane, opposite the church.

Manor Waste, the open space on the south side of High Street, is opposite the fine old Red Lion Inn, the first licensed house in Wendover. This inn has connections with Oliver Cromwell who is believed to have stayed here in 1642. Rupert Brooke was another visitor here, and Robert Louis Stevenson resided here in 1875, whilst he was writing *An Autumn Effect*. At the bottom of the High Street is the Clock Tower, built in 1842 by Mr Abel-Smith, the Lord of the Manor, and it was restored in 1985 by Wendover Parish Council, when it was reopened by Mr Lionel Abel-Smith, the present Lord of the Manor. The Clock Tower contains a cell where in Victorian times the village constable could lock up drunks or troublemakers. At the top of the High Street is Bosworth House, formerly part of a monastery, and now containing an antique shop, and the old archway for coaches to pass under. This brick and timber house dates from the early seventeenth century, though it was refronted with brick at a later date. There is a fifteenth century pillar piscina in the wall of the gateway, and wall paintings inside the house.

Wendover is accessible by bus or train, and is a good starting point for Walks 6 and 7 for anyone using public transport.

Walk 6 – Wendover Woods

Located on OS Landranger 1:50 000 sheet 165 and
Explorer 2 Chiltern Hills North 1:25 000.
Length of walk is 11 miles, plus 3 extra if starting from
Wendover station.
Time required is 5–6 hours.
Terrain – undulating, with several steep climbs and
descents.
Starting point is at grid ref 888092 and is reached from
the A4011 Wendover to Tring road, 2 miles north of
Wendover and 1 mile north of the RAF camp at Halton.
Turn left if driving south, or right if driving north, on
the road signposted to St Leonards, Cholesbury,
Chesham. Take the forestry road off to the right at the
Wendover Woods noticeboard, pass the pay and display
machine, and note that the gates close from one hour
after dusk until dawn. Drive along this road as far as the
main parking area, with children's playground,
information board and toilets, and in summer there is
likely to be an ice cream van. There are picnic sites,
barbecue sites and many footpaths in these woods,
suitable for a good family day out.

This circular walk starts and finishes in Wendover Woods, but
in between are a few miles of farmland and the Iron Age fort
at Cholesbury. Wendover Woods cover almost 400 hectares
(1000 acres), and were formerly owned by the Rothschild
family as part of the Halton House estate, but then became
part of Halton RAF camp and subsequently have been managed by the Forestry Commission since 1939. Planting in the
1940s and 1950s was mainly beech, though with some conifers,

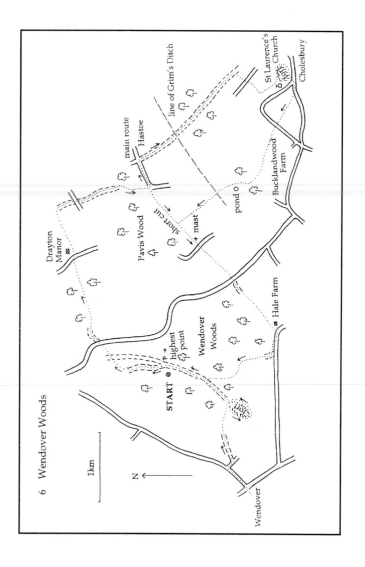

6 Wendover Woods

1km

N ←

Wendover

Drayton Manor

Pavis Wood

START ⊗ P + highest point

Wendover Woods

Hale Farm

main route Hastoe

line of Grim's Ditch

short cut

+ mast

pond

Bucklandwood Farm

St Laurence's Church

Cholesbury

but some older and larger trees remain from the Rothschild era. In those days the woods were used for shooting, riding and picnicking. Multi-purpose forestry is the modern aim of the Forestry Commission in Wendover Woods, with provision for leisure and recreation, as well as extracting 2000 tonnes of timber each year. Animals and birds are numerous, and the rare firecrest nests here regularly. Grey squirrels, glis glis (an edible dormouse, introduced into this area by Lord Rothschild) and deer have become so numerous that they have become a nuisance and numbers have to be controlled by the wild life rangers.

These woods contain the highest point in the Chilterns, at 267 m (876 ft), marked by a cairn. A gravelled path leads to this summit, which is flat and nondescript rather than a real peak. The path passes a barbecue point, and a wooden carving of an owl on the way to the stone cairn, which has a plaque to say it was erected by the Parish Council, the Forestry Commission, the Chiltern Society and the RAF, to commemorate the Silver Jubilee of Queen Elizabeth II in 1977. There are many other walks and trails through the woods. Daniel's Trudge starts from the car park on the north side of the road at 892102, and has a steep descent and a zigzag climb, passing a group of lynchets; Aston Hill Ramble is through beech woods and a yew glade; Beech Hanging Walk goes through the beech woods on steep slopes; Hale View Walk is to a viewpoint looking over the Wendover Gap; and Boddington Bank is included in our walk.

Start the walk by heading back on the road we followed on our arrival, but a few yards beyond the playground area leave the tarmac and turn left at the yellow arrow along a broad track going downhill, soon to join another track coming from the left, where there is another post with a yellow arrow and a concrete drainage channel running across the track. About 30 m beyond that take the main path going right, still descending. Follow the stony track to a cross paths, where a path comes in from the left between flint walls, but we turn right here to climb up steps, and follow the path up to the main driveway. Cross straight over and keep going uphill, fork right when the path splits, and at the broad horizontal grassy track turn left. Soon reach a narrow path going right to the triangulation point at 260 m (852 ft) on the top of Aston Hill, and it is possible to go right to visit this if you wish to collect trig points, but the walk goes straight along the broad level track, through a gate, passing the Chalet on the left, to reach the road by Aston Hill Lodge.

Cross over the road on to a stony track, but first walk to the car park on the left, to admire the vast views over the plain, with Tring Reservoirs clearly visible. Follow the footpath sign along the stony track, passing the Forestry Commission notice saying 'No Entry for Unauthorised Vehicles', and 'No Riding Please'. The track soon emerges from the woods, with woods still on the left, but a field behind the hedge to the right. At Long Meadow Farm and the entrance to Aston Hill Place, the footpath goes to the left of the track, but still straight on, with a wooden fence to the right of the path. Pass through an asymmetric wooden barrier and keep straight ahead, with a wire fence to the left of the path, descending slightly now. A path comes in from the left and the land can be seen slightly sloping down left to an open field, and the impressive Drayton Manor is ahead, down at the bottom of the scarp.

Descend steadily to a narrow road, turn right and after about 100 m turn left along a narrow footpath. Drayton Manor is to the left. The path leads out into an open field, and straight ahead the traffic can be seen on the A41 near Tring, and a tree-lined scarp we shall soon be climbing is visible over to the right. At the end of the field continue straight on along the next field to the right of the hedge. Reach a broad track and turn right, following this to a narrow road, and keep straight ahead, as the track continues past Bridleway Cottage. The track is between lines of trees, and passes a footpath going right and a bridleway comes in from the left. Just keep straight on along this fairly stony path, and reach the edge of the woods, where paths go right and left, but continue ahead, and climbing.

Ignore small paths going off right and left, until a major fork near the top of the climb. Go left, following the blue arrow and continue to climb, but our path soon levels off and reaches a narrow road, and on our right is the entrance to Pavis Wood.

SHORT CUT

For the short cut route, turn right through the gate into Pavis Wood to follow the Ridgeway (see Walk 5). A notice board here gives information about Chiltern Woodlands. (1)

Walk along the fairly horizontal track with the edge of the woods visible a few metres to the left, and occasional views opening up to the right, towards Bittam's Wood, Bradnidge Wood and Coombe Hill on the next ridge. This is not the Coombe Hill with the monument, overlooking Ellesborough, but another hill of the same name. This word coombe is a geographical term for an armchair shape hollow. (2)

A footpath comes up from the right to join the gravelled path we are walking along, and then we reach cross paths. The path coming in from the left here is the route used by the longer walk which has taken in a visit to Cholesbury fort.

Keep straight ahead, passing a few small pits to the right of the path, and reach a narrow road. Turn left along the road, notice the radio mast on the left, and after about 30 m turn right, following the Ridgeway sign through an iron kissing gate and into a field cluttered with old farm vehicles and untidy barns. The path leads across the middle of this field, past a marker post in mid-field, and on to an iron kissing gate. Go through, and along the left margin of the next field to another iron kissing gate and a narrow road. Go straight across to the stony track, passing a house on the left, where the track deteriorates to a broad path and goes on into the woods. An open field is seen to the left for a short distance. Reach a cross paths, where a small path goes off left, and a broad track goes straight ahead into a Forestry Commission area where horse riding is by permit only. In between these two routes is our path going left, and it is located to the right of a sunken trench. Walk on the higher path, with the sunken path about 3 m down to the left, but gradually the trench diverges from our path. Our path descends steadily and, at the bottom of the slope, before beginning to climb again, we turn left on a path leading towards the open field visible through the trees. Just before reaching the open field, turn right along the sunken path which leads down and to the edge of the woods. This path can become muddy, but there is a drier path on the field margin to the left, if required.

Reach the road, with Hale Farm on the left and Hale Farm Cottage to the right. Walk straight along the path or use the path just inside the field to the right. This path goes over a stile at the end of the field and continues as a narrow path through trees, then over a stile at the end of the field and along another narrow stretch between fir trees to the end of the houses. Turn right here on the Forestry track heading up into Wendover Woods. After about 40 m fork left off the track and take the narrow path closely following the boundary of the large field on the left. Soon begin to climb and the path leads through to a broad stony track, with a recently cleared area to the right, and down into the valley. Follow the gravel track and at a cross paths where one path comes up from the right, and another goes off to the left, there is a marker post for the Firecrest Walk. Turn left here and follow the Firecrest Walk for the remainder of the climb back to the car parking area on top of the hill. In addition to the firecrests, another rare bird which may be seen here is the crossbill, feeding on the pine cones, but much commoner are various tits and woodpeckers. Different types of habitat have been created by opening up the woodland with glades or wide rides where more light can get in. Along the margin of the woods there are other habitats where the agricultural land and the woods meet, and many birds and animals thrive here.

We go past marker post 8 which is very close to the edge of

the wood and the large field to the left, and at marker 9 there is a seat with good views into the field and across the countryside. This location is called the Valley Overlook, and looks out over a well managed landscape, with farming on the lower areas with richer soils, and forestry on the thinner soils on the chalk hills. Note that the edge of the woods is not just a bold straight line, but has curves to enhance the appearance of the landscape.

The Firecrest Walk next leads across the broad stony track, and at post 10 is the hide, from which it is sometimes possible to see the firecrests. (3)

Continue climbing steadily, with a steep slope down to the right. Pass marker post 11, where the path is beginning to level off, and then come out on to an open area of grass. The Firecrest Trail goes over to the right edge of this grass and the path continues through the trees, but we go straight ahead through a few trees to reach a stony track.

At this gravel track, turn left in order to walk around the old Iron Age camp on the top of Wendover Hill. Follow the track until it ends at a circular stony patch, which is the turning space for cars. Go straight on past the wooden barrier gate to a notice with information about the Boddington hill fort. (4)

A white arrow on the top of a marker post indicates the route ahead, which is the Boddington Trail around the hill fort. The path is fairly level, and passes through a variety of trees, including a few conifers, found in the old hill fort. At an information board there are good views out over the Vale of Aylesbury, especially in the winter months. As this fort has not been excavated, the description of the way of life is based on research in other forts. Housing, clothes and pottery are all mentioned, as well as the metal items which the inhabitants were able to make or obtain.

Continue along the path to reach the end rampart, and then the path turns left along the top of this embankment, which is the end of the fort. Follow this embankment along the east side of the fort, and soon reach the end of the stony drive seen earlier, and the circular turning space. Go on to this stony drive, and follow it as it leads back to the starting point at the top of the Wendover Woods.

For anyone who STARTED FROM WENDOVER, turn left out of this turning space, through the wooden barrier gate again and go past the information notice about the Fort Walk along the muddy track for about 100 m, then go right downhill to retrace your steps into Wendover. It will feel very steep at the end of the walk.

THE MAIN WALK

If not taking the short cut, do not turn right into the woods, but turn left along Gadmore Lane, signposted to Ridgeway and Hastoe. Hastoe is a tiny hamlet which was part of the Tring estate, and it is situated on the top of a small hill, near where the old route of Akeman Street bends to avoid this hill. At a staggered cross road turn right, not on Church Lane, but on the bridleway passing between the large buildings of an old farm complex, which have been recently modernised into magnificent dwellings. Walk along the broad stony track, ignoring the footpath going off to the right, and passing a few houses on the left. The track is lined with wild flowers and blackberries along the verges and continues out across open fields. A cross paths is where the track crosses the line of Grim's Ditch (see Walk 9), some evidence of which can be seen to the right. Near Hastoe the ditch is up to 3.5 m wide and 2 m deep. The track leads on into the woods and can become very wet.

Keep straight on beyond another cross paths in the wood, then an open patch on the left where there are several magnificent tall beech trees. Reach an open area on the right, with several horse jumps and eventing obstacles in it, and then reach a cross paths, where the bridleway goes straight on, and we turn right here to go over a stile. Walk alongside the hedge on the left of the field, and notice there are a few jumps in the hedge, enabling horses to leap from one field to the next. At the end of this field go over the stile, with a movable top pole, out on to the road and turn left for a few yards. Then go right over a stile and along a narrow path leading past a garden and over a small stile into woods with an open field on the left. At the end of this field, go left over the stile and along the field margin with a dressage practice area through the hedge to the right. Go over the stile at the end of this field and follow the path through woods, with an open field just to the right, then there is one more stile and an area of scrub before reaching a line of very tall beech trees. These are situated on the embankments of the Iron Age fort at Cholesbury. (5)

Turn left along the ditch between two embankments and walk on a carpet of leaves and mast, round in a semi-circle as far as a garden. The path bends right here, up on to the embankment, and passes over two stiles in quick succession, then along the left margin of a small field to a stile by an iron gate. Go over this, and along the stony driveway to the village hall (1895) and a wide grassy area and the road. Turn right along the road passing the lovely old manor house with its colourful garden, and then turn right again, on Parrotts Lane. One hundred metres along here turn right towards the church, and notice the plaques on the gates telling that these are the villagers' memorial to those who died in the Great War.

After visiting the church, retrace your steps past the Old Vicarage to the road and turn left for a few metres, then go right across the grassy area to reach the road opposite Sandpit Hill Cottages. Turn right, and after about 200 m, when the road bends left, go right over a stile by the gate. Walk along the right margin at first and then head towards the gate in the middle of the fence at the far end of the field. Beyond this, go diagonally left to the margin of the field to reach a stile about 20 m beyond a wooden kissing gate and hidden beyond a bend in the hedge. Go over this and follow the left margin of the field to another stile and out on to a surfaced driveway. Walk

between the houses, through a gate and up to a narrow road, where the aptly named Stone Cottage is on the left.

Turn right here along the road for about 200 m, and go left over a stile and across the middle of the field to a gap in the hedge opposite. Continue across the next field heading to the right of the red brick houses, and cross a stile on to the road. Straight across is a stony track, the way ahead, which we follow to the farm buildings of Bucklandwood Farm. Pass to the right of the main buildings and farm yard, with a few barns and a small pool to the right of the track, and keep straight ahead along a field margin to the edge of the woods.

In the woods are several paths but we head diagonally right ahead, go towards the open space soon visible on the far side of the wood. Our path is soon joined by another coming in from the left, and an open space and a pool can be seen to the left of the wood. The embankment which is damming the pool is just to the left and, once past this, look for a split of paths, as we need to go left to keep close to the left side of the woods. The fork is near a tree on which a white arrow is pointing straight ahead. Fork left here on a path which is going up slightly, whilst the path straight on is just descending slightly. Our path leads parallel to the edge of the woods and the pool in a north-westerly direction.

Emerge from the woods and walk straight on along a field margin, with farm buildings down to the right. Cross a surfaced track, the line of Grim's Ditch, go over a stile and then through a very large field, heading towards the woods. Over to the left is the radio mast and four old grey breeze block barns. Walk into the woods and after about 30 m reach a T-junction with a gravel track which is the Ridgeway bridleway. Pass the pits on the right, and continue with the route described under the short cut section (just over half way down on page 115).

Highest point in the Chilterns marker stone

If starting from WENDOVER STATION OR TOWN CENTRE, walk down the High Street and pass the Tourist Information Centre in the old Clock Tower building. Go straight on past the Information Centre and walk along the Tring Road, up the hill past the Coldharbour Cottages, as far as Colet Road. Turn right here and then first left along Barlow Road. At the end of this road, keep straight ahead along a stony track sign-posted Public Bridleway. There are houses through the hedge to the left, and an open field to the right. The track begins to climb, and then levels off to reach a house at the end of the drive. A bridleway goes off right and immediately splits. We take the left fork. After about 30 m reach a cross track, and go straight ahead on a footpath with no horses permitted, and begin to climb steeply up through the woods. The steep ascent climbs a well worn broad path, with an erosion gully in the middle, and becomes slippery after rain, with some bare chalk. Good views of the RAF camp can be seen through the trees to the left in winter. At a cross path, a red marker post indicates that this is the Fitness Trail. Go on about 10 m to a broad track and turn left. At a wooden barrier gate is a notice about Boddington hill fort on the right, and you could turn right here and join the walk for the Boddington Trail or go straight on to get to the real beginning of the walk. If the latter is chosen, go straight on to the stony track beyond the barrier gate, passing a notice for the Fitness Trail to the left, and begin to climb slightly. Pass a picnic area on the left, then a barbecue area and just keep going along this track to reach the main car parking area and information centre with toilets, and the main starting point of the Wendover Woods walk.

On completion of the walk retrace your steps through the wooden barrier gate and past the information notice about the fort, along the muddy track for about 100 m and go right downhill to retrace your steps into Wendover.

(1) A notice board giving information about Chiltern Woodlands mentions that Pavis Wood covers 35 hectares (87 acres) and is semi-natural woodland, growing on the Chiltern escarpment. Some parts of it have not been managed and have been left to natural evolution of plant growth, but elsewhere there has been planting to try and introduce variety to complement what is growing naturally. Much damage was done in the storm of 1987. Oak has always been important in the forests and in the medieval period was crucial for ship-building, over 300 oaks being required for each vessel. In later times, with the growth of the furniture industry, beech trees became more important, for the green wood which could be bent and worked, straight from the tree. Areas of hazel were coppiced for small sticks and poles. Bodgers (see Walk 13) worked in many of these woodlands.

(2) Coombes are arm-chair shaped hollows found on hill sides, especially escarpments. They are particularly common on the scarps of the South Downs in Sussex and the North Downs in Kent, as well as the Chilterns. They are probably formed by the process known as solifluction or soil creep, which would have been particularly active during the colder conditions of the Ice Age. Repeated freezing and thawing of soil and top layers of rock would gradually break up the surface material and it would slide downhill with gravity, especially where well lubricated with water or ice. In areas of rock weakness considerable amounts of material could slide downhill to leave hollows behind. These hollows are the coombes, and they will often have small terracettes on their sides (see Walk 5). Steep back walls of coombes may become hangers, although these can form on scarp slopes as well (see Walk 1). The coombes are similar to but generally smaller than the corries or cirques found in glaciated areas such as the Lake District. These larger features were cut by ice, not by the freezing and thawing of water particles.

(3) The firecrests may be seen in the Norway spruce which is

where they generally nest. Listen for their call note which sounds something like *zis*, and is repeated several times, generally becoming faster and faster. They nest high up in the crowns of the Norway spruce, in a delicate nest of moss and grass. The felling plans for this area will ensure that new Norway spruce are regularly planted in order to try and retain suitable habitat and nesting sites for this quite rare bird.

(4) Boddington hill fort is an oval-shaped fort, enclosed by a single bank and ditch, probably dating from the early Iron Age about 500 BC, although the site was probably occupied before that time. It was not only a defensive site, but also contained a settlement, as food remains and some pottery have been found here. There has been no excavation into the interior of this site. A map of 1768 shows Calloway Farm at the eastern end of the fort, and at that time the interior of the fort was open land divided into three enclosures. In 1954 the buildings were demolished and the land was planted with trees. It is planned that the trees will mostly be removed by the end of the century and the land left in a semi-open state.

(5) The old British camp at Cholesbury is a late hill fort, probably from the first century BC, and was deserted at about the time that Roman villas were set up in the Chiltern area. It is oval in shape and covers an area of about 6 hectares (15 acres). The flint St Lawrence's church with its small wooden tower is within the defences. These generally consist of double ramparts and a ditch, with mature beech trees on the ramparts. There are two small ponds within the earthworks. The drive to the church goes through a gap in the defences. On the north side of the fort are two banks and a ditch in between, and an extra bank and ditch were added in the south-east. In the west the defences stretch out to the north-east to form a small roughly triangular shaped small extension. Excavations in 1932 found a few pieces of hand made pottery probably from the second century BC, and also some Belgic-style pottery from the first century AD.

Walk 7 – Coombe Hill and Chequers

Located on OS Landranger 1:50 000 sheet 165 and OS
Explorer 1:25 000 map 2.
Length of walk is 6 miles, or 10, if starting from
Wendover.
Time required is 3 hours, or 4–5 from Wendover.
Terrain – an undulating walk with occasional steep
climbs, ending with the very steep ascent up to the
monument on Coombe Hill.
This walk can be linked in with Walk 8, if required.
Starting point is grid ref 852063, and can be reached
from the B4010 Princes Risborough to Wendover road
via Great Kimble and Ellesborough to Butlers Cross. At
Butlers Cross take the narrow road leading southwards
and after about one mile turn sharp left and this leads to
a car park.

We pass through woods and farmland in the early part of the
walk, then move on to the real highlights by walking around
the edge of the Chequers Estate with good views of the Prime
Minister's country residence. After passing through more
woods, including an unusual yew forest, near an old pre-
Roman fort, we reach the delightful church at Ellesborough
and end on Coombe Hill, the highest viewpoint of the Chilterns, with outstanding views all round.

STARTING FROM WENDOVER
If using public transport, a start can be made from Wendover
which has bus and train services, and this will add about 4
miles to the length of this fairly short walk. Walk out of town
over the railway bridge near the station on the road to

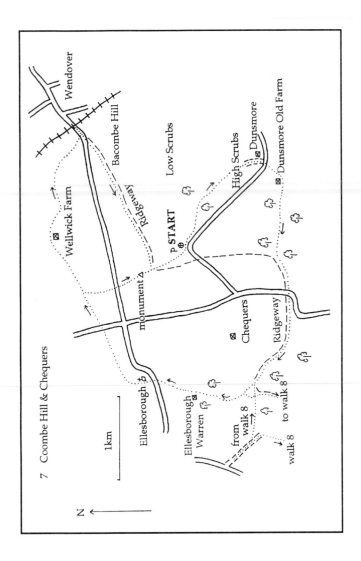

7 Coombe Hill & Chequers

N ←

1km

Wendover

Bacombe Hill

Wellwick Farm

Ridgeway

Low Scrubs

Dunsmore

High Scrubs

Dunsmore Old Farm

monument

P START

Ellesborough

Chequers

Ridgeway

Ellesborough Warren

from walk 8

to walk 8

walk 8

Ellesborough, Princes Risborough and the Kimbles. Pass a few houses on the right, and the road begins to climb slightly. When it bends right, take the broad track going straight ahead. After about 20 m it splits and the notice mentions that this is Bacombe Hill (1). Fork right following the Ridgeway sign, and when the path splits again in about 30 m near an Information Board, take the left fork, still following the Ridgeway sign. After another 30 m at the black kissing gate, keep straight ahead, following the acorn, to reach a few wooden steps up into an open chalky area with good views over to the right. At the end of the Bacombe Hill Nature Reserve, go through an iron kissing gate into some trees, and then on to another more open area. Cross a major cross paths where a bridleway goes down to the right and another goes up to the left, and go straight ahead through a gate and up to the Monument. Pass the National Trust sign and walk on to the open and often windswept top of Coombe Hill. Turn left at the monument and walk on the broad level area of grass, to lead through to a car parking area in the trees.

THE START

From the car park, walk towards the road and turn left into the woods passing the National Trust 'Low Scrub' sign. A clear path leads between beech which must have been cut down and pollarded a few years ago. The ground is carpeted with blue-bells in the spring. The main paths are marked by yellow arrows on trees, and at the first cross paths with arrows pointing left and right, turn right. At the next cross paths go straight ahead, and ignore a few narrow paths turning off the main route. At a cross paths where the wood opens out into a grassy glade, turn left following a yellow arrow, and keep on this path to a T-junction just before a large wire fence and a few houses. Turn right here along a broad path, which can become muddy. Cross a driveway which leads over a cattle grid, and keep straight ahead with the large wire fence still on the left, and a barbed wire fence on the right. Pass a cross paths, with a stile going right and gate going left, and keep straight ahead. There are old jumps for horse-training in the woods to the right. Pass an open field to the left of the woods, and then go over a stile and straight on. The path splits with a left fork going through a garden, but keep on the main track, passing along the right side of some houses. Stay on this track which becomes a surfaced drive, and passes between the houses of Dunsmore village.

At the road, we can notice the track straight ahead which leads to the former Black Horse pub, now a private house, and to the left of the track is a small church, but we turn right along the road, signposted Kimble 3½, P.R 5½. Pass the duck pond on the left, and a wooden house on the right, then turn left over a stile. The path immediately splits, but take the right fork, leading across the field to a stile, and then down through another small field, with the buildings of Dunsmore Old Farm down in the hollow straight ahead. Pass over a stile and along a narrow path between fences down to the buildings. Another stile will lead into the farm yard.

Go straight ahead, with fine old flint buildings and garages to the left, and stables of Dunmore Livery on the right. A stony track leads gradually uphill, and a yellow arrow and footpath go off to the right, but keep straight ahead on the track, following the blue arrow and bridlepath. At a major cross paths, with five ways, go slightly left of straight ahead following a yellow arrow. The main track with a blue arrow goes slightly right of straight ahead.

Continue to climb steadily through mixed woods, mainly beech. The path then levels off and divides in two, but soon rejoins, and reaches a cross paths where the Ridgeway comes in from the right. Go straight ahead on the Ridgeway footpath, and begin to descend. As the descent becomes steeper, Brockwell Farm can be seen on the hillside opposite and then the main drive to Chequers (2) comes into view, with the house visible away to the right.

Pass a major cross paths, with South Bucks Way (3) going left, but we keep straight ahead. A footpath runs to the right of the track for a short distance but soon rejoins. Growing alongside the path here is a mass of woodruff, with its dainty white flowers and rings of green leaves resembling ruffs around the stem. Pass a wood shed on the right and some houses on the left, then arrive at the road.

Go straight over, then through an iron kissing gate and across the field on the Ridgeway path. At the end of the field go through a kissing gate, and cross the main drive (Victory Drive) into Chequers, with the lodge houses and gate just a few yards to the left. The drive is lined with beech trees, an idea initiated by Winston Churchill in the 1960s.

After two more iron kissing gates, ascend slowly up through a field to the edge of Maple Woods, with Brockwell Farm in the hollow to the left. At the woods turn right and follow the path along the margin of the woods, with good views of Chequers away to the right, and the monument on Coombe Hill beyond.

At the end of the field, pass through another iron kissing gate, and fork right to walk along the margin of Whorley Wood, with trees to the right and an open field to the left.

EXTENDED WALK. For anyone combining this walk with Walk 8, go straight ahead at this point, across the field, following the Ridgeway (see the bottom of page 142 in Walk 8).

MAIN WALK CONTINUED
Near the end of this field the path joins a track, passes through a gate and reaches a surfaced driveway. Go straight across this and ahead along a broad track through a small wood. Emerge from the wood and bear slightly left, following the path across the middle of the field. At the end of the field follow the public footpath sign and go down some steps into dense box woodland. (4)

Up to the right of the path is a very steep wooded slope, and the steep slope continues down to the left of the path. This is Ellesborough Warren, a densely wooded coombe or hanger (see Walk 1). The path levels off, between boarded sides, which are presumably reducing the erosion of this path. Go over a stile and straight ahead, emerging from the wood. Up to the right is a steep grassy slope leading to the summit of Beacon Hill (225 m), where there are relics of a Neolithic round barrow, and down to the left is a flat grassy area, beyond which is the site of the castle of Cymbeline or Cunobelinus, the King of the Britons. (5)

The path leads on to a stile and across the next field heading towards the church in Ellesborough. Leave the field through a wooden kissing gate and turn right along the path. Pass the thatched Church Hill cottages on the left, and the eighteenth-century Dame Dodd almshouses on the right. Cross over the road and walk into the churchyard, where there is a sculpture of the crucifixion. The path ahead is along the left side of the church. (6)

The church has a large graveyard. Leave from the far end of this yard, by going down a few steps and over a stile. Walk across the field, but turn right just before reaching the stile, and follow the field margin. In the corner of the field, cross two stiles and walk along the narrow surfaced road past a thatched and flint cottage and a few more houses. We are now on the Aylesbury Ring footpath, which has a duck for its symbol (7).

When the drive bends right, go straight ahead along the footpath between a bungalow and a field. Then cross the middle of an open field, with clear views of the Monument up to the right. Leave this field over a stile which has a notice mentioning the Parish Paths Partnership between Ellesborough Parish Council and Buckinghamshire County Council to maintain and improve footpaths. Continue along a narrow path between wire fences and fields, crossing over three stiles and reaching a road. Turn left following the yellow arrow and after

50 m turn right to go over a stile and along the left margin of the field to another stile. Beyond this, continue straight ahead on a grassy track and then along the margin of the next field, with the fence just to the right and open field to the left. Go over the stile at the end of this field, then turn right and go up the margin of the field.

FOR ANYONE WHO STARTED IN WENDOVER keep straight ahead after this stile, across the middle of the field, still using the Aylesbury Ring footpath with the duck symbol. Go over the stile at the end of the field, cross the middle of the next field, then over a stile and alongside the left margin of the next field. At the end of this small field go over two stiles in quick succession to pass to the left side of the buildings, including the fine old flint and brick Wellwick Farm, part of which dates from 1450, though the main building is later. The weathered crest of the Brudenells is above the door, and it is thought that Judge Jeffreys may have stayed here, when holding Assizes in Aylesbury.

Once beyond the buildings head right to the field margin beyond the big barn, go over the stile and pass between the barn on the right and a house on the left. Cross the driveway into the field but immediately turn left to follow the field boundary for about 30 m, before turning right at a telegraph pole to follow the line of an old field boundary between two open fields, heading initially towards a green barn about a quarter mile away. At the end of this field, where the hedge for the next field begins, go over the stile and turn left to walk alongside the wire fence. Climb the stile at the end of this field and head diagonally right across to the far side to reach the corner of the cricket field. Walk along the right side, and at the end of the cricket field turn left through a kissing gate to walk past the pavilion and on to a new footbridge over the bypass and the railway. Once across the railway turn right along Station Approach to reach the main street through the town centre.

MAIN WALK CONTINUED

To reach Coombe Hill and return to the starting point of this walk, having turned right, walk up the margin of the field to a stile and then on to the golf course. The path leads straight ahead over the course to pass to the right side of the club house and out to the road.

Cross the road and enter the National Trust land around Coombe Hill. The path splits here and we take the right fork through the wooden gate. A few metres beyond the gate this path splits and the broader bridleway goes straight on, but take the left fork, the footpath, which begins to climb immediately. Climbing through the trees is quite steep but becomes very steep for the final ascent up the grassy slope. The monument (8) is at the top and the views all round are impressive. The summit reaches 260 m (852 ft) and is nearly the highest location in the Chilterns, only being exceeded by a point in Wendover Woods, from where there are no views.

From the monument walk straight ahead along the level patch of grass, passing footpath signs with the acorn of the Ridgeway which come from right and left to cross our route. Keep ahead along the grass to the trees in the distance, and the car park is just through these trees.

(1) Bacombe Hill is a 25 hectare (65 acre) reserve described as a rich chalk downland, with scrub and coppice, including some semi-natural woodland. It contains a rich variety of plants and animals, and has magnificent views over the Vale of Aylesbury. Management of the landscape is organised by Buckinghamshire County Council who attempt to preserve the delicate balance for plants, animals and humans.

(2) Chequers is an imposing sixteenth-century house, built by Sir William Hawtrey who was jailer to Lady Jane Grey. The name was probably derived from De Scaccario, the name of the first tenants of an earlier house built on the site in 1187. The Hawtrey family owned Chequers from the thirteenth to the

sixteenth centuries, and it was altered considerably in 1565 by Sir William. The West Wing was rebuilt by Sir George Russell in the late eighteenth century. It was given to the nation by Lord Lee of Fareham in 1917, for use by the Prime Minister as a country retreat and also as a place to hold meetings. Lord Lee and his wife restored the house to some of its former Elizabethan style.

(3) The South Bucks Way is a long distance route extending 23 miles from Coombe Hill to the Grand Union Canal near Denham. For a few miles it follows the River Misbourne, one of only four rivers which cross the main part of the Chilterns (the other three being the Bulbourne, Chess and Wye).

(4) Although often seen in parks box only grows wild in a few locations now. Some quite large trees have grown here, mixed in with other deciduous trees. Box is slow growing, with very hard wood, and is the only native wood which is too heavy to float in water.

(5) Cunobelinus or Cymbeline, the King of the Britons, was killed by the Romans. Although now covered by a small plantation, ramparts and ditches can still be traced, and a tumulus on the site contained Roman and older relics. Also in the woods are the remnants of a motte and bailey castle from Norman times, but there is no public access. The name of the nearby villages, the Kimbles, is thought to have been derived from this King.

(6) The twelfth-century flint-faced church of St Peter and St Paul has a fine Norman tower and battlements. There are interesting wall paintings and some old floor tiles in the chancel (made at Tylers Green near Beaconsfield), as well as memorials to the Hawtrey family. This church is used by Prime Ministers whilst visiting Chequers.

(7) Aylesbury Ring is a joint project of Buckinghamshire County Council, Aylesbury District Council and local Ramblers' Associations, and is fully waymarked. The 31 mile route circles round Aylesbury and is never more than 5 miles from

the town. It passes the Aylesbury arm and Wendover arm of the Grand Union Canal, and three houses formerly owned by the Rothschilds at Aston Clinton Park, Eythrope Park and Halton, as well as Waddesdon which is still owned by the family.

(8) The monument on Coombe Hill is a memorial to 148 Buckinghamshire soldiers who died in the Boer War 1899–1902, and was erected in 1904. It was almost totally destroyed by lightning on 29th January 1938, but was rebuilt in the same year.

There is a toposcope viewfinder, donated by May Warren on behalf of her family in remembrance of Denis James Robert William Warren 1929–88, a beloved husband, father and grand-father. Views include Brill Hill (13 miles away), the Cotswolds (55 miles), Ivinghoe Beacon (9 miles), and Wittenham Clump (19 miles). Closer landmarks include Aylesbury church (5 miles), the new bypass at Wendover, Halton House in the Wendover Woods, Beacon Hill with its small clump of trees and Ellesborough church with the Manor House in front of it.

The area of downland around the monument was presented to the National Trust in 1918 by the Viscount Lee of Fareham. The downland covers an area of 43 hectares (106 acres) and is rich in flowers such as ragwort, scabious, birdsfoot trefoil, harebell, bedstraw, St Johns wort, knapweed, some of which are very short on open grass, but grow taller in the shelter of bushes. Common centaury is a special flower in the Bacombe reserve. Many trees and bushes grow on the top of Coombe Hill, including several wayfaring trees.

Beacon Hill from Ellesborough

Buckinghamshire – Princes Risborough

Walks 8 and 9 can both be started from the station in Princes Risborough. This delightful market town is a very busy centre with many attractive buildings. The Market Hall in the centre of the town dates from 1824, and has a council room upstairs above the open ground floor which was used for the markets. Along Church Street are Corner Cottage, Vine House and several other old houses, though many have changed functions in recent years. On the right just before the church is the Manor House, a seventeenth-century red brick mansion with a noted Jacobean staircase. Now owned by the National Trust, it can only be visited by appointment with the tenant. Adjacent to it is the flint-faced St Mary's church with its fine steeple and a most beautifully kept churchyard. Behind the church is The Mount, an earthworks, possibly a relic of a Saxon camp. Another church of interest is the Catholic church of St Teresa of Lisieux, a modern circular building located on the Aylesbury road out of town. There used to be watercress beds at Princes Risborough, fed by the springs which come out from beneath the chalk of the Chiltern scarp. The name of Risborough is derived from the Old English *hris* which means hills covered with scrub.

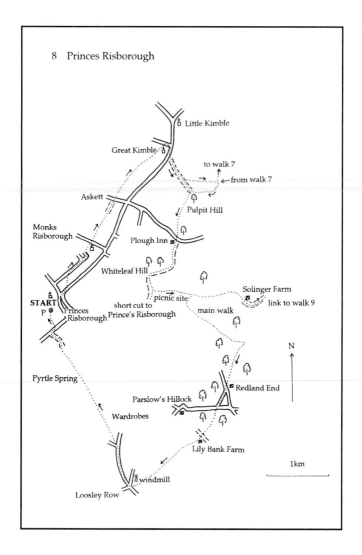

8 Princes Risborough

Little Kimble

Great Kimble

to walk 7
from walk 7

Askett

Pulpit Hill

Monks
Risborough

Plough Inn

Whiteleaf Hill

picnic site

Solinger Farm
link to walk 9

START
P

Princes
Risborough

short cut to
Prince's Risborough

main walk

N

Pyrtle Spring

Redland End

Parslow's Hillock

Wardrobes

Lily Bank Farm

1km

windmill

Loosley Row

Walk 8 – Princes Risborough

Located on OS Landranger 1:50 000 sheet 165 and OS Explorer 1:25 000 map 2.
Length of walk is 10 miles, or 11 if starting from the station.
Time required about 5 hours.
Terrain – includes two ascents of the Chiltern scarp as well as a couple of shorter climbs.
A possible extension for a long day out could make this into a 17-mile walk by including the Coombe Hill/Chequers Walk (Walk 7).
Starting point is at grid ref 806036, easily reached along the A4010 from Wendover or the A4129 from Thame.

This walk passes through the attractive villages of Monks Risborough, Askett and Great Kimble before climbing up the scarp to the woods and nature reserve of Pulpit Hill and Grangelands. After Lower Cadsden and the climb to the top of Whiteleaf Hill, we cross farmland and woods towards the Chiltern Society windmill at Loosley Row before descending back into Princes Risborough.

Start from the Mount car park adjacent to the church and swimming pool in the centre of Princes Risborough. If starting from the station, walk away from the station to the main road. Turn right, and after about 20 m cross over to turn left along Manor Park Avenue which will lead you through to the car park. Walk past St Mary's church to the town centre, and just beyond the church on the left is the Manor House. Turn left in the Market Square and walk to the traffic island at the end of the main street. Turn right along Aylesbury Road, passing the church of St Teresa, and after about 50 m turn left into a park. Cross over to the far side and out on to Wellington Avenue, then turn right and soon pass Icknield County Middle School on the left. When the road bends left, turn right on Dunsmore Avenue, and where this becomes Dunsmore Ride, go right through a gap in the fence and follow the path on the left side of the grassy area. This leads past the Old Dovecote, with the church of St Dunstan over to the right. Go over to the right for an interesting detour to visit the church, and the old village of Monks Risborough just beyond. (1)

Just beyond the dovecote is the road and here we turn right for a few yards, and then beyond the first houses turn left on a footpath between fences and gardens leading through to a stile. Go over the stile and a small stream, then cross to the far left corner of the field to a stile, a small paddock and then another stile. Continue along a tree-lined path with houses and gardens on the left and an open field to the right. At the junction of paths, turn left through a wooden gate, with a brick wall on the left side, and this path leads to a surfaced driveway passing between houses and out to the road. This is the village of Askett and contains some lovely seventeenth-century half-timbered houses, including several with thatch. The gardens are very colourful in summer and the village has all the features required for a picture postcard. At the road is the magnificent Askett Farm and across the road is the village pub, the Crowns.

Turn right along the road for a few yards, but soon cross over and turn left on the footpath by the outhouses of the Crowns. Go over a stile and follow the right side of the field. The path leads on to a stile where the path splits, but ignore the left fork and keep straight ahead along the right margin of this next field to another stile, and keep straight on to yet another stile and beyond. A brick building is up to the right, and ahead to the left is the Old Grange, which dates from the fifteenth century and belonged to Missenden Abbey. It was moated but only part of the moat remains, and the old timber and weather board barn was built in 1793. At the end of the next field, go over the stile in the corner, and turn left through the fence into the next field. This is now the Midshires Way, a 225-mile footpath, cycle route and bridleway through the Midlands, linking the Ridgeway in Buckinghamshire with the Pennines in Derbyshire. The way leads on to a stile at the far side of the field. Keep straight on following the yellow arrow and North Bucks Way. (2)

Pass a small summer house, crossing a drive and over another stile. Keep straight ahead across the next field, over a stile and then go straight ahead along a less worn path following the white arrow rather than taking the main path which heads slightly right across the next field. Stay near the fence on the left of the field. Over the fence can be seen evidence of old moats, and remains of medieval settlement when Great Kimble was much larger. The path leads on to a stile at the far end of the field, adjacent to an iron gate, and then goes on through a small field, between a pond on the left and a garden on the right. Pass the large house on the right and then an enormous old barn from the fifteenth or sixteenth century which was possibly the original church house. Reach the stile and turn right along the narrow road, to walk between the flint houses (one with an old well) and school, up to the church. (3)

At the road we turn right, but if there is time and you have the interest it is worth making a left turn at the Bernard Arms to visit the thirteenth-century church of All Saints in Little Kimble, less than half a mile away. (4)

Turn right for about 100 m along the noisy A4010 from Great Kimble church, cross over and go to the left of Cymbeline's Cottage, along the stony track which is both the Midshires Way and North Bucks Way, and pass between houses, the last on the left having a small swimming pool. The track begins to climb steadily between large hedges and fields.

POSSIBLE EXTENSION

After a quarter mile, reach an old iron kissing gate to the left, and this is the way to turn if the walk to Coombe Hill and Chequers (Walk 7), for an extra 7 miles is desired. For this, go through the kissing gate and take the path across the middle of the field, passing a few scattered trees. Fields near here have been managed by the BBONT as a Nature Reserve (5), and have not been ploughed for many years, hence a variety of plants have thrived. This field is rich in bird, flower and butterfly life in spring and summer. To the right of the path is a small knoll (Chequers Knap) and to the left is a deep dry valley which leads downhill to Great Kimble. The path divides and we take the right fork going slightly uphill, though not up to the top of Knap. Meet a well worn path coming from near the top of Chequers Knap and follow it as it goes downhill slightly. This is the Ridgeway which skirts round the head of the dry valley (Great Kimble Warren), climbs up slightly, to go straight on past a stile leading over to the left, just before reaching a cross paths. Here there is a stile going left and an iron gate ahead. Go through the gate, but ignore the path straight ahead across the field, as this is the route to be followed on the return journey. Instead take the path going diagonally left, and this will lead across the field to the far corner, where it will join a path coming on the field margin alongside the edge of Whorley Wood. From here follow Walk 7 via Ellesborough, Coombe Hill and Chequers.

At the end of this 7-mile extension to the walk, after walking around the field with good views to Chequers, and reaching the point where the route comes through an iron kissing gate and then turns right along the margin of the woods, do not turn right, but go straight ahead across the field, following the Ridgeway sign. This will lead across to the iron gate seen earlier, and once through this, turn left and follow the fence on the left for 20 m. Near the cattle drinking trough, fork right, away from the fence and admire the views right, looking eastwards across the plain. The path soon splits and we take the left fork, following a white arrow on the tree, and climb a little into the woods, with some magnificent beech trees. A few yards into the wood is a stile over a wire fence, and at the cross paths just beyond, turn right, and this path leads alongside the wire fence to the right. It becomes a sunken path going downhill, through woods, passing an iron gate on the right and a few steps where the Ridgeway footpath comes in from the right. After about 20 m the path splits, and we take the left fork, which is the Ridgeway footpath, and have now rejoined the original route of the walk.

CONTINUATION OF THE MAIN WALK

If not going to Coombe Hill and Chequers, ignore the iron kissing gate on the left and continue along the track, steadily climbing. Pass a stile and path leading off to the right, and soon pass another stile on the right by a wooden gate. The track has narrowed by now but just keep straight ahead along the clear well worn path, climbing slightly to a major cross paths. Turn right here, following the Ridgeway footpath sign, and ignoring the Ridgeway bridleway which goes straight ahead. The North Bucks Way goes for 35 miles back the way we have come.

We are now rejoined by anyone using the extension walk to Coombe Hill.

Descend a few steps to a stile, with a wooden kissing gate to the right of it. Go straight on into the field, and emerge from the trees to admire wonderful views all round, with the plain to the right, and Whiteleaf Hill and Stokenchurch radio mast ahead. Pulpit Hill is to the left, and if you are feeling energetic, climb over the butts of the old rifle range and up the grassy slope to a stile and into the woods.(6)

This section of the walk has a variety of trees, very colourful in the blossom season, and also birds and flowers, with white, blue and yellow butterflies. Walk straight on, through a wooden kissing gate to a major cross path. The Ridgeway turns right here for a few yards, but we go straight ahead. Pass through a gate in a wooden fence, and on the right notice a stile to the right and two cattle drinking troughs, but just keep straight on along the grassy path, descending steadily. Admire the great views back left to Pulpit Hill and straight ahead to Whiteleaf Hill, with a golf course club house just visible on the hillside below the woods.

Follow the worn path downhill through the scrubby vegetation, until on the right we notice a large garden and house. Just past the garden is a wooden gate, but do not go through this, as 10 m further on is another gate which will be a better route to follow as it enables us to avoid walking along a narrow but often busy road. Once through the gate, on the right is an old notice board with information about the Grangelands Nature Reserve. (7)

Follow the path through woods to the road, cross over and turn left to reach the Plough Inn. This is the only pub situated on the Ridgeway, and is the pub where, until a few years ago, they used to bake a cherry pie in the shape of a coffin on 17th June to commemorate John Hampden, as his body rested here on its way to the funeral (see Walk 9).

The Ridgeway sign points off the road to pass in front of the Plough, with picnic tables at the front and a garden at the rear. Just beyond the Plough turn right at the Ridgeway Bridleway sign, but this drive soon splits and here fork left following the Ridgeway Footpath sign. Pass through an iron kissing gate and start climbing, following the yellow arrow and acorn. Fork right but keep on climbing, to reach a cross paths. Keep straight ahead through magnificent beech trees as the path steadily climbs on a ridge, with deep valleys down to the right and the left. The path bends round to the right, then levels off, but has another short climb to a wooden kissing gate, and out on to the grassy patch (8) which is the flat summit of Whiteleaf Hill, above the top of the white cross, which is an area of chalk exposed by removing the vegetation cover. Remains of ancient settlement have been found on this hill top. (9)

The way ahead is to turn left, but before doing so, walk to the top of the scarp. The cross is just below, and there is the magnificent view across Princes Risborough and miles of rural countryside. The earliest record of the cross is in 1738, when shown in a view from Wain Hill, and the first written record is in 1742. There may be an earlier reference to it in a Charter of 903 when a boundary mark was recorded here, and in the time of George IV an Act of Parliament said that it had to be cleared and kept in good condition by the Hampden estate. The origin is uncertain and it has been suggested that it was an early Christian fertility symbol, or a marker for an ancient trackway, but is more likely to be a seventeenth- or eighteenth-century folly, or to have been created by medieval monks from Monks Risborough or from Missenden Abbey. The 24 m (80 ft) cross is about 22 m (72 ft) wide at the top, widening to about 91 m (300 ft) at its triangular base. An information board gives some history of the slope and surrounding landscape. (10)

Turn left following the Ridgeway, and walk through a wooden gate. Ahead is the car park and picnic area which could be used as an alternative starting point, if desired – just walk towards the summit of Whiteleaf Hill from the car park, but before reaching it, turn right at the cross paths mentioned here. To return to our route, before reaching the car park turn left at a cross paths off the Ridgeway to continue the walk, following a blue bridleway sign.

It is possible to take a SHORT CUT back into Princes Risborough, which reduces the walk by 4 miles. This involves walking through the car park where an information board tells that the Whiteleaf Cross area is an 11-hectare (27-acre) site overlooking the Chiltern scarp. The hill has ancient barrows and in the woodland there is evidence of coppicing. In former centuries the oak trees were used for making ships for the navy and in later years the beech became important for furniture.

The short cut takes us across the road from the car park, through a small wood, continuing along the Ridgeway. Go through an iron kissing gate and walk along the edge of a field and then at the far end of the small field turn right, and take the path leading downhill to the bottom of the field, and then through a kissing gate on to a narrow and steep path. Descend quickly through trees and shrubs, straight on at a cross paths, over a small stile and along the field margin for two fields. At a major track, turn left along the Ridgeway, and then turn right at the road and into Princes Risborough.

CONTINUATION OF MAIN WALK

For the main walk, pass through the gap in the wooden fence and take the path into the woods, with the open field to the right. The broad path is fairly level, though two or three footpaths go left and steeply downhill. Views left are limited in summer, but in winter the deep valley can be clearly seen. The path splits and a yellow arrow points left along a footpath, but we keep right following the blue arrow. At a cross paths, with arrows painted on the trees and posts, turn right, and the open field is still to our right. Walk along the edge of the wood, pass a path turning left, and continue to the end of the wood, where just beyond the gate is a cross paths, and Green Hailey Farm is to the right.

Turn left here at the cross paths, along a track, which soon leads to a path between fences, with an open field to the right, and Sergeant's Wood to the left. The path begins to drop into a valley, and then enters a wood (Kingsfield Wood), continuing to descend. A four-ways split is reached just inside the wood, and our route is straight on along the broadest and clearest path, between fences with one strand of wire. There is another parallel path to the right of this route. Keep along this straight path, passing an area of fine tall beech trees on the right and an area of conifers to the left. Descend to a hollow, which is often damp in the bottom, and on up the other side. Cross a stony track and continue to rise slightly, still with two parallel paths. Cross an earth track, and straight on through a dark coniferous wood, to reach a major cross paths.

Turn right here, still in the wood, with the line of Grim's Ditch (see Walk 9) just to the right. Soon emerge to an open field, and follow the right margin. At the end of the field, go over the stile and straight ahead into the woods, which are light and mainly beech here. A ditch and embankment of Grim's Ditch are clearly visible 20 m to the right, and several beech trees are growing on the top of the embankment. A path comes in from the left and we keep straight ahead, soon to cross the ditch and then walk along the embankment. Climb a stile to reach the road at Redland End and go straight ahead, along the minor road signposted to Lacey Green, passing a few houses and then between woodlands, with ditch and embankment still visible to the right.

At the T-junction we go straight ahead over a stile and into more woods. Before doing so, a detour of a few hundred metres to the right leads to Parslow's Hillock, the location of the famous inn, Pink and Lily. (11)

The path from the T-junction begins to descend, with an erosional gully in the middle of the path. Two paths come in from the left, but keep straight on, passing a flint and brick house to the left, and then walking along a stony driveway to a narrow road, Lily Bottom Lane. Turn left here for a few metres and then right, alongside the brick wall of Lily Bank Farm. Climb slightly into a few trees, and as the broad path levels, look for a footpath going right over a small stile. Cross the field to a stile in the hedge on the far side, and then on to the far right corner of the large field to a stile between two gates, and ahead along the left margin of a field. Go over another stile, cross a track and over another stile and along the margin of a small field, and then another stile, track and stile into the next field. Head diagonally right to a gap in the middle of the hedge, and over the stile and straight across the middle of the next field, to come alongside a hedge for the last few yards. Go over the next stile and along the right margin of the field, and then another stile and one more field, with the windmill over the hedge to the right. At the end of this field, go over a stile and on to the road, by a bus shelter. Turn right, and pass the entrance to the windmill (12) and then the Whip Inn, on the corner of Pink Road.

Go on past the pub and the cross roads, keeping straight along Wood Way. Use the footpath on the left of the road and begin to descend. The pavement ends and although there is a narrow verge for most of the way, take great care walking along this road. A narrow road joins from the left and there are a few flint and brick houses (including a new development) near this junction. When the road bends sharply to the left, Wardrobes Lane goes off to the right, and our path ahead goes between these two roads. Climb a small stile and take the path across the middle of the field, passing beneath the electricity wires. At the end of the field go over the fence and diagonally left across the next field to a small stile on the left margin. A tennis court can be seen over to the right. Once over the stile, turn sharp right to follow the hedge. At the end of the field, cross a stile, the drive (leading to Wardrobes) and then another stile, to go straight ahead along the field margin, with good open views away to the left. When the hedge bends right, just keep straight ahead and soon drop down to a hollow. Cross the stile and climb up the other side, and at the top of the climb there are good views of the wooded scarp to the right, and the spire of Princes Risborough church ahead. Keep straight on to a stile and then along the margin of the next field, with a fence and fragmented hedge to the left. Drop steeply down into a dry valley, and at the bottom of the hollow some fine chestnut and other trees are growing to the right. This is Pyrtle Spring, at the junction of the chalk and gault clay, though no water has been seen flowing on my recent visits. Continue to the end of the field, where a broad track is reached, the Ridgeway. Cross this and keep straight ahead along a field margin and the path leads out on to a road which is the edge of Princes Risborough. Follow this road gradually downhill, and at the main road turn right. There is a pedestrian crossing, which may be necessary if it is a busy time of day, and just beyond the crossing is the Sorting Office and Park Street. Turn left along this road, and at the end of this cul de sac, keep straight ahead on the footpath which leads to the car park by the church.

(1) Monks Risborough contains a row of beautiful old cottages with gardens to match. Flint Cottage is one of several old thatched buildings, and it is worth walking to the corner to see the stonework on the wall of Monks Thacky. The house called Churchways at the end of the lane leading to and from the church has an exposed section of wattle and daub wall showing behind a glass panel. The church of St Dunstan seems large and light, and has a large section of exposed flint wall at the west end. The building dates from the thirteenth and four-teenth centuries, though some work was started in the twelfth. Outstanding features include the rood screen from about 1500, with pictures of nine of the Apostles on it, as well as carvings of flowers and leaves. On the floor in front of the Apostles are medieval tiles from the famous tilery at Penn which supplied many churches as well as Windsor Castle and the Tower of London. The tower is fourteenth-century and contains six bells. There is a twelfth-century Norman font, and fifteenth-century pew ends with slightly weird but interesting carvings of figures and heads. Can you work out what they portray? The windows include the unusual Fragment Window, made up from the pieces of glass uncovered in the churchyard in 1807. The 1971 sculpture of St Dunstan, by Maureen Coatman of Askett, is based on the legend of his encounter with Satan, in which he is

about to twitch the Devil's nose with some tinker's tongs. Above the church door in the fifteenth-century porch there is an earlier reminder of the story, with a pair of blacksmith's tongs which converge on a face carved in the wood, to show how Dunstan overcame the Devil. Also near this door is the stoup, where the Holy Water was kept in order that villagers could make the sign of the cross before entering the church.

Before returning to the dovecote to continue the walk, be sure to admire the garden of the Old Rectory to the east of the church. This is the source of a spring which feeds a stream, and now creates a marvellous environment for a water garden full of colourful flowers.

Hollows in the field around the dovecote are relics of medieval fishponds. In the dovecote, the birds were kept as a source of food, especially for the winter months, and the nests were in recesses on the inside walls. The building dates from the sixteenth century and is a Grade II Listed Building which was restored by the local council with volunteer labour, in 1983.

(2) The North Bucks Way is 35 miles in length, from Great Kimble on the Ridgeway to the county boundary of Buckinghamshire and the Grafton Way at Wolverton just north of Milton Keynes. The North Bucks Way was created by the Ramblers Association in 1972, and it crosses the Vale of Aylesbury near Eythrope Park and Waddesdon Manor, and goes over Quainton Hill which gives panoramic views all round.

(3) The name of Great Kimble is probably derived from Cunobelinus or Cymbeline (see Walk 7). The church of St Nicholas is situated on a small hill and has a tower with masks and faces on it. The oak screen across the tower arch is a memorial to Robert Hampden and there is another Hampden memorial, with a copy of the famous John Hampden protest.

(4) All Saints church, Little Kimble, contains a Norman font, has some thirteenth-century tiles on the floor, and fragments of medieval glass, but the main treasure are the wall paintings,

the finest in the county. These wonderful wall paintings are part of the complete wall covering which was educational in origin. In the days before books were available, and when most people could not read, the paintings were an attempt to inform parishioners of Biblical stories, which the priest could refer to in his preaching. Eleven of the saints can be identified, most outstanding being St Francis preaching to the birds.

(5) The Chequers Reserve is managed by BBONT in an agreement with the Chequers Estate. It covers an area of 33 hectares (83 acres) and is part of the Kimble Warren SSSI, with woodland down in the coombe and grassland on the valley sides. The grassland is maintained by grazing and poisonous plants, notably the ragwort, are removed by volunteer workers. The grassland is noted for its variety of plants, such as rock rose, wild thyme and squinancy-wort. Deadly nightshade, *Atropa belladonna*, is found here, too.

(6) Pulpit Hill is covered with woodland, mainly of beech but with areas of whitebeam as well as other deciduous and some coniferous trees, and it is rich in wild life. It is managed by the National Trust. On the summit, near the steep edge overlooking the plain, there are remains of a small hill fort extending over 1.6 hectares (4 acres). It has a single ditch and bank on the west side, where there are very steep slopes, but on the eastern side is a double bank as the gradient is quite gentle. The main entrance was on the east side. There are paths on the hill top, which can also be reached from the car park at grid ref 834046 on the narrow road east of Lower Cadsden.

(7) Grangelands Nature Reserve is an SSSI, covering 11 hectares (27 acres) with areas of chalk grassland and scrub, and is managed by BBONT, together with Buckinghamshire County Council. It contains a rich variety of plants, with up to thirty different species being found in a square metre. Bird's foot trefoil, quaking grass, sheep's fescue, glaucous sedge and dwarf thistle are amongst the specialities here, and insects are abundant. The land was ploughed during World War II and

then was grazed for a few years. When grazing ceased, the scrub took over, and volunteers from BBONT have recently cleared some of the reserve, often by hand. Fences have been erected round some of it and grazing has been reintroduced, with the support of Buckinghamshire County Council and English Nature. Butterflies thrive in this reserve, including the marbled white and chalk hill blue.

(8) The area of chalk grassland just above the cross is well worn and trampled down by all the visitors. A few flowers such as bird's foot trefoil, selfheal and salad burnet can be seen here. In the area of longer grass on the edge of the woods other flowers include rock rose, field scabious, thyme, marjoram and cowslip. The four remaining juniper trees on the hill top are on the edge of the grassland near the cross.

(9) On top of Whiteleaf Hill (90 m high and 200 m north of the cross), are two Bronze Age round barrows, with beech trees growing on them, and there is a Neolithic long barrow about 50 m to the east of the cross. The kidney shaped long barrow just above the cross was excavated in 1934–39 by Sir Lindsay Scott, and was found to contain a wooden burial chamber with the remains of a middle-aged man, many of whose bones were arthritic. A second burial place was found at the southern end of the barrow, and animal bones, flints and Neolithic pottery were found.

(10) Near the cross, areas of juniper bushes have been killed by overshading, but the chalk grassland has survived in places. The geology of the hill is mainly chalk, capped by a thin layer of clay with flints along the summit of the ridge. It is the Chilterns Countryside Management Project team from County Hall in Aylesbury who manage the site. Work as part of the Chilterns Project has cleared areas of wood and scrub woodland to help preserve wild life, and during the last three years the grassland has been cut in an attempt to simulate the natural grazing of the chalk turf. This is quite difficult, but is an important part of helping to preserve a variety of flora, though

it is not as good or effective as having traditional grazing. It is planned that some sheep will be brought in during summer months to help with this process.

Woodland management is part of the project and there are many variations of woodland type on the hill. Semi-natural woodland occurs in places where the tree cover has been continuous since 1600, with beech, ash and oak on the higher land and on the acid soils of the clay with flints. Ash, sycamore, and whitebeam are commoner on the slopes, with yew and holly in places. Recent planting to replace damaged trees has included all those tree types, but also hazel and cherry.

On the scarp face to the north of the cross there is woodland which has grown on what was formerly a grassland area. This happens naturally, but was encouraged by tree-planting during World War II, in order to prevent the cross from being used as a navigational aid by the enemy. This area of secondary woodland is mainly ash, whitebeam and beech, with yew and holly, as well as several spindle, hawthorn and wayfaring trees.

(11) Several of the windows in this old inn, the Pink and Lily, were blocked up to avoid window tax, but it is more famous for its links with Rupert Brooke. He is most noted for his poem 'The Soldier' with those famous lines:

> If I should die think only this of me:
> That there's some corner of a foreign field
> That is for ever England.

He also wrote a serious poem entitled 'The Chilterns', but his famous effort on this pub is more lighthearted:

> Never came there to the Pink
> Two such men as we I think
> Never came here to the Lily
> Two men quite so richly silly.

It has been suggested that the other such man referred to could have been Winston Churchill. The pub was named after Mr

Pink, a head butler at the Manor House, and Miss Lily, a chambermaid from Hampden House, who ran the inn together.

(12) The Chiltern Society windmill is open to visitors from May to September on Sundays and Bank Holiday Mondays, 2.30–5.30 p.m. It dates from the seventeenth century and is thought to be the third oldest windmill in Britain. It was restored by the Chiltern Society under the direction of the engineer Christopher Wallis, son of Barnes Wallis. It is probably the oldest surviving smock mill in Britain. The name smock mill is thought to originate from the similarity in shape of these mills to the smock overall worn by farm workers. Only the upper part of a smock mill turns round, unlike a post mill as seen at Pitstone (Walk 5). Some of the machinery in this mill probably dates from 1650, when it was built. It was brought to Lacey Green in 1821 and ceased to work at the beginning of World War I. It was used as a weekend cottage for a time, and in World War II was a watch tower used by the Home Guard.

The Chiltern Society windmill at Lacey Green

9 The Hampdens

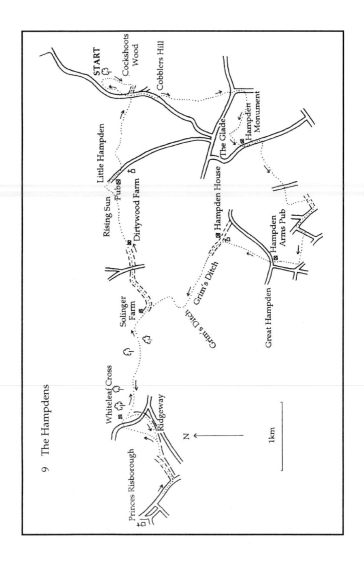

Walk 9 – The Hampdens

Located on OS Landranger 1:50 000 sheet 165 and on OS Explorer 1:25 000 map 2.

Length of walk is 10 miles.

Time required is 5 hours.

Terrain – undulating with a few short hills.

From Princes Risborough the starting point in Cockshoots Wood (grid ref 873043) can be reached via narrow roads through Great Hampden, but it is easier to approach from the A413 Wendover to Great Missenden road. Two miles south of Wendover turn right at Emerald Valley Nurseries where the signpost points to Picnic Site and Cobblershill. Go over the railway line and when the road splits take the left fork which is Cobblershill Lane.

The nearest train service is at Princes Risborough, and the walk can be joined from there – as described later in this section.

This walk passes through the two villages of Great and Little Hampden in the heart of delightful countryside – a walker's paradise. Much of the walk is on the Hampden estates, which probably helps to explain the fact that such a delightful rural atmosphere has been preserved only 40 miles from London. The beech woods and the rolling hills and vales have the feeling of places the world has passed by. John Masefield rented a farmhouse near Great Hampden in 1909 and the area provided the inspiration for his poem 'The Everlasting Mercy'.

The car park and picnic site were donated to the County Council by the Little Hampden Estate and are an excellent starting point for this walk. Like many woodland areas there are numerous paths through the woods. Two paths lead from the car park into the woods, and we take the one on the opposite side of the car park from the road, following a yellow arrow and a white arrow on the post at the edge of the car park where the path begins. Do not follow the path on the right side of the car park, viewing from the road side, which has the blue arrow.

Climb up into the woods, and where the path soon splits at a tree with two yellow arrows, ignore the left fork but just keep straight ahead. At a cross paths where five or six routes meet, ignore the broad tracks to right and left, but go straight ahead on a bearing of 160°, along a narrow path marked by yellow arrows on the trees. The path leads on through the beech trees, many of which are quite young, and then bends round slightly to the right, but just follow the clear path with yellow arrows on trees, with a bearing of 180°–190°. After being joined by a path coming in from the left, the path becomes broader and soon an open field can be seen to the left. We are now nearly parallel to the edge of the woods. When there are woods on the left, instead of the open field, we reach a cross tracks with five ways, and here we take the second left turn to follow the yellow arrow on the tree, on a bearing of 220°. After about 30 m the path splits, and we follow the yellow arrow straight on at about 260°, and soon see a garden on the right, and then we emerge from the woods at a house with a driveway. Turn right here and after about 50 m reach a narrow road and turn left.

Note that it is often useful to have a compass handy when walking through woodland, as all sense of direction can be easily lost, and new tracks or paths are not always clearly shown on OS maps.

The South Bucks Way (see Walk 7) which we have followed for the last 50 m goes straight across, and we shall return on that route in 3 or 4 hours, but before that, turn left along the road to pass Cobblers Hill Farm on the right. When the road splits, take the right fork, which is Cobblershill Lane, and when this lane bends right, turn left past an iron gate and a public footpath sign, to walk between two hedges. After about 30 m bend right to walk along a field margin with the hedge to the right. At the end of this field, walk into the wood, the path staying close to the margin of the wood, with an open field on the right and views down to Hampden Bottom, a large dry valley followed by the road from Princes Risborough to Great Missenden.

Emerge from the wood and go straight ahead along the left side of the hedge, with an open field sloping down to the left, and another field on the right side of the hedge. The path leads along the margin of this large field and then across the middle of the next field, which is very flinty. Descend towards the road at a junction and go straight across along a narrow road.

This rises gently and winds between hedges. At the end of the first field on the right, turn right up four steps, and follow the narrow path between a garden on the left and hedge on the right, and then straight ahead on the margin of a field. Over to the right is the large white building of Court Field House. Go over a broken-down stile and into Pepperboxes Woods, managed by the Woodland Trust, which is gradually being turned into a more broad-leaved wood, as the larch are being removed. Soon reach a cross track, but carry straight on, following white arrows on the trees. When the footpath splits at a T-junction turn right, and at the cross paths go straight ahead, with an open field to the left of the path. Go over the stile on to the Glade, a long narrow grassy avenue, with views left up to Hampden House a mile away, and right down to the Lodge Gate Houses, known as the Pepperpot Lodges. These were built as one-room houses but have been extended. The Glade is a lovely avenue of trees, with beech and oak and a fine show of white blossom in May.

Having seen the Glade, retrace your steps over the stile and along the footpath with an open field now on the right, and back into the woods to the cross paths. Turn right here, staying close to the right edge of the woods, and reach a stile into a small field. Walk along the right side of this field towards the Monument, surrounded by a grassy area and a small hedge.

This is a memorial to John Hampden, erected in 1863, but the inscription is difficult to read because of the effects of weathering. (1)

Turn left along the road, passing Honor End Farm and Honor House, and after about 200 m, at the end of a small wood, turn right, through a small iron gate, and walk along the margin of the field. At the end of this field turn left, with the hedge on our left, and walk to the stile at the far end of the field. Go over the stile and along the margin of the next field, where skylarks may be heard singing. There is much rich farming land around here, but careful land management as well as areas of set aside have encouraged the bird life, as well as insects, flowers and animals. Just before the end of the field go left to follow the path through a short stretch of woodland and down to a minor road. Cross straight over and climb up into the woods. Emerge from the woods, and walk along the right side of the hedge on the margin of a large field. Beyond the end of the hedge, reach a cross paths and turn left, across the middle of the field. At the end of this field go over a stile and along a narrow path between two fences, over a stile into a small wood and then over another stile to reach a track. The stiles are quite high, designed for tall walkers.

The Old Rectory is just a few yards to the left here, but turn right to walk to the narrow road, and turn right again on the surfaced road. When the road splits take the left fork, and turn left again at the next road junction.

After nearly 200 m along this road, turn right, following the footpath sign into the woods, Hampden Coppice. Go through a small wooden gate and past the stone marker post with a horseshoe on it, and climb gently into the woods. At the cross paths go straight ahead and just before the gate and the stile at the edge of the woods, turn right. This path soon splits but take the left fork which runs along the left edge of the wood. Go over a stile and on to the cricket pitch.

Walk round the left side of the pitch and at the road turn left, with the Hampden Arms a few metres to the right. Cross over the main road and straight ahead along a surfaced track leading to a few houses. Where the surfaced road ends, go through a wooden kissing gate and along a grassy drive, with a larch wood to the left and open field to the right. Keep straight ahead through a large open field, cross a drive and continue to a small kissing gate. Walk along the left side of the next three fields, passing to the left of a small pond and reach the church. Pass to the left side of the church and out onto a driveway, but it is well worth pausing for a visit into the church of St Mary Magdalene. (2)

Turn left along the drive and on the right is the magnificent Hampden House (3), and on the left is the old stable block. Walk on through a gate, and along a straight driveway, following the line of Grim's Ditch. (4)

The route is along a driveway as far as the next gate and then goes through into an open field. Just keep straight ahead and, shortly, go through a gap in the fence on the right where horses have to keep straight ahead. The path continues parallel to the bridleway along a line of deciduous trees, with a line of coniferous trees over to the right. When a barbed wire fence blocks the path, move slightly to the left but continue ahead in the same direction, with the bridleway now to the right of the footpath.

At a cross paths turn right off the straight path, and pass a stile into some deciduous woods very rich in bluebells. Shortly cross a track but go straight on following a yellow arrow, with the edge of the woods and an open field a few yards to the right. After a level stretch, the track begins to descend and bend slightly to the left, then descends more steeply, still in the woods. Pass the bottom of the hollow and then begin to climb, at a stony track go right, and after ten yards go over a stile and on to a farm track. Turn right.

ALTERNATIVE STARTING POINT

At this point, Solinger Farm is to the left, and anyone walking up from Princes Risborough station will join the circuit here.

There is a pleasant 3-mile walk from Princes Risborough station to join the circuit through the Hampdens, making a total walking distance of 16 miles. From the station walk into the town centre (see Walk 8), and turn right at the old market building. At the end of High Street turn left, and at the traffic island turn right along New Road, passing the Fire Station. Walk uphill and out of town, and just beyond the speed derestriction sign the Icknield Way crosses the road. Turn left along this track, which is the Ridgeway. Once past the houses, look for the right turn, at the Ridgeway information board, and follow the Ridgeway sign. Walk up the field margin, climbing slightly, with good views left to the white cross and Whiteleaf village. At the top of the field is a patch of scrubland and the slope is becoming much steeper. At the patch of trees, ascend a few wooden steps. The Ridgeway path goes straight up some more steps, but turn left here, and continue along the fairly horizontal path into the woods.

The path soon splits; take the right fork, although there are several possible routes which go to the far end of this narrow strip of woodland. At the far end is a narrow road, and the path ahead is directly opposite, with the bottom end of the cross a few yards to the left. Climb quite steeply, and at the top you will reach a stony track, signposted the Ridgeway. Go straight across, following the bridleway sign, and proceed along a clear path through the woods. Pass three yellow arrows pointing left, but keep straight on, following the blue arrow to a major cross paths, with white arrows painted on trees and posts. Keep straight ahead along a narrower path, into an area of fir trees. At a T-junction with a broader track, turn left, following a line of telegraph wires. The path is joined by a path from the left, and 20 m beyond this the path splits, and here we take the left turn off the main track. White arrows on the trees point the way, and this leads through to an open field with wonderful views ahead. Turn right along the margin of the field, with the wood (Sergeants Wood) to the right. This leads to Solinger Farm, and the path passes to the right of the buildings, and on to the surfaced driveway, and so on to the Hampdens walk.

For the return journey, we pass the left side of the farm, and where the driveway ends and turns right into the buildings, our path goes straight on through a wooden gate and along the field margin with the woods to the left. At the end of the first field, take the path into the woods. The narrow path is marked by arrows and soon reaches the broader track. Turn right here and after 20 m fork left to follow the line of telegraph wires. Look out for the path leading off to the right through an area of coniferous trees and back to a major cross paths. Go straight on here, with an open field to the left, until you reach the Ridgeway and the gravelled track near the top of Whiteleaf Hill. For a variation on the outward journey, turn left here to the car park and picnic place. Cross straight over the road from the car park, through a small wood, continuing along the Ridgeway. Go through an iron kissing gate and walk along the edge of a field, and at the far end of this field turn right, and take the path leading downhill to the bottom of the field, and then through a kissing gate on to a narrow and steep path. Descend quickly through trees and shrubs, straight over a cross paths, over a small stile and along the field margin for two fields. At a major track turn left along the Ridgeway, and then turn right at the road and into Princes Risborough.

MAIN WALK AGAIN

Having turned right, follow this track which becomes stony and leads through to a minor road. Cross straight over and along the track to Dirtywood Farm. Just before the farm yard

turn left off the drive, as a permitted diversion leads round the left side of the buildings to avoid going through the gardens. Beyond the farm the path leads alongside the hedge and uphill to the woods. The path in the woods levels off and to the right of the path is an old chalk pit. An open field soon becomes visible to the left, and then the path emerges from the wood, and gradually passes over the top of an exposed and open agricultural landscape, and after two more fields, reaches the next area of woodland.

The path leads into the woods and at a junction of paths turn right on to a track which is part of the South Bucks Way and leads out of the woods and into the parking area of the Rising Sun, Little Hampden's pub, which gives a friendly welcome to motorised visitors or walkers without boots. To the left is the driveway of Hampden Manor Preparatory School, but we walk on along the village street. The village only consists of farms, a church, the pub and a few houses, and is one of the quietest and most isolated parts of the Chilterns. At the village green turn left to follow the South Bucks Way, but before doing so, walk on along the road, passing two farms and visit the thirteenth-century church (5), one of the smallest in the county.

Follow the signpost and over the stile by the gate, into the woods. A notice provides information about Sir Leonard Figg, the estate owner.

After 100 m fork right off the broad track along a clearly marked footpath. This is a mixed woodland with a few wild cherry trees looking colourful with blossom in the spring. Emerge from the wood and walk along the margins of two open fields, the first with a hedge to the right and the second with the hedge to the left of the path. Climb up towards the woods, and then over the stile and slightly right of straight ahead as the path climbs steeply up through woods. At a cross

The author walking towards Great Hampden church

paths go straight ahead, and soon leave the woods over a stile to go diagonally right over a small field. At the end of the field are two small stiles in quick succession which lead on to a track. Turn right here and walk along to the road. The South Bucks Way goes straight ahead here, but turn left along the road. Pass the wooden house called Old Garden on the right, then an iron gate and a track beyond. Stay on the road, but before it begins to bend right and descend, go right over a wooden stile at a public footpath sign. Head into the woods, through a coniferous area containing some larch as well as evergreens, and occasional yellow arrows on the trees show the way. Go through a more open patch of beech to a cross paths, where a yellow arrow points straight ahead, but blue/white arrows point right and left. Turn left here along a major path, following a blue arrow bordered with white. Arrows on the trees show the way and, at a post with a pale blue arrow on a white disc, bear right and then begin to go downhill to another blue/white marker. Descend more steeply now and bend left, still descending, to reach a broader track with a blue arrow on a post. Go left here and the path soon begins to level, as we reach the car park.

(1) The inscription on the Hampden memorial reads:

For these lands in Stoke Mandeville
John Hampden was assessed at twenty shillings Ship Money
Levied by command of the King
Without authority of law
4th August 1635.
By resisting this claim of the King
In legal strife
He upheld the rights of the people under the law
And became entitled to grateful remembrance.
His work on earth ended
After the conflict in Chalgrove Field 18th June 1643
And he rests in Great Hampden church.

Great and Little Hampden parish was part of the Hampden family estates from Saxon times. Its most famous member, John Hampden (1594–1643) was a leader of the resistance to Charles I and his rather arbitrary form of government. In 1641 Hampden, then MP for Wendover, refused to pay Charles I's unpopular ship tax on some of his land. He took his case to court, but lost and, although ordered to pay up, he still refused. This refusal was one of the factors which helped to start the Civil War. During the Civil War he raised and commanded a regiment, the Buckingham Greencoats. He was regarded as a possible successor to the Earl of Essex as Lord General of the Parliamentary Army, but was wounded at the battle of Chalgrove Field in Oxfordshire, possibly an unintentional self-inflicted wound.

There is a John Hampden Society, one of whose main aims is to make the character and achievements of a great seventeenth-century Parliamentarian better known. The society publishes a quarterly newsletter called *The Patriot*, the name he was often known by. There is a bronze statue of him in the Market Square in Aylesbury.

(2) The church of St Mary Magdalene contains a fine thirteenth-century font, as well as some stained glass and several interesting memorials. On the south wall of the chancel is a Purbeck limestone memorial to Elizabeth, wife of John Hampden (1634). In the south aisle is a monument to Richard Hampden (1662), and the north wall of the chancel has a monument with a relief of the battle of Chalgrove Field. The eighteenth-century memorial to John Hampden was erected by his grandson.

(3) Hampden House is on the right, and on the left is the old stable block, modernised and used as offices. The house, now also used as offices, has an E-shape, facing south, and the central part of the house is the oldest. Parts of the house date from the fourteenth century, but most was rebuilt in the seventeenth, with further changes in the eighteenth century. The Hampden family lived here from the fourteenth century.

It is reported that when Queen Elizabeth I visited Hampden House, a section of Grims Ditch was filled in to level the road to make her journey easier. She commented that there were too many trees in the view from her room, and a wide avenue was cleared overnight whilst she slept. This avenue became known as the Queen's Gap, now the Glade, and the two lodges (Pepperpots) were built later.

(4) Grim's Ditch. The date of this earthwork is unknown, possibly from the Iron Age or alternatively from Saxon times. One of the most distinct sections of this ditch passes close to Hampden House, in a dog-leg direction. It was probably used as a boundary between the common grazing land and small enclosures. The line of the ditch is in places so straight that it must have been dug at a time when the countryside was open and not wooded.

(5) The thirteenth-century church has walls of flint rubble, and is one of the smallest in the county. In the churchyard are several gravestones by Eric Gill who lived at Pigotts nearby (see Walk 13). The church has a timber-framed porch and there is an upper storey, a priest's room, above the porch. The altar is Saxon but the main treasures inside are the thirteenth-century wall paintings.

Buckinghamshire and Oxfordshire – near Stokenchurch

Walks 10 and 11 are close to Stokenchurch and can be reached by anyone using the public bus service to Stokenchurch. The church is St Peter and St Paul, and is built on the site of an Anglo-Saxon timber and thatch church. The chancel and part of the nave date from the twelfth century, but both were rebuilt in the fourteenth and fifteenth centuries. The font is thirteenth century. There are two fifteenth-century brasses on the chancel wall, and they show the Morley brothers, probably ancestors of the residents of the house now called Mallards Court, derived from the name Morley. The church is built of flint and clunch, though partly faced by a gravel covering, and the tower is shingled and has a large clock. A cobbled path leads from the lych gate to the main door. The church survived the attention of the Roundheads, probably because of the influence of Adrian Scrope, from the Wormsley Estate, who was one of the men who signed the warrant for the King's execution. Another famous inhabitant of Stokenchurch was Hannah Ball (1734–92), a friend of John Wesley, and founder of the first English Sunday School, in High Wycombe in 1769.

The village was probably named after the church in the stocken, that is a stockade or fence. Stokenchurch fair was a big wool fair in the Middle Ages, though in later centuries horses took over from sheep. In the nineteenth century the major activity became chair-making and the village grew at this time. There was also some brick-making. It was a coaching station on the turnpike road in the seventeenth century, and Charles II stopped at the hotel here in 1680, which was renamed the King's Head in his honour, though this was later changed to the King's Arms.

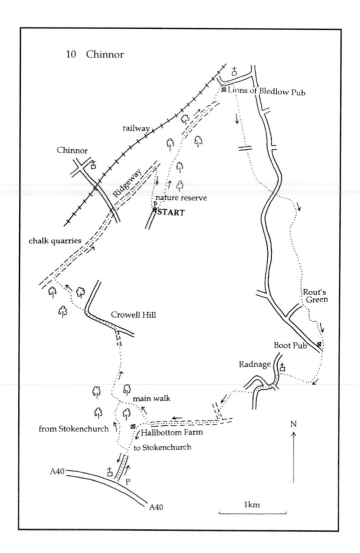

10 Chinnor

Lions of Bledlow Pub

railway

Chinnor

Ridgeway

nature reserve
P
START

chalk quarries

Rout's
Green

Crowell Hill

Boot Pub

Radnage

main walk

from Stokenchurch

Hallbottom Farm

to Stokenchurch

A40

P

A40

N

1km

Walk 10 – Chinnor

Located on OS Landranger 1:50 000 sheet 165 and on OS Explorer 1:25 000 maps 2 and 3.

Length of walk is 11 miles, or 12 if starting in Stokenchurch.

Time required is 5–6 hours.

Terrain – typical Chilterns, with several climbs out of valleys, and one ascent of the scarp.

Starting point is grid ref 767003 which can be reached from the B4009 Watlington to Princes Risborough road near the M40 Junction 6. Leave Chinnor following the signpost to Bledlow Ridge and Steam Railway, go up Chinnor Hill along Hill Road, near the top of the steep climb turn left along Red Lane at a sharp left bend, and when this road bends right, go left along Hill Top Road, marked No Through Road. The car park is on the edge of the Nature Reserve, managed by the County Naturalists' Trust. An alternative starting point can be in Stokenchurch (see p 176).

The walk passes through woodland and across farmland, much of which is arable, and visits the villages of Bledlow and Radnage with their interesting old churches. Do not miss the water gardens at Bledlow with their amazing lush growth of vegetation. Chinnor Hill has a BBONT Nature Reserve and at the foot of the hill are the pits of the Rugby Cement company. The village of Chinnor has a moated manor house, and the church has two fourteenth-century stained glass windows, as well as some brasses and carvings on the mouldings. The large Rugby Cement works is adjacent to the village.

Flowers are abundant, even in the car park, with ladies

smock in spring and a lot of blackthorn around here, with magnificent flowering in May. Set off and follow the direction of a blue arrow, passing the information board of the Berkshire, Buckinghamshire and Oxfordshire Naturalists' Trust Reserve at Chinnor Hill. (1)

Walk past the information board on the broad stony track which soon changes to a grassy track. To the left of the path is a viewpoint looking down the scarp and over Chinnor. An information board explains some aspects of grassland management (see Walk 11). The path begins to descend, with a wire fence on the left, passing a chalk pit, where another useful information board tells us that the origin of the pit was probably a local farmer seeking lime to improve the fertility of some of his fields. The pit is now a sun trap and excellent habitat for a variety of plants and insects, which means also for butterflies and birds.

The path follows the county boundary here, with Oxon to the left and Bucks to the right, and bends left slightly and descends, passing close to a wooden house in the woods on the right. There are parallel paths here, one deep and often muddy, and a drier and higher path to its left. Masses of spring flowers grow in this area, with violets, ground ivy, primroses and wild strawberry. The two paths join near the bottom of the slope, descending between gardens to join the Icknield Way-Ridgeway. Turn right for a few yards along the Ridgeway, passing a house which until about 1925 was a pub called the Leather Bottle.

Up to the right on the scarp of Wain Hill is Bledlow Cross which probably dates from the seventeenth century. Wain Hill was formerly spelt Wynnal, and the small hamlet here is now called Hempton Wainhill. Just beyond the house the Ridgeway turns right, but we go straight ahead (now in Bucks) on the Swans Way and Midshires Way, a stony track with open fields on the right. Where the track bends right, go left on the footpath across the middle of a field, passing close to a telegraph pole.

Over to the left is the railway line from Chinnor to Princes Risborough, part of the old Watlington branch line which opened in 1872 and carried passenger trains until 1957. (2)

Reach the road at the pub, the Lions of Bledlow, and turn right, passing a farm on the left and houses on the right. This is Bledlow village, and after 100 m our path turns right. But before leaving Bledlow, walk on a little further to visit the church and the gardens just beyond. (3)

The path passes between fences and gardens, and then goes over a stile and along the left margin of a large field, over another stile, to continue on the left margin of this field. There are good views of the wooded scarp over to the right. At the end of this field go over a stile, across a track and over another stile, and straight ahead, across the middle of an open field. This descends slightly to two stiles, separated by a narrow strip of trees, and then climbs up through the middle of the next field. Good views of the Whiteleaf cross can be seen over to the left, both from here and later on in the walk.

At the top of this field cross over two stiles and through a few trees, then turn left along the field margin. This is the Ridgeway again. Go through a kissing gate and turn right along the hedge, which leads us to a kissing gate at the minor road, Wigan's Lane. Pass through another kissing gate on the opposite side of the road, walk on through a small field, and another kissing gate, into a larger field. After about 100 m turn right at a cross paths, leaving the Ridgeway which continues straight ahead here.

At the end of this field, the path splits, and we turn right just before the gate to follow the hedge which is the field boundary. Bend left on reaching the track and this leads towards Old Callow Down Farm. Pass to the right of the buildings, including a magnificent house and garden, and on to the path which becomes sunken between two lines of trees. Walk on through a small farmyard and on a narrow path between lines of trees, to emerge on the path with a field to the left, and a view of a hillside beyond. Wild flowers are abundant on this section and there may be skylarks singing in the field around here. The path reaches Neighbours Wood on the left, with open fields to the right, though the path is sunken, restricting views. A carpet of bluebells and celandines grow in the wood to the left.

Emerge from the wood, to pass a bungalow on the left and go along a stony driveway passing a few houses of Routs Green. Twenty or thirty metres after joining a surfaced road, turn left, passing between houses and gardens, and after 100 m, where the road bends left, go right along the narrow footpath between gardens and then into a small wood. Go over a stile and follow the left margin of a small field to a kissing gate, beyond which is a stile and a patch of rough ground. The left margin of this will lead to a house and a stile. Go over this on to the driveway track and turn right. At this point if you look left there is a good view, including the Chiltern Society's windmill at Loosley Row.

After about 70 m along the drive, turn left just past the last house, on to a narrow footpath between a fence and a hedge. This leads to a stile and then a narrow path, with a hedge on the right, and at the end of this field go over a stile and the hedge is now on the left. Reach a stony drive and walk out to the road. The Boot Pub is a few yards to the right.

Cross straight over the road and follow the footpath between gardens, go over a stile and walk on between fields, where there are lovely views up the valley to the left (which leads down towards High Wycombe and contains Colliers Lane further up the valley). At the edge of a small wood the path splits and we take the right turn. Reach a stile and beyond this the path begins to descend through brambles and undergrowth, but soon opening out to a grassy area, with cowslips in spring, and a view ahead to the telecommunications tower near Stokenchurch. On the descent stay close to the right side of the grassy area, and bend right near the bottom along a narrow grassy area, with the bottom of the slope and a patch of woodland now to the left. Follow the margin of this woodland and ahead of you is a large expanse of a grassy downland slope. Where the woodland on the left ends, turn left to a stile. A path is arrowed straight ahead but our route is diagonally right to a stile in the hedge on the side of a large field. Go over this rather fragile stile and an arrow points towards the church tower of Radnage at the opposite side of this field. A stone stile over a flint wall leads us into the churchyard, and we walk along the left side of this small flint-faced church with its squat tower. (4)

The church driveway leads down to a minor road and here we turn left, passing Two Yews Cottage on the left, and the trees in the garden explain the name. Where the road splits, fork right towards Bennett End, and at the next split fork left, which is really straight ahead, and is also signposted to Bennett End. As this road climbs, just before a house on the right, go right over a stile and along a footpath between hedges. After the next stile, go right, along the right margin of the field, climbing steadily. At the end of this field go slightly right on to a surfaced drive and then walk past the buildings on the left and soon see a wooden gate straight ahead, with a stile alongside. Go over this, cross a drive and over another stile, and turn left. Follow the left margins of this small paddock and reach a stile to go over into a larger field. Turn left and start going downhill, and diagonally across the middle of a large field, passing close to a telegraph pole in the middle and aiming to the left of the large barns down on the valley floor.

At the driveway turn left, and after 100 m or so, turn right along the track leading along the floor of the magnificent dry valley. This is Colliers Lane, which is followed by the county boundary, with Bucks to the left and Oxon to the right. Colliers Lane received its name because of the charcoal made in the nearby woods. It was also used as a drove road, in order to avoid the tolls on the turnpike, now the A40. Follow this track for half a mile and the track splits and becomes grassy and less clear, where a hedge comes in from the left. The left fork goes more or less straight ahead to Hallbottom Farm, a large white house, on the route to be followed by anyone going back to Stokenchurch.

ALTERNATIVE – ROUTE BACK TO STOKENCHURCH

Walk on the grassy drive towards Hallbottom Farm, but just before reaching the hedge round the garden, turn left, and start climbing. Walk alongside the field margin with the garden to the right and the open field to the left, and at the top of the garden and past the tennis court, go right over a stile. Head diagonally up to the far right corner of the field, and notice the clear view right to the Stokenchurch telecommunications station. Go over the stile at the top of the field and out on to a surfaced drive. Turn left here and follow this back into Stokenchurch, passing Mallards Court on the way.

MAIN WALK

For the main walk, fork right here to follow a line of isolated trees, oak and ash, and the path will soon lead into the margin of the woods, where footpath numbers may be seen: CR11 right, S82 left. Keep straight ahead along S87, a broad track just in the edge of the woods, with an open field to the left. This is an area rich in bird life and with masses of bluebells in spring.

ALTERNATIVE START – FROM STOKENCHURCH

Coming in from the left here is the route for anyone starting at Stokenchurch. If driving to Stokenchurch, leave the M40 at Junction 5. There is parking near the King's Arms Hotel. If using public transport there are regular bus services from Amersham, Chesham, Oxford, Cambridge and High Wycombe, so access is fairly easy.

From the centre of Stokenchurch, walk along the edge of the grassy area at the side of the King's Arms Hotel opposite the Post Office and the Royal Oak. Just behind the King's Arms is

Park Lane, leading to Longburrow Hall. Take this narrow road, and when it turns left into Longburrow Hall and Park, with a playing field area, keep straight ahead on what has become a stony track. Follow this track and just beyond Mallards Court on the left is a footpath sign and a stile. Go over here and stay near the left margin of the field, and begin to descend slightly. At the end is a stile which leads on to a path into the woods. Ignore the right turn after about 10 m, but at the next junction turn sharp right through the wood, to a surfaced driveway which leads to Hallbottom. The path splits and we take the left fork to go over a stile and down across a small field. Go over another stile and straight across the middle of the next field, climbing up steadily. At the end of this field keep straight ahead along the left side of a hazel hedge, to reach another stile and the edge of the woods. The path in the woods leads downhill slightly and meets the major track down in the valley. This is the route of the walk and turn left here, along S87.

MAIN WALK

Just keep straight ahead, passing the path coming in from the left, and look out for the path going up to the right, with CR12 marked on a tree. Turn right along this path which is clear, though narrower than the main track along the valley bottom. There are numerous fragments of flint on this path which soon crosses a track, but continues ahead climbing steadily. When the path begins to level off, an open field can be seen to the left. Wild garlic (*Allium ursinum*) grows here with the bluebells in spring, to make a colourful and aromatic carpet.

The path then descends slightly into a valley which is to the right. The path is joined by a broad path coming in from the right, but just keep straight ahead along an elevated path to the left of a sunken path in a trench. Then we pass barns on the left, there is a garden on the right, and we reach the farm track. This leads out to the road, where we turn left, passing the entrance to Crowellhill Farm.

Follow this road for 300 m and where the road bends right, go straight ahead into the woods where there is a clear track, and a white arrow on a tree confirms the route. There are oak trees on the clay with flint deposits at the top, and some old clay diggings for making bricks may be seen. The path soon begins to descend steeply and will reveal views of the plain in winter, but the scarp is densely wooded, with many young trees growing here, and views will be restricted in summer. There are whitebeam and some yew here, as well as beech. It is all right walking down the steep scarp until you realise that there is an ascent sometime to climb back up to the starting point in the car park. This is a stony path, and can be slippery, or dusty in dry weather. The path is very eroded and gullied in places, and there is an old embankment descending through Crowelhill Wood and coming in from the left. A path joins from the left, and then we begin to level off, in an area of many small trees, spindle, crab apples, hawthorn, blackthorn, roses with hips – different types of trees from those on the scarp.

At the bottom of the slope is a major cross paths, where we turn right along the Ridgeway. Pass the Ridgeway Information Board and walk northwards on a broad stony track, between hedges. The scarp can be seen up to the right, and the quarry workings of Rugby Cement Company are to the left. (5) The dense hedges along this track are rich in fruits and flowers at various seasons, with blackberries, elderberries and old man's beard being prolific in early autumn. Pass a broad track going up to the right, but keep straight ahead. The hollows in the quarry to the left may contain some water, but there is a larger pool to the right, where the digging has gone down to the water table.

POSSIBLE ALTERNATIVE START AND FINISH
Reach the minor road and, at this point, anyone starting from Chinnor using public transport will join the walk, by coming up the road from the left, from the village of Chinnor, and will

also leave on completion of the walk by going back into the village.

MAIN WALK

Cross the road and keep straight ahead along the Ridgeway, and there are now fields to right and left, with a playing field and football pitch in the field on the left, and the church in Chinnor can be seen beyond this. (6)

At a cross paths keep straight ahead along the Ridgeway, passing a sign saying Bridleway: No Motor Vehicles. Pass a house on the right, and soon reach an entrance to the BBONT Chinnor Hill Nature Reserve, with two information boards, one on scrub control (7) and the other with general information about the Reserve (1).

Walk along the grassy path, passing the picnic tables, and keeping parallel with the Ridgeway through the hedge. Soon rejoin the Ridgeway by descending a few wooden steps, and walk on, up a slight ascent to reach a major cross paths. Turn sharp right here off the Ridgeway, almost doubling back, and begin to climb up the scarp. The narrow path through the trees and bushes has been eroded into a trench, and chalk is visible on both sides. The path climbs up and, when it begins to level, notice the soil is darker. We pass a house on the right, Windy Ridge, and continue along the driveway which leads us back into the car park and starting point.

(1) The Chinnor Reserve covers an area of 28 hectares (70 acres), with an area of Chiltern escarpment and woodland. Beech is very common but oak and ash are also plentiful, with some areas of hazel where coppicing has taken place. Clay with flints covers the top of the hill to create a more acidic soil and environment, whilst chalky scrub and grass occur on the alkaline slopes below. The mixed scrub includes hawthorn, privet, buckthorn, spindle. Grassland areas support wild thyme, rock rose, candy tuft, and several types of orchid. Areas

of grassland are grazed by sheep occasionally to help control the scrub development. This Nature Reserve has been designated an SSSI and, in addition to its wild life, contains two Bronze Age burial mounds and three ancient sunken tracks down the scarp. The Reserve has been supported by the Rugby Cement Company.

(2) The railway followed the line of the Icknield Way and goods traffic continued until 1961 when the track from Watlington to Chinnor was removed. The section from Chinnor to Princes Risborough remained in use for the cement works until December 1989 when the entire line was finally closed. The Chinnor and Princes Risborough Railway Association was formed in August 1989 to preserve the 4 miles of this line which had survived, and already Chinnor and Wainhill stations have been restored, with regular trains running throughout the summer, especially at the weekends. The service is run entirely by volunteers.

(3) The name of Bledlow is derived from Bledda's Grave or Bledda's Hill, or possibly bloody hill. Its famous river is the Lyde, which rises from the springs, the biggest in Bucks, in the great coombe beyond the eastern end of the church. The water was formerly used for two mills, Bledlow Mill and North Mill. The position of the church on the edge of the coombe is referred to in the well-known local rhyme:

> They that live and do abide
> shall see the church fall in the Lyde.

The springs were used to feed watercress beds, and are now surrounded by the magnificent Lyde Garden, with a wonderful variety of plants. Dense greenery grows here in a very sheltered hollow, and there are seats and walkways in the gardens, and around the springs and pools. The gardens were laid out in the

Sunken path in Chinnor Woods, going back up the scarp to the end of the walk early 1980s by Lord Carrington, who lives in the Manor House across the road. There are other lovely houses in the village, with thatched roofs and timber frames, and several with small Tudor bricks in herringbone pattern.

The flint church of Holy Trinity is of Norman origin, and contains a Norman font. Part of the church may date from the twelfth century but mostly it is thirteenth. The south door is one of the oldest in Buckinghamshire. There are several old wall paintings, including the medieval painting above the south door showing the Angel of the Lord, and Adam and Eve who are digging and spinning. Windows in the chancel date from the early fourteenth century and there is a fifteenth-century beam in the roof. Outside the church are wrought iron gates which celebrate the coronation of Edward VII. Notice the tower where the clock is offset to the right. A large sarsen stone has been incorporated in the building as foundation for one of the buttresses on the north wall of the tower. Some very tall trees line the front of the churchyard, and daffodils and primroses are magnificent in spring. The church is often open on Sunday afternoons in the summer, and at other times a key may be available from the Old Cottage.

(4) St Mary's church, Radnage dates from the thirteenth century, though with many changes in later centuries. It is built of flint rubble with limestone dressings, and is noted for its thirteenth-century wall paintings. Other unusual and interesting features are the medieval tiles beneath the Addison window, and the font, thought to be Saxon. Over the tower arch is the thirteenth-century painting of the Tree of Life, which has been recently repainted. In the churchyard are several old gravestones, including one which is claimed to be that of the man who killed the last wild bear in England. In reality, the supposed bow and arrow on this stone is an hour glass and scythe. The grass in the churchyard is not always cut short, as plants and insects are encouraged here, to create a mini-nature reserve.

(5) The cement works was founded by W. E. Benton in 1908, producing up to 250 tons in a week using five beehive lime kilns. Changes and improvements in the kilns increased production, reaching an output of 4500 tons per week in 1958. In 1963 the Chinnor works was acquired by the Rugby Cement Company, and increasingly modern and efficient machinery has been used. About 1600 tons of chalk are quarried daily, and this will produce 880 tons of cement. The raw material is from 58–98% pure calcium carbonate, and has to be washed and converted into a slurry. The rock exposed at Chinnor is Lower Chalk (see Introduction page 13) which is softer and greyer than the Middle Chalk which forms the escarpment. As chalk needs to be mixed with some clay, the presence of the impurity is an advantage, and the natural rock is almost perfect for making cement.

(6) The church of St Andrew dates at least from the thirteenth century, and early in the fourteenth century much of the church was rebuilt, the aisles were widened and the tower was built higher. It has a saddle-back roof, and in the tower beneath are bells which have been ringing peals since the sixteenth century. A new Churchill bell was dedicated here in 1965. The church is one of the largest in the county, and much of it has been restored since 1863. When approaching from the lych gate, look at the first wall of the church that you reach, and there you will notice fragments of red tiles in between the flints. These are thought to be of Roman age, and were picked up and used by the local builders when they were building these walls. The rood screen is of oak, worked locally over 700 years ago, and is one of the oldest screens in England. The famous Chinnor medieval brasses have been fixed to the chancel walls, though three were missing when I last visited. The foliated cross, from about 1320, on the north wall commemorates William de Leicester who rebuilt the chancel. It was still there when I visited, and close inspection revealed the head of a priest in the middle. The wonderful oil paintings by Sir James Thornhill

have been here since the eighteenth century. These were the designs for Joshua Price, the glass painter, to copy, when he was creating the north rose window in Westminster Abbey.

Chinnor is an old village, and an Iron Age settlement was set up on the chalk slope as early as the fourth century BC. There is also the site of a Roman villa at the foot of the chalk, and an Anglo Saxon barrow along the Icknield Way is from the sixth century.

(7) Scrub control was necessary because this area had become overgrown with bushes and small trees and other invasive plants which were shading out and killing off the grassland and small flowers. Scrub has been cleared in places to open up sunny glades and larger areas for grassland to thrive. Primroses can grow in spring, and marjoram, cowslip and common spotted orchids grow here. Butterflies are more numerous where there are open spaces in the woodland. Ringlet, meadow brown and skipper butterflies are particularly mentioned on the information board. Birds likely to be seen include four types of warbler, the kestrel, which does well because of the large numbers of mice and shrews, and the redwings and fieldfares which come to eat the berries in winter.

Walk 11 – Stokenchurch

Located on OS Landranger 1:50 000 sheets 165 and 175 and on OS 1:25 000 Explorer map 3.

Length of walk is about 8 miles, with an extra mile walk round the National Nature Reserve on Beacon Hill, if required, and also a mile round the Sculpture Trail. Using public transport and starting from Stokenchurch will add a further 2 miles.

Time required is 4–5 hours.

Terrain – quite hilly with several potentially muddy patches.

The starting point of the walk is reached from Junction 6 on the M40, then follow the A40 sign towards Stokenchurch. Turn right on a minor road at the top of the scarp, where a signpost points towards Christmas Common, and a brown sign points to the Sculpture Trail. A few hundred metres along this road, take the first right, at the narrow road signed by an upright sarsen stone, and drive on to the parking place at grid ref 733966. Notice the other sarsen stones in the car park.

Most of the walk is in Oxfordshire, though Stokenchurch is in Bucks. The county boundary is very irregular, passing close to the telecommunications station, Lower Vicar's Farm and the car parking and picnic area in Cowleaze Woods. Starting from a National Nature Reserve, we pass through woods, downland and farms as well as going beneath and over the top of the M40, and find huge contrasts between the busy road and the peace and quiet in the heart of the woods. Keep an eye open for red kites in this area.

Go through the end of the car park past the notice board and

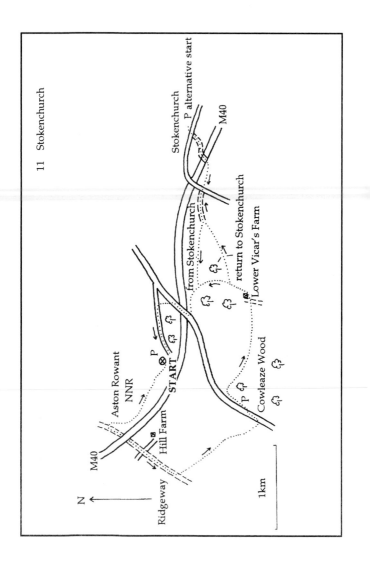

11 Stokenchurch

on to a small concreted area with magnificent views out across the very noisy M40 and the Thames Valley beyond. Drop steeply down the Chiltern scarp, some of the path having been stepped. Parts of the path can be muddy and become slippery after heavy rain, as always happens on chalk slopes. The chalk particles also become very clingy and will stick to your boots. The fences and kissing gates are all in good repair here.

At the bottom of the slope emerge into the open where the path then splits. Keep left, along the bottom edge of a delightful grassy slope, with flowers in the summer months and possibly with sheep and lambs. This leads round to the edge of the National Nature Reserve (1) and down on to the Ridgeway (see Walk 5), which here is not on to the ridge. Turn left along this broad track, and pass beneath the motorway, where there is a raised footpath, to avoid the pool which is frequently present in the subway.

Go straight ahead, and notice up to the left the lovely dry valley and coombe (see Walk 6), in the other part of the National Nature Reserve. Crops grow on the lower land and grassy scrub is higher up the slope. At a cross tracks you will see Hill Farm to the left, with the scarp beyond, and to the right the narrow road which leads to the village of Lewknor. Keep straight ahead, passing the Ridgeway notice board, with informative comments about the Code of Respect. After 200 m, leave the Ridgeway via a small gap in the hedge on the left, and follow the path across a flinty field, over a stile and into the woods. Pass through a small scrubby woodland, excellent for birds and flowers. At the edge of the small wood, pass over a stile and turn left along the field margin.

Follow the field margin for three fields, climbing over two stiles and begin to ascend the scarp. Away to the right can be seen the chimneys of Didcot Power Station. The path becomes a track, which can be very muddy, and climbs steeply up to the road. Turn left along this minor road, and soon reach the parking and picnic place of Cowleaze Wood. (2) The highest point of this wood reaches 253 m (830 ft), one of the highest points in the Chilterns.

At the far end of the parking area is the beginning of the Sculpture Trail (3), well worth following the circuit of 3 km. Many of the sculptures are on the main paths, but others are less obvious. The location of the sculptures and a map of the paths can be seen on the information board at the northern end of the car park. In addition to the delights and interest of the sculptures, there is also a War Memorial in the woods, to the crew of a 51 Squadron Halifax, killed in action on 31st March 1944.

Whichever you choose, our onward walk is by following the path to the left side of the information sculpture, passing between two colourful picnic tables. The path is soon joined by one coming in from the left, but keep straight on, near the left-hand margin of the wood. The wood is mainly deciduous but does contain a few coniferous trees along this path. The ground is covered by bluebells in the spring, and an abundance of birdsong may include bullfinches, several varieties of tits, and jays. The broad stony path stays close to the left margin of the woods, and soon reaches a cross path where the telegraph wires cut through the wood. Here is sculpture number 2, Sophie Horton's Rural Industry, made of cast concrete and forest floor looking like the chimney of a kiln or brick works. Further along our path, where a narrow worn footpath goes off to the right, is the location of Paul Amey's Fish Tree, sufficiently realistic to be easily missed. Made of welded steel and cast resin, it almost integrates with the natural environment.

Just before reaching the end of the wood is Richard La Trobe Bateman's Bench, of oak and stainless steel, soaring up towards the sky. If you have enjoyed the sculptures turn back into the woods to walk the full circuit, but otherwise go on with the walk. The way ahead is over a stile at the end of the wood.

Enter the Wormsley Estate (4) and take the path which goes

straight across the field, and steeply down into a dry valley, at the bottom of which is the impressive flinty complex of Lower Vicar's Farm. Woodland covers many of the slopes around here, and there is much evidence of recent planting. The tower of Stokenchurch mast is over to the left.

At the bottom of the field, turn left along the farm track. After 50 m turn right off the track, pass through a few trees, and over a stile to the right of the farm buildings with traditional flint walls and a large wooden barn on a flint lower wall. Walk diagonally left, across the grassy field, over a stile and into the woods – Langley Green Plantation – and follow the path through the woods, which are rich in bird life. The path is clear, but several of the trees are marked with white arrows as well, to emphasise the correct route. Climb slightly through the woods to a cross paths, and turn left to continue the walk to Aston Rowant National Nature Reserve.

ALTERNATIVE

For anyone who started from STOKENCHURCH and wishes to return there, do not turn left, but go straight ahead, along footpath L20. Continue climbing slightly, but once over the top of the hill, begin to descend quite steeply. Go over a stile and out of the wood, turning left for a few metres before turning right, across the middle of the field, with good views of the lovely flint buildings of Reed's Farm on the left. Leave the field over a stile and, as the path splits, take the left fork (S3), crossing the stony driveway, and then head steeply up the wooded slope through South Remlets Wood. This leads through to the track where you turn right to walk across the open field and retrace your steps into Stokenchurch.

MAIN WALK CONTINUED

Having turned left (L19) in the wood, follow this clear path to be soon joined by a path coming in from the right (L21) which is the route to be used by anyone starting from Stokenchurch.

FOR ANYONE STARTING THE WALK FROM STOKENCHURCH

Leave the centre of Stokenchurch near the King's Arms Hotel. Cross over to the Four Horseshoes, and walk along the A40, with Ye Fleur de Lis pub across the green to the left. Turn left along the stony track named Cricket Ground and walk past the cricket pitch to the footbridge over the M40. From the footbridge the path leads between houses and gardens to a narrow road. Turn left here and after a few metres turn right along Mill Lane, at the side of house numbered 73. This leads to a main road, cross it and just keep straight ahead along Mill Lane, and the track then becomes the driveway to Reed's Farm. Pass between hedges at first and then across an open field, descending towards the woods. Just before reaching the wooden gate, S3 leads off left (this is the return route). Take S1 over the stile to the right of the gate and diagonally cross a small grassy field, with views to Reed's Farm down to the left. Leave this small field and walk into North Remlets Wood on a path leading through small trees, largely hawthorn. Go over a stile, keep straight ahead, and then go over another stile before descending through an area of larger trees down into a valley. The climb up the other side is gentle at first. Pass through a grove of large beech trees and begin to climb more steeply, on path L21. On a level patch at the top of the climb is an area of recent planting and then a T-junction with a clear path is reached. Turn right here on L19 to join the main walk.

MAIN WALK CONTINUED

This is in Langley Green Plantation, which contains many beech trees. The drone of motorway traffic will become audible, and we soon reach the edge of the Wormsley Estate. At the road, climb on to the embankment, turn right and walk over

Reed's Farm, in the walk from Stokenchurch

the bridge above the M40. There is a good view of the cutting on the left, which takes the M40 through the edge of the Chiltern Scarp and down on to the plain.

About 150 m beyond the bridge, turn left on the footpath (L32) going up a few steps into the wood. Go over the stile and pass through a small larch wood and then out on to a narrow road. Turn left along this road, soon to pass a footpath sign pointing right into the woods of the Nature Reserve on Beacon Hill, but keep straight on and follow the road to the car park, unless you intend to walk all round the Reserve.

(1) The Aston Rowant National Nature Reserve is partially on the top of the Chilterns, but also on the scarp slope. The name is derived from the Rohant family, and from East tun meaning the east settlement. The Reserve covers an area of 104 hectares (258 acres) and includes Beacon Hill, at just over 250 m (800 ft) one of the highest summits in the Chilterns. The M40 was opened in 1973, and its construction split the Reserve in two. Both sections contain areas of grass downland, scrub and beechwood, typifying the Chilterns as they were.

The information on a National Nature Reserve notice board in the car park mentions the woods and the chalk grassland. 126 species of plants have been recorded on the Reserve, and in one square metre there may be up to fifty different species. It also mentions that red kites exist around here (5) as well as hawfinches, and there are badgers and deer in the woods. Violets, wood barley and large white and slender-lipped helleborines can also be seen. More than one third of the total area is grassland, and English Nature uses a flock of sheep to graze this to help maintain the grasses and small flowers and prevent scrub from taking over. The downland flowers include frog orchid, fragrant orchid, Chiltern gentian, dwarf thistle, dropwort, clustered bellflower, and the wild candytuft which grows in areas of bare soil created by the rabbits. The areas of scrub in the Reserve are cut in rotation to keep them under control, and also to provide differing types of vegetation cover. Hawthorn grows very successfully, and areas of pure hawthorn may be completely removed, whereas the juniper, which is not common, is encouraged as it attracts a few different varieties of insects.

(2) Cowleaze Woods cover just over 29 hectares (70 acres) and were largely planted by the Forestry Commission between 1957–66. They contain a mixture of broad-leaved and coniferous trees, with the coniferous growing much faster than the broad-leaved. The coniferous include all three common varieties of larch, the European, Japanese and hybrid, but it is planned that the coniferous will gradually be removed, as a small source of revenue. This will also give more space for the remaining trees, and the wood will then consist mainly of oak and beech.

(3) The Sculpture Trail is a joint venture between the Forestry Commission and the Chiltern Sculpture Trust, and work began in summer 1991. It is the third sculpture trail to be created in England's forests, the first being in Grizedale in the Lake District in the 1970s, and the second in the Forest of Dean. Some sculptures are occasionally removed and new ones are added from time to time, and occasionally the sculptors can be seen working on new projects on the site where they are to remain. Each work is related to its location in some way, even though a variety of materials are used, not just natural and local materials, as has been the case in the other two sculpture trails. Larch beams, oak and beech wood, tin, steel, and even a polypropylene carpet are amongst the materials used, but my favourite is Nature Girl, a painted bronze figure.

The Information Centre is made of thuja and larch, and beneath its shelter is a map of the paths and sculptures. Walk along the main path to the right of the information centre and this will lead to Nature Girl, a painted bronze by Laura Ford; the untitled pink granite by Hideo Furuta; and the Forest Floor, a polypropylene carpet and wood by Anya Gallaccio. These

will provide a sample of what can be seen, and you may then wish to walk on for a circuit of the wood, or simply retrace your steps to the information centre.

(4) The Wormsley Estate was owned by the Scrope family for 400 years and then by the Fanes through female succession. It was sold in 1984 and it was on this estate that a new cricket pitch was created by Paul Getty in 1990. The area of the estate is more than 810 hectares (2000 acres), of which half is woodland and half is farmed. Major clearance and replanting has been carried out in the woodlands following the 1987 and 1991 storms. The farming is mixed arable and pastoral, and both the farmland and the woodlands are managed positively with an eye to conservation and amenity. The public rights of way pass through a mixture of woodland, pasture and arable land.

(5) Red kites are regular sights, floating around overhead. They were formerly widespread in Britain, but became extinct due to persecution by the end of the nineteenth century. A few pairs survived in mid-Wales, and in recent decades have recovered and increased their numbers to over a hundred pairs. During the years 1989–94 a reintroduction project was undertaken by English Nature and the RSPB in two carefully selected areas, one in northern Scotland and the other in southern England, and young birds were brought from Spain and Sweden. They spread out from the immediate areas, but seemed to return for the summers and certainly for breeding. The success of this scheme so far can be shown by the fact that there are over 200 kites in southern England, mostly in the Chilterns, and in 1994, twenty pairs in southern England reared thirty-seven young. Some of the young born here in previous years bred for the first time.

The kites spread in northern Scotland too, and so there are now three areas in Britain with successful kite colonies. In

Drive and large barn at Lower Vicar's Farm

order to build on this exciting development and ensure the long term survival of kites in Britain, more colonies are required. In 1995 the release of young kites in two new areas began, one in the Midlands and the other in Central Scotland. It is hoped to ensure that red kites will be a permanent feature of the British bird population.

Buckinghamshire – near the Wycombes

Walk 12 – West Wycombe

Located OS Landranger 1:50 000 sheet 175 and 165 and
OS 1:25 000 Explorer map 3.
Length of walk is 8 miles.
Time required is 4 hours, but with so many features of
interest on the way, a whole day could easily be spent in
this area.
Terrain – includes two steep climbs and small areas of
potentially muddy paths.
Starting point is at the western edge of West Wycombe
village where there is free parking adjacent to a large
garden centre. Situated on the A40 between
Stokenchurch and High Wycombe it is easily accessible
from the M40. Grid reference of the starting point is
826947. An alternative starting point for anyone using
the railways could be at Saunderton station.

There has been a village on the site of present day West
Wycombe for a thousand years, and it grew up on the main
route from London to Oxford which later became the A40.
Houses were built on both sides of the old through route. The
village can still be overwhelmed by traffic, in spite of the
construction of the M40. West Wycombe is now a National
Trust village, containing a wealth of architectural interest, with
buildings dating from the sixteenth, seventeenth and eighteenth centuries, and very few later additions. So the buildings
have been preserved in a time capsule, with Renaissance,
Queen Anne, Georgian and Tudor buildings to be seen within
250 m of each other. Many of the buildings were decaying

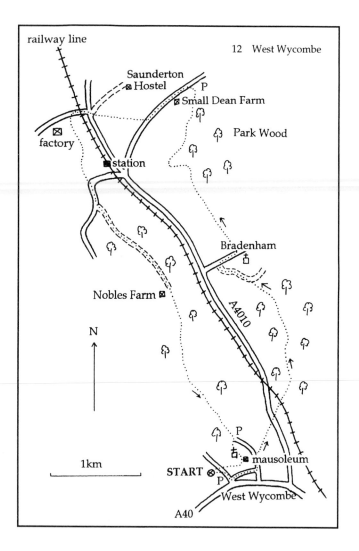

railway line

Saunderton
Hostel   P

Small Dean Farm

Park Wood

factory

station

Bradenham

Nobles Farm

A4010

N

1km

P

mausoleum

START   P

West Wycombe

A40

when Sir John Dashwood offered the village for sale in 1929 in small lots. The Royal Society for Arts acquired several of them from the West Wycombe Estate and began repair work. These buildings were taken over by the National Trust in 1934.

The walk takes in the National Trust village of Bradenham, some delightful and typical Chiltern scenery of hills, valleys and woodland, as well as all the features associated with the Dashwood family in the West Wycombe area.

Leave the car park, ignore the signpost to the church, Mausoleum and caves up the hill, and walk along Chorley Road, back to the A40. Directly opposite is the entrance to West Wycombe Park, the home of the Dashwood family and now in the care of the National Trust. (1)

Turn left along the main road to walk through the village which contains an assortment of interesting old buildings. Some of the cottages have tiled roofs which are steep, as they were probably thatched originally. The Swan Inn has a fire mark above the door, which showed that the inn was insured. In the eighteenth century when fire engines were operated by insurance companies, the firemen would only attempt to put out fires insured by their own company. The Black Boy yard was formerly used for the coaches, when it was a coaching inn, and the George and Dragon was another old coaching inn. Several of its windows have been blocked, possibly because of the window tax from 1696–1851. There were eight coaching inns in the eighteenth century. A fascinating architectural leaflet about many of the buildings is available from shops in the village.

Just before one of the shops there is an archway on the left called the Church Loft and we turn left here. Before doing so it may be of interest to walk on further to look at other buildings, especially Crown Court on the right which contained eleven tiny picturesque cottages in the eighteenth century. At the far (east) end of the village on a patch of grass is an eighteenth-century milestone, erected by Lord de Despencer (Francis

Dashwood) in 1752. From the City (London) is 30 miles, from the University (Oxford) is 22 and from the County Town (Aylesbury) is 15 miles.

The Church Loft dates from the fifteenth century and was a rest house for pilgrims. Our route takes us through this to Church Lane and on up the fairly steep hill. Church Lane has an old furniture factory, with wood store and tool room downstairs, and workshops upstairs. Several buildings on Church Lane have dated bricks in their walls, inscribed with the names of the builders. Pass a few houses, including the Rectory on the right, until you reach a narrow road coming in from the left, from the caves.

About 30 m beyond this junction go right through a kissing gate into a field. Go diagonally across the field to the far corner down to the road, with the woodland we are heading towards directly ahead on the hills over the other side of the valley. Down to the right as we cross the field are the buildings of Flinthall Farm, surrounded by a hedge. Cross the road, the A4010, and walk alongside the edge of the field to the railway line. Pass through a kissing gate, cross the railway line and go up a few steps and then through an iron gate. The path into the woods is between barbed wire fences and climbs steadily.

Pass an open field to the right and then the path levels off and bends to the left away from the margin of the woods. When the wood opens out slightly there are views downhill to the left, and in the more open patches the road or railway might be seen in the valley, with the tree-capped hillside beyond, which is the line of our return route on this walk. Wild roses and honeysuckle grow well in this part of the woods. Join a track coming in from the right, but just keep straight ahead. The path splits, with white arrows as markers on a tree. Ignore route 14 which goes off right, but keep ahead along path number 13, which soon begins to descend. This is an area of recent planting, still with undergrowth, small plants and many wild flowers. Descend into a small valley, climb steeply up the other side, having crossed a grassy track in the bottom of the hollow. The path levels off, and there are quite a few fir trees on the right. Where the path splits and the broader grassy track goes straight on horizontally, we go off to the left, on the narrow path descending and leading into a good stand of beech trees. Then the path descends more steeply, with an open field to the left, and soon emerges on a stony track, with a brick wall straight ahead. Turn left and follow the track alongside the wall which is the boundary of the Bradenham Manor gardens. The track bends right and the Manor House becomes visible, with a tennis court and a croquet lawn. Emerge at the cricket pitch and village green, with delightful flint houses along the road on the far side of the green.

A National Trust notice board in a small parking area by the green gives local information. (2) The National Trust rents many of the houses to tenants, local people wherever possible.

Follow the track past the pavilion and along the left side of the pitch, turn right at the narrow surfaced road and walk on to the major road. Our route ahead is to the right, but first turn left to admire the flint houses, including the Old Forge, and at the main A4010 is the Red Lion.

Turn back here and retrace steps, passing a farm complex with a large old barn, the Old Post Office on the left, and the cricket pitch on the right of the road.

Leading up to the main gate of Bradenham Manor (3) from the green is a cobbled driveway, though it is no longer used. Alongside the Manor is the church of St Botolph (4).

Opposite the church is a driveway alongside an old chapel, which is now the Youth Hostel. Turn left along this driveway and when this ends, go over the stile and along the margin of a small field. After another stile is a larger field and keep straight ahead. Across on the left is a wooded ridge, our return route, and to the right are wooded slopes with a radio mast

just showing above the top of the hill. The broad path leads across beautiful countryside, passing between open fields. At a cross track is a simple log seat, and we keep straight ahead, beginning to climb slightly to the top of the field, with the wood now to the right of the path.

Pass through a wooden kissing gate and follow the margin of the field, with a fenced and hedged wood to the right. This is Park Wood, managed by the National Trust. The large buildings of the engineering factory down in Saunderton can be clearly seen to the left. Pass another of the simple log seats and continue along the margin of the woods until reaching a wooden kissing gate where the path goes into the woods. Follow the clear path, which soon is joined by a broader track coming in from the right. Keep straight ahead and when this track splits, ignore the right turn and keep straight on. When the path splits again, take the left fork going downhill, which is marked by an arrow with a horseshoe on it. The path soon narrows from track width, and down to the left can be seen Small Dean Farm. A small gate on the left leads to the footpath down to this farm, which is a slight short cut if required.

A muddy patch is reached in a hollow, and the path climbs up a few steps to join a broad footpath (with a No Riding sign) coming in from the right. Continue along the track with the horseshoe symbol, until reaching a junction of four paths, where our selection is the left fork, with the edge of the woods just to the left. Emerge at a small car park, where there is a National Trust information board. This car park could be used as an alternative location for the start of this walk.

Turn left along the narrow road, and walk between a fine flint house on the right, with Small Dean Farm on the left. The farm has some magnificent buildings including a huge old barn and a grain store on staddle stones, and the short cut

Bradenham Green

footpath, mentioned above, emerges on to the road just beyond the main farm buildings. The road begins to climb and once over the brow and descending, where the road bends left, look for the footpath on the right. Walk along the left side of a hedge, not over the stile on the right of the hedge. Follow the field margin and, as it bends round to the left, look for a gap on the right, and at a marker post go through into the next field. A long diagonal path cuts across the field to the far right corner and to the road, and up on the right can be seen the green tower on top of Saunderton Hostel. At the road, cross over and turn right, then after 30 m turn left along Haw Lane, following the sign to Bledlow Ridge.

Pass beneath the railway line, and just beyond the house on the left, and before reaching the factory (Molins International Precision Engineering), turn left along a broad grassy track following a public footpath sign. At the end of the factory and the wire fence on the right, the path bends diagonally to the right, and reaches a hedge which is then followed on our left. The field slopes up to the right, but we stay down on the level. At the end of the field, go through a gap in the hedge and walk along the bottom of the next field with a hedge to the left and sloping ground going up to the right. This leads through to a narrow road and we turn right to continue the walk.

Only 300 m down to the left is Saunderton railway station, suitable for anyone using public transport for this walk. This is the Marylebone to Princes Risborough and Aylesbury line, with regular services during the week, but no trains stop here on Sundays.

To continue, walk along the narrow road, and at the driveway going off left to Nobles Farm, leave the road and take the footpath just inside the field margin to the right of the surfaced driveway. Climb up the hill which becomes very steep parallel to the drive, or walk on the farm drive if you prefer. At the top of the climb is a major cross paths and our route is straight ahead to Nobles Farm. Pass three open fields on the right and a small open field on the left, with views down into the valley. The surfaced driveway ends at the magnificent flint buildings of the Nobles Farm complex which have been modernised.

At the farm buildings is a footpath pointed to the left, but this goes down to Bradenham, and we go straight ahead along a grass and flinty track, with woods to the left and fields behind hedges to the right. Go straight ahead through a wooden gate and along the track, now with woods on both sides. Fir trees on the right and then also on the left, make a variation from the predominantly deciduous woods seen on the walk.

Reach a major cross paths, keep straight ahead along the broad horizontal route in an area where wild flowers are abundant, especially in the cleared areas. A path comes in from the right and, soon after that, pass an open field on the left, and then back into woodland for the final few hundred metres. Noise of traffic may become audible down to the right, and then the gold ball on top of the West Wycombe church tower becomes visible straight ahead. Reach an iron gate and shortly beyond that is the large grassy parking and picnic area. The National Trust notice says that the West Wycombe hill top is closed to vehicles from sunset to sunrise.

At the far end of the grassy area is the church of St Lawrence (5), a flint building with a tower and a gold ball on top. There was an Iron Age British camp where the church stands. Just beyond the church, on this fascinating and historical hill top is the Mausoleum, built in 1765. This hexagonal building of flint and Portland limestone was constructed roofless, the idea based on Constantine's Arch in Rome. Decoration which can be seen through the gateway includes several friezes, vases and columns, and there is also the tomb of Lady Despencer, an ancestor of the Dashwoods.

From the main entrance to the Mausoleum is a grassy slope going steeply down the hill. The long straight road below is the A40 leading out of West Wycombe towards High Wycombe and London. It was originally built by Sir Francis Dashwood when he diverted the Oxford turnpike in order to extend his park. The broad grassy path leads downhill, and good views open up of the yellow house in West Wycombe Park. Turn right at the wooden steps and look on to the roof tops of West Wycombe. At the small road turn right, passing the entrance to the caves (6). Follow the narrow road, West Wycombe Hill Road and pass the Victorian school on the way back down to the A40 starting point.

(1) West Wycombe House and Park were donated to the National Trust in 1943. The grounds only are open in April and May, Sunday and Wednesday, from 2–6 p.m., and at Easter and on May Bank Holidays on Sunday and Monday. House and grounds are open in June, July and August, Sundays–Thursdays, from 2–6 p.m.

The Dashwood family owned the village and the estate from 1698. The 2nd Sir Francis Dashwood (1708–81), who became Lord Despencer, was a very enigmatic figure – a Jekyll and Hyde type, famous and notorious. He was a distinguished politician, both as Chancellor of the Exchequer and as Postmaster General. He rebuilt West Wycombe House, redesigned West Wycombe Park, and rewrote the Book of Common Prayer. He also redesigned West Wycombe church and yet he was best known for the foundation in about 1755 of his Hell Fire Club. This was notorious for orgies and drunkenness – or was it merely the high spirits of young aristocrats? He rebuilt the house in the 1750s in Palladian style, with columns, fine ceilings, tapestries and furniture. The Park surrounding the house was landscaped by Humphry Repton, and contains a swan-shaped lake. The River Wye, from which Wycombe takes its name, rises in the park and was dammed to create the lake. There are several temples, including one designed by Revett who also designed parts of the house.

(2) The National Trust acquired the land and several buildings including the Manor House and the Red Lion in 1956, under the will of Mr E. E. Cook. Bradenham used to be a centre for cutting sarsen stones (see Introduction page 15 and Walk 18). Bradenham is a Saxon name, meaning home in a broad valley, or possibly just Brada's homestead. The green was part of a much larger common, and the woods surrounding it were probably a deer park and a vital source of venison. There is still a Park Wood nearby, and a section of Grim's Ditch runs through this wood along a south-easterly trend.

(3) The main entrance to Bradenham Manor now comes off the road, rather than across the edge of the green, and the Manor is now the Grant Thornton National Training Centre, running residential accountancy courses from Mondays–Fridays. This brick-built house with its hipped roof dates from 1670, but in an earlier building on the site Queen Elizabeth was entertained in 1566. Isaac d'Israeli lived here, and he enlarged and modernised the house in the early nineteenth century. He died in 1848 and a tablet memorial to him and his wife can be seen in the church. The Manor was the home of his son Benjamin who later bought Hughenden, near High Wycombe. The Manor was the basis of the house Hurstley in *Endymion*, one of Disraeli's novels, and he also wrote *Sybil* and *Coningsby* whilst living here. A gate through the garden wall leads into the churchyard, and Isaac d'Israeli is buried there.

(4) The church is dedicated to St Botolph, but has a different location from most St Botolphs which are generally found outside the gates of towns. It is a small and quite simple twelfth-century church, made of dressed flint and some freestone on the outside, but with undressed flint and clunch on the inside. The tower is fifteenth century and contains three bells, two of which were cast in the thirteenth century, amongst the oldest in England. The clock is early seventeenth-century. In the tympanum is a memorial to St Botolph with three flying swans and a model of the church. The lych gate was erected by

the parishioners of Bradenham in 1920 and is inscribed with the words 'Lest we forget'.

(5) The fifth-century Iron Age British camp covers about 1.2 hectares (3 acres) and is located in a good place to command the valley below. The inner vallum forms the boundary of the churchyard. The bank is about 3.4 m in height on the north-east side, but on the south-east side was damaged by the building of the Mausoleum. In St Lawrence's church is a painting on the ceiling of the chancel of the Last Supper by Giovanni Borgnis, an Italian who also painted several ceilings in West Wycombe House. The interior of the church is a copy of the third-century Sun Temple at Palmyra near Damascus. The font depicts a snake creeping up it to attack the doves around the bowl. Behind the altar are oak carvings by Grinling Gibbons. When Sir Francis rebuilt the church on the hill top in 1751, he heightened the tower and added the great ball, covered in gold leaf. The ball is hollow and has room inside for six people to sit on a circular bench. The church is open in June, July and August, and the church tower is open on Saturdays, Sundays and Bank Holidays from April to September.

(6) The caves are on the site of a quarry, and were dug out by Sir Francis Dashwood between 1745–52 to give employment and income for farm workers who had been unemployed because of poor harvests. The stone was used for building the main road to High Wycombe when it was straightened by Sir Francis. The caves were hollowed out as a secret place to hold meetings of the Hell Fire Club, which were thought to involve black magic and orgies. Passages and chambers extend beneath the hill, and several statues are placed at strategic positions in the caves. One of these is of the famous American Benjamin Franklin, who came and stayed with Sir Francis whilst in

Bradenham church and Manor House from across the valley

England. Sir Francis built a mock Gothic-style ruin at the entrance to the caves and just inside this the present Sir Francis Dashwood built an underground cafe in 1995. The caves are open weekends throughout the year, and on weekdays from March to October.

Entrance to the caves and cafe, West Wycombe

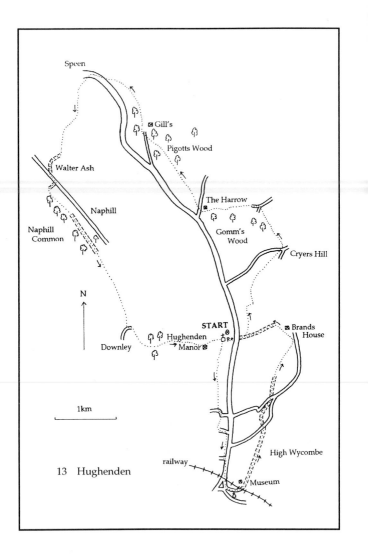

Speen

Gill's

Pigotts Wood

Walter Ash

Naphill

Naphill
Common

The Harrow

Gomm's
Wood

Cryers Hill

N

START

Downley

Hughenden
Manor

Brands
House

1km

13 Hughenden

railway

High Wycombe

Museum

Walk 13 – Hughenden

Located on OS Landranger 1:50 000 sheets 175 and 165 and OS Explorer 1:25 000 map 3.

Length of walk is 9 miles, or 13 if the tour of High Wycombe is included.

Time required is 4 hours, or 6–7 for the longer option.

Terrain – mostly flat, though with a few slight hills. The paths are clear and well worn, though on the edge of Naphill Common there are so many that it could become confusing.

The starting point is at grid ref 864955 on the A4128 2 miles north of High Wycombe. There is ample parking alongside the church in the grounds of the estate of Hughenden Manor.

From the former home of Benjamin Disraeli this walk crosses hills and valleys in an area of great rural charm to the north of High Wycombe, as well as including a stroll round this town to see its modern face and discover a little of its historical importance as a routeway and an industrial town.

The first church in Wycombe was built by Thane of Bradenham and consecrated by Wulfstan who was Bishop of Worcester from 1072–92. Some of the building materials came from the Roman villa which was situated on the Rye, the large open area east of the town centre on the valley floor near the River Wye. The church was extended in the thirteenth century, the old tower was taken down in 1509 and the present tower added in 1522. Amongst many interesting links with the town's history are the Dove window near the organ, installed by Dame Frances Dove, Headmistress of Wycombe Abbey School, and the Petty Memorial window. This commemorates William

Petty, Lord Shelburne, the Prime Minister in 1783 who negoti-
ated with Benjamin Franklin at the end of the American War
of Independence. In the town centre outstanding buildings
include the Guildhall (1757), and the Little Market House or
Shambles (1761). This octagonal shaped building is known as
the Pepperpot, and was built to a Robert Adam design. Nearby
is the Red Lion, where Disraeli spoke at the Wycombe election
in 1832. The town was formerly known as Chepping Wycombe,
the word *chepping* (a market), being derived from *cheapen*, the
Old English for to buy or to sell.

SHORTER WALK

If taking the 9-mile walk, without visiting High Wycombe,
start from the church of St Michael and All Angels, walk back
to the road, over the cattle grid, across the small stream, the
River Hughenden, which dries up occasionally. Pass the Lodge
and then turn left along the main road. After about 30 m cross
over to walk along a stony track, which soon deteriorates to a
footpath between hedge and fence. What a relief to get off that
road! After just over 100 m, look for a gap in the hedge on the
left, and go over a small stile which may be overgrown in the
summer.

FULL LENGTH WALK

If walking the extra 4 miles to include High Wycombe in a 13
mile walk, set off from the church and walk down the valley
across the wide open field, passing to the right of the cricket
pitch, with good views of the house up to the right. Walk
alongside the stream, passing a pool created by damming. In
the nineteenth century several small weirs were built to help
trout-breeding. Go over the stile at the end of the Hughenden
Estate, and continue down the valley, on the right side of the
stream, heading towards a tall chimney. Walk along the road,
with Harrison & Sons on the right. When the road bends left,
past Harrison's car park, go straight ahead along the footpath,

passing to the left of the tall chimney. At the road turn left, passing CompAid and Broom Wade, and then turn right along the footpath with the factory on the right and the tiny stream on the left. This is the short-lived Hughenden (or Hitchin) River, which goes underground as it reaches the Wye valley, having risen from springs about a mile north of Hughenden church. At the next road turn left, and then right at the main road. At the railway bridge where the road splits, fork left into the town centre, passing the Chiltern Shopping Centre and approaching the church.

You may want to look around the interesting buildings in the town centre before leaving High Wycombe on the road to the north of the church. Once past the church on your right and the line of shops on the left, turn left along a broad surfaced path going uphill between houses, and then over the railway line. Turn right on Priory Avenue to visit the old Castle and Museum, where there is an exhibition of old chairs. The Museum is situated in a magnificent flint house, in the grounds of the old Castle. (1)

Take Greenway, the road alongside the Museum, and continue uphill away from the town centre. At the end of the Greenway, cross over the road and go up the steps on to a surfaced footpath which is known as Benjamin's Path. This leads between houses on the right and the huge cemetery on the left. Climbing steadily all the time, some good views open out to the left, across High Wycombe to the radio mast on Great Tinker's Hill, and the Isaac d'Israeli Monument, a memorial to Benjamin Disraeli's father, erected by his daughter-in-law in 1862. Climb steadily to reach a road, but cross it and just carry straight ahead, along a narrower path. This is soon joined by a path coming in from the left, but just keep ahead, on a sunken path, with trees on both sides. At the next road go straight across towards the Green Hill Wood sign, but walk a few metres along Brands Hill Avenue, where a footpath leads into the trees along the backs of the houses. The clear and broad path goes alongside the edge of gardens to the right, with a field to the left. Once beyond the houses on the right, playing fields will be passed, and over to the left is a large white house, Brands House. Do not go over the stile to the road, but turn left over a stile into the field. Stay near the right margin of this field and pass the front of Brands House. Go over the stile at the end of this field and straight ahead across a stony track to walk along a broad path with a house just to the left. The track narrows but remains a clear path through trees, and begins to go downhill between hedges. As the valley bottom and the road become visible and the Hughenden Estate can be seen on the other side of the valley, look for a stile in the hedge on the right about 150 m before reaching the road, and this is where we join the 9-mile route from Hughenden church.

SHORT (AND LONG) ROUTE CONTINUED

Once over the stile, the path leads on the field margin, with a hedge to the left, and open fields on both sides of the path. Pass a barn to the left of the path, but keep straight on to the end of the field. Turn right here, with the hedge on the left-hand side, and begin to climb slightly. Less than half-way up the field, go left over a stile, on to a narrow path between fences and lines of trees, with fields on both sides. The settlement of Hughenden Valley can be seen down to the left. The path is level at first, but then begins to climb and bend slightly to the right, going into woods and then passing some gardens on the left. Leave the woods through an iron kissing gate, and walk along the right side of a small field, through an old wooden gate, another field, an iron gate and along the right margin of another small field. After the gate at the end of this field is a small patch of rough ground, a wooden kissing gate and a second patch of rough ground, before reaching the road on Cryers Hill.

Cross over the road (A4128) and turn right. Just past the

school turn left along a narrow path between the school and a house. Once past the school playground and playing field, bend left for a few metres and then right, to emerge in an open field, with a big hedge and trees just to the right of the path. At the end of the field go right slightly, but more or less straight ahead, with Gomm's Wood (2) to the left and a wire fence and open field to the right. At the end of the wood go over a stile and straight ahead on the right side of the field by a wire fence. At the end of this field pass through an old iron kissing gate, straight across the drive, over a small stile and pass through a few trees. Then cross another drive, go over a stile and turn left, to walk along the left margin of the field, by a wire fence and trees. Wonderful views now open out to the right, looking northwards. At the end of the field go over a stile on to a narrow path between fences, passing to the right of a hut with a cross on it and a large white house. At a cross paths, where a path comes from the woods on the left and goes across the field on the right, keep straight ahead, and soon begin to descend between barbed wire fences, with woodland on both sides. This leads steeply down to the houses in a small modern development. At the houses go straight across the road, and on to a narrow path between gardens, to a stile and then into the pub yard and car park. It is the Harrow, an attractive flint pub, with a large garden.

Just to the left is a road junction with North Dean and Speen along one route, and Hampden and Aylesbury along the other. We turn towards Hampden, but only for a few metres, as we really just cross the road, past the post box, to an iron kissing gate. The path heads across the middle of the very flinty field, climbing slightly towards the end of the field. Go over the stile at the end of the field and up a steeper slope, across another field, with trees 30 m to the left, and at the top of the slope, the trees of Piggott's Wood can be seen ahead.

Go over a stile and on to the clear path which leads into the woods, through a few magnificent beech trees at first. The

wood opens out for a time, and the land can be seen sloping down to the left. Just keep ahead, and emerge at a narrow road where we turn right to pass a small house with a stained glass studio and show room on the left. A few hundred metres along this road is the farm complex which was once Eric Gill's community (3) and is now used as a music camp. But we do not go so far, as after about 200 m along this road, when it turns right, we go left along a broad track, signposted public footpath. At the wooden building, where the main track goes straight on, turn right along a clear path into the woods. An open field is just visible a few metres to the right of the path. This path leads through to a stile at the far end of the wood, and beyond the stile we follow the right margin of the field, which slopes steeply down to the left where a row of houses can be seen. There is a narrow strip of woodland just to the right, beyond the wire fence. At the end of this field go over a stile to the right, and join another path coming along from the right.

Continue more or less straight ahead, through a wooden gate, along a path between hedges, with trees to the left and an open field to the right. After about 50 m go over a stile and into the field. Follow the hedge on the right at first, but then head diagonally across towards the bottom left corner of this field, where a small stile leads us through a small old fashioned meadow rich in wild flowers and butterflies, and then down to another stile and a road.

We do not turn right along the little road, Spring Coppice Lane, but go across to the slightly larger road and turn right to walk on up the hill. Pass the Scout Hut on the right, and Speen Baptist church on the left, a flint and brick building dated 1813. In the lych gate of this church is a memorial to the men of Speen who lost their lives in World War I.

Hughenden front garden

Continue up the hill, and just past the 30mph sign is a footpath going off to the right. Across the road is a surfaced driveway where we turn left. About 20 m along this, just before Pye Croft, a footpath goes up a few old wooden steps and passes between gardens to a stile. Beyond the stile, cross a small paddock, then another stile and continue along the right margin of the field, with houses and gardens to the right. Go over another stile and along the right margin again, with a few larger gardens to the right. Keep straight ahead, which really requires a few yards left first, before going along the margin of the field with a hedge on our right side. Follow this hedge as it goes downhill to the margin of the woods.

Beyond the stile the track immediately splits. Take the right fork, to follow the right margin of the woods, with open fields down to the right. Descend to the end of the wood and to a cross paths at the bottom of the valley. Go over a stile and straight ahead, climbing across a small field, then over two stiles and into the next field. Climb up the left margin of this field to a gate at the far end, but ignore the white arrow pointing straight ahead. Once out of this field, do not go straight ahead along the hedge, but cut diagonally left across the middle of the very flinty field towards a tree and a line of hedge in the hollow ahead. In the middle of the field, the hollow is a small dry valley, and from the bottom ascend slightly alongside the hedge. At the far side of the field turn right along the edge of the field, with the backs of houses on the left. At a stony track, turn left, and follow this between playing fields on the left and houses and gardens on the right. This is part of Walter's Ash.

At New Road, cross over and turn left, and just beyond the small pond on the right, and nearly opposite the entrance to RAF High Wycombe, turn right on the short road between houses to a footpath leading into the woods of Naphill Common. Once in the woods, turn left along a broad path running parallel with the houses and their gardens. Keep straight ahead, passing houses, bungalows and then more houses, but when the houses have just come to an end, at a cross paths turn left. After 20 m pass over an old low boundary embankment, and bearing slightly left, walk on until reaching a stony drive. Turn right along this and follow it as it passes a house on the left, then a few more houses, before arriving at a small green with several houses around the left side of it. Walk to the right of the green, and at a large oak tree the drive splits. Down to the left can be seen a main road, but turn right here and go back into the woods.

After about 50 m is a major cross paths, and the stony drive goes straight ahead, but we turn left along a public bridleway, which is a broad avenue between trees.

We are now following the blue arrow indicating a bridleway. This route is parallel to the houses about 50 m to the left, and goes straight on through these woods for more than a mile. This broad track does have some muddy patches. Pass a cross paths, where a house is clearly visible to the left, but keep straight ahead, following the blue arrow. We pass another cross paths, then a cross tracks, and then pass an open patch with bracken and a few trees. Keep going ahead, following the broadest path. At another cross paths by a small pond bear right to pass the pond, and then bear left. At a cross tracks, which is really a driveway to Cookshall Farm to the right of our route, go straight ahead, still following a blue arrow. Carry on through the woods, although we are now near to the right edge of a narrower strip of woodland. Houses are still to the left, and open fields are 30 m to the right. Ignore a footpath (No 6) going right over a stile and into a field. Keep straight ahead, passing another small pond to the left of the path, and a path going off right, shown by a yellow arrow. Go on beyond a cross paths, and soon arrive at a narrow road. The field across the road is the Downley cricket pitch, which becomes a football pitch in the winter.

Turn left along this narrow road, and at the T-junction, the de Spencer Arms is up to the left, but we turn right along a stony track, with houses on the left. When the track bends left, go straight on across a grassy patch, with houses away to the left. Follow a clear path as it leaves the open grassy area to go downhill into the woods. A broad path descends to a meeting of five paths at the bottom of the slope. This is also the edge of the Hughenden Manor Estate and a National Trust notice board can be seen.

Turn left and go past this notice board, and where the path splits, take the left fork to go down the valley. Emerge from the woods and take the path between wire fences and open fields, walking down a dry valley. Walk into the woods and go straight ahead, following a blue arrow. The path splits and we take the left fork which begins to climb slightly and winds its way up through the woods towards Hughenden Manor. (4)

Walk out on to the driveway, with the house to the right and the stable block, shop etc on the left. Continue down the drive and then take the path between the church and Church House (5) back to the starting point. Excellent teas are served in the Stable Block cafe whenever the Manor is open.

(1) The castle was built on the site of an Iron Age hill fort, with commanding views over the valley. The castle mound is covered by trees, but good views all around are possible in winter when the leaves have fallen. In the Museum is an account of the fascinating history of the furniture industry, which already existed in the eighteenth century. In the early 1800s changes in farming and in paper-making, the major occupations at that time, resulted in many people being out of work. Improving communications with London and the local timber resources helped the development of the furniture industry. In 1875 there were 120 furniture factory workshops in High Wycombe, and the number was still increasing. The speciality chair was the Windsor, but many other varieties were produced, and sent to London and to many countries

overseas. Much of the chair industry was in the hands of small domestic manufacturers. The bodgers who turned the chair legs and stretchers often lived in the woods in simple huts, felling their patch of trees between November and March. Before 1914 furniture was the only big employer in the town.

(2) Gomm's Wood has been managed under the council's Wycombe Woodlands Strategy since 1990, protecting it for future generations. It provides opportunities for involvement in conservation and management, with footpath improvements, coppicing and the creation of glades and other differing habitats for plants and insects. The 14 hectares (35 acres) contain woodland of varying ages, scrubland and some chalk grassland.

(3) Gill's Place is in Pigotts Wood. Eric Gill, sculptor, engraver and author, was born in Brighton in 1882. He was articled to a famous architect, W. D. Caroe in London, but soon found the modern thinking in architecture was not to his taste. He converted to Catholicism in 1913 and set up craft and religious communes, first at Ditchling, where he began to build up his reputation in stone lettering. His first exhibition came in 1911. In 1924 he moved to Capel y Ffin in the Black Mountains for four years, and was then at Pigotts from 1928–40. He used the farmhouse and other buildings, including a chapel where he is buried. Although he worked on sculpture and some wood, as well as writing books, his main fame was for his lettering in stone. Amongst his most famous sculptures are the Stations of the Cross in Westminster Cathedral, and the carving on the prow front of Broadcasting House.

(4) Hughenden Manor was the home of Benjamin Disraeli from 1848 until he died in 1881 and many of his possessions remain on show in the house. There is an attractive garden and surrounding parkland. Owned by the National Trust since 1947, the house and garden are open to the public on Saturdays and Sundays during March, and on Wednesday to Sunday (and Bank Holiday Mondays) from April to October. Disraeli

and his wife, Mary Anne, came to live here in 1848, having bought the house from John Norris. This was close to his former family home at Bradenham, so he knew the area, and he was MP for High Wycombe. The house is surrounded by a park in which Disraeli loved to stroll. Milton described the house as sitting 'bosom'd high in tufted trees'. On a hillside in the park is the obelisk, erected by Mary Anne and dedicated to Disraeli's father Isaac. Disraeli restored much of the house and with Mary Anne made the garden, in which he came out to rest from the rigours of high political life in London.

(5) The church of St Michael and All Angels is located in a most beautiful setting in the park and serves surrounding settlements from the outskirts of High Wycombe to Speen and Naphill. It is mainly Victorian, though a church was first built on the site in the twelfth century. The chancel is the oldest section. The church was in bad repair in the nineteenth century and much restoration work took place before the end of the century. There are many memorials to Benjamin Disraeli, especially on the north side of the chancel and at his tomb in the churchyard at the eastern end of the church. The memorial in the chancel is unique, as it was erected by Queen Victoria, who was known to think highly of Disraeli. The Queen visited Hughenden to lay a wreath a few days after his death, another unique act from a reigning monarch. On the tomb in the churchyard is the name of Mrs Brydges Willyams, not a relative, but an admirer. She offered to make him her heir if she could be buried alongside his tomb. This money helped to finance changes in the house and the park. The north chapel contains many interesting relics and effigies, and on the north-west pillar is the old key of the church. This has a small circle in the handle which was for couples to use as a wedding ring, if they could not afford to buy one for their ceremony.

Hughenden House from the back garden

The old sixteenth-century houses alongside the church were occupied by six monks and a prior in pre-Reformation days. Later they became the vicarage, and subsequently almshouses. Restoration work has retained the original pre-Reformation appearance.

Oxfordshire into Buckinghamshire

Walk 14 – Watlington

Located on the OS Landranger 1:50 000 sheet 175, just extending on to 165, and on OS Explorer 1:25 000 map 3. Length of walk is 12 miles if starting from Watlington, but only 9 miles if beginning from the National Trust car park, grid ref 709935.

Time required is 5 hours for the full-length walk.

Terrain – includes one steep ascent and one descent of the scarp, with several short hills in between. Much is through woodland and paths can become very muddy. Starting point is at grid ref 692945. It is easily reached by leaving the M40 at Junction 6 and driving southwards on the B4009, passing the villages of Lewknor and Shirburn. In the centre of the town turn left on to Hill Road where there is a free car park.

Watlington is a very old small town, located on the Icknield Way, the ancient route which followed the foot of the Chiltern scarp. As a major turnpike did not pass through here in later centuries, it did not prosper as much as some other old market towns. There are stone houses dating from the sixteenth and seventeenth centuries, and although several fronts were replaced in the eighteenth and nineteenth centuries, the rear and insides still reveal their original age. The impressive Town Hall dates from 1664, built by the Stonor family. This Town Hall was very influential in helping the growth of the town, but has now become a major obstacle to modern day traffic. The church of St Leonard is situated at the end of Church Road and Church Lane across meadowland, nearly one

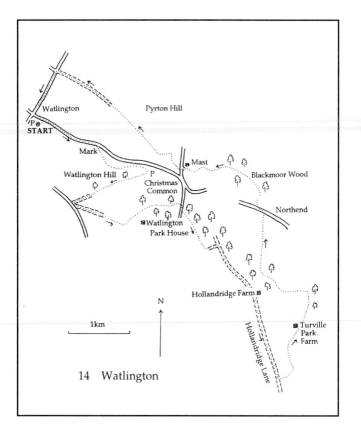

Watlington

Pyrton Hill

P
START

Mark

Watlington Hill

P
Christmas
Common

Mast

Blackmoor Wood

Northend

Watlington
Park House

Hollandridge Farm

Turville
Park
Farm

N

1km

Hollandridge Lane

14   Watlington

mile from the town centre. It is flint-faced and built on the site of a former castle. A railway line formerly ran through the town, but it is now dependent for public transport on its bus links with Oxford and occasional services to Wallingford or Henley.

This walk from Watlington begins with a climb up the scarp alongside the famous Watlington Mark, and undulates its way through woods and valleys, following the old route of Hollandridge Way for more than a mile, before returning past isolated farms and through the small hamlets of Christmas Common and Northend. The walk is mainly in Oxfordshire.

Walk out of Watlington towards the scarp, passing the Carriers Arms and using the pavement on the right side of the long straight road. There are houses on the right, but open views ahead and over to the left. A radio mast is visible up on Christmas Common. Pass Watlington Hospital on the right, and the Mark will soon become visible. Just beyond the Ridgeway which crosses this road, go right on to a path adjacent to the road, and walk into the trees. Begin to climb quite steeply and pass the National Trust sign for Watlington Hill to reach an open grassy patch, with flowers for much of the summer. Most of the flowers are yellow or purple. Pass through a kissing gate and walk alongside the Mark, where small erosional gullies can be seen in the exposed chalk. Long views open up over the plain, to the church in Watlington or towards Didcot Power Station. Above the Mark is grassland with bushes, and we climb to the top of the hill, then bear slightly left along a wide grassy path between gorse and hawthorn, with a mast straight ahead. This leads out to the road, and turn right uphill to arrive at a NT car park. Over in the far right corner of this car park is the onward route.

This car park at grid ref 709935 is an alternative starting point, and is reached by driving out of Watlington on the narrow road passing the village car park. There is a beacon on the left, nearly opposite the right turn into the car park. On the way up, this road passes the Watlington Mark, where the vegetation has been removed to expose the chalk. (1)

Leave the car park from the opposite corner to the entrance and follow the track just on the edge of the woods, through a kissing gate and on down the hill. This track can be muddy after rainy weather. Pass through another kissing gate and the view opens out to the left and straight ahead. On the right are many yew trees, relics of an old yew woodland on Watlington Hill. (2) Our route continues on down to the bottom of the hill, where we pass through another kissing gate and over a stile, and the path leaves the woods to continue beneath an avenue of small trees. Pass over two stiles and keep straight ahead to the right of a house and on to a track. Turn left here to walk along the track, with a view left up a grassy field with the mast on Christmas Common at the top, and to the right is another grassy slope with two masts of a WT station (6991) at the top.

Where the stony track bends left towards Lower Dean House, go straight on through a few trees, over a stile, and into a grassy field to ascend the scarp slope. Pass a lone tree, protected by an animal-proof fence, and walk on up to the top and a gate into the woods.

Just continue for a few metres into the wood, with a house to the right in the trees, but turn left, out of the wood and into a small field. This is covered with a carpet of snowdrops in the early months of the year, and up to the right, the upper storeys of Watlington House can be seen. The field creates a gap in the woodland, in order that residents in the house can look out west across the plain. The house was occupied by members of the Stonor family (see Walk 15) in the past, and then it was let to other Roman Catholics as tenants (3).

Cross the field and enter the woods again and follow the clear path, marked with directional arrows painted on trees. As in the earlier woods, a variety of birds will be seen or heard. There are many wild flowers in spring and, as usual in the Chilterns, a lot of beech trees.

Pass the NT sign which informs us we are leaving Dean Wood, and at the track which leads right to Watlington House, turn left and walk out to the road. The houses to the left are in the small village of Christmas Common. (4)

Turn right along the road and after about 150 m go left into the woods. The track soon splits, where we take the right fork, passing the sign saying No Horses, and soon bending right around the edge of Queen Wood. Follow close to the margin of the wood on the left and open fields to the right, with a horse gallop circuit with jumps around the edge of this field. Bend left on approaching the end of the wood and at a track turn left for 50 m. At the cross way of tracks, where straight ahead leads into Forestry Commission land, turn right along Hollandridge Lane, passing the notice board which says 'In the interest of wild life please keep dogs on leads'. There is certainly an abundance of wild life around, including deer in the woods which come out to feed in the fields. The track is near the edge of the woods, with fields just a few yards to the right. The view then opens out to the left as well, and better views can be seen on both sides.

Just beyond the point where the Oxfordshire Way footpath crosses our route, pass Hollandridge Farm, which dates back to at least 1282. The farm has a collection of early eighteenth-century flint walls in the buildings and a very large barn. The track becomes a little firmer from here on as we progress southwards to pass Whitehill Shaw, a small wood on the left. The word shaw is derived from an Old English word meaning a copse.

Hollandridge Lane was formerly the main Watling-ton–Henley route and in places exposed tree roots show the wear and tear, and hence the age of this track, especially where the clay with flints has been worn away down to the chalk. We leave this track by turning left at a major cross paths, where there are a few houses and the hamlet of Pishill to the right. Go left along a line of trees and downhill to a large open barn, and

over to the right can be seen a grassy slope with a variety of trees, part of the parkland of Stonor House. At the bottom, turn left along a track leading northwards between fields and along the floor of a dry valley. This passes the fine buildings of Turville Park Farm and goes on up the valley. Just beyond the farm, there is a wood on the slope to the right, and after bending left, the path stays in woodland, still on the bottom of the dry valley, which, in spite of its name, can be damp even in summer. On reaching a cross paths nearly a mile beyond Turville Park Farm, turn right and follow the track climbing gently to the edge of the wood, passing two small groves of redwood trees.

Leave the wood through a small gate and follow a shallow dry valley across the middle of the field, passing one oak tree in the middle, and go on up Launder's Valley, which is followed by the county boundary, towards Northend. Go through a newish gate, with a high handle which can be reached by riders from horseback, and along a track. When it splits turn right following the bridleway sign, through another new gate, and bend left through the woods (rich in snowdrops) to reach the road.

Turn left along the road, pass the county boundary between Buckinghamshire and Oxfordshire with Boundary Cottage adjacent to it. Just beyond the last house on the right and before reaching the road sign with the village name on it, turn right along a track towards Woodside. At the end of this driveway, climb over a stile, cross a narrow field and then over another stile to enter Blackmoor Wood. This contains some holly, a lot of beech, interesting bird life, wild flowers and there may be sightings of the shy fallow deer. A boundary bank in this wood was the boundary between woodland which was used for timber and the old common land. Small hollows

Hollandridge Farm

in the wood are the old pits from which lime was extracted for the fields.

The path winds through the trees, with white arrows showing the way, and gradually begins to go downhill. The wood extends to the bottom of the dry valley, but before getting right down to the bottom, reach a T-junction and a major track. Turn left here along a broad path, and soon begin the climb up to the top of the valley side. There is evidence of recent planting here, as well as clearance work, and this ancient wood contains trees of all ages.

This is the last climb of the day, and up at the top bend left, then emerge on to a track, turn right past the mast (Ministry of Defence property), to reach the road. Turn left here, and if going back to the car park, turn right at the cross roads and walk along the road to the car park. If going down to Watlington, just before reaching the cross roads turn right along the Oxfordshire Way footpath. Go over a stile and along the left margin of the field, and then over another stile and continue along the margin of the next field – still fairly level walking. Near the end of this field, ignore the stile on the left margin but bend over to the right corner of this field, to a stile which leads on to a broad track. Turn left on this and follow it through the woods, going downhill.

Emerge from the woodlands to see good views ahead across miles of the plain, and to the right is a deep dry valley and Pyrton Hill beyond, rich in butterflies, grasses, shrubs and flowers (including cowslips in spring and in summer the pyramid orchid, and common St John's wort which is quite similar to ragwort).

Continue down the valley, passing houses and buildings on the left, including Pyrton Hill House and a timber yard. The track becomes a narrow surfaced road, and the verges have an abundance of wild flowers in spring and summer. Willow warblers and yellow hammers sing here in the summer and a red kite may be floating around overhead. Cross the Ridgeway and keep straight ahead along the Oxfordshire Way. As the road levels off on the plain, the number of wild flowers in the verges decreases with the change of soil type, from the chalk of the hills to the sands and clays of the plain. The old parish of Watlington had a long narrow shape, stretching from the plain up on to the hills. This was to ensure that it obtained its fair share of different soils. The neighbouring parishes of Shirburn, Pyrton and Lewknor were all similar in shape.

At the main road, turn left and walk back in to Watlington, passing the cricket pitch on the right.

(1) It was thought for a long time that this Watlington Mark was more than 2000 years old, possibly even 2500 years old, and a pointer for the summer equinox, or a Celtic fertility symbol. Good stories maybe, but the truth is even better, as the accepted story is that it dates from the eighteenth century and was made as a rather eccentric whim. Mr Edward Horne lived in Greenfield, a house out on the plain, and from his window he could see the squat tower of Watlington church and behind it the steep slope of Watlington Hill. In order to improve on this view he had the mark cut out of the hill side in 1764, so that it would appear to be the top of the church tower, giving it the appearance of having a spire. The mark is 82 m (270 ft) long and 11 m (36 ft) wide.

(2) About 43 hectares (108 acres) of Watlington Hill are managed by the National Trust, a gift from Lord and Lady Esher. The chalk hill is covered in places with flint and clay deposits which enable both acid-loving plants as well as the usual chalklands plants to thrive in certain places. Trees include whitebeam, dogwood, hawthorn and wayfaring trees, as well as the yews, some of which have trunks up to nearly 2 m (over 6 ft) in diameter. The top of the hill is up to the right, and reaches a height of over 220 m (720 ft) and gives excellent views across Oxfordshire. It is one of the most westerly and southerly hills of the Chilterns.

(3) Watlington House. Richard Earl of Cornwall created Watlington Park in the thirteenth century and in 1632 William Stonor bought the park from Charles I. Thomas Stonor lived there in the 1670s but it was then let to Roman Catholic tenants until being sold to John Tilson in 1758. Tilson did some building in Palladian style in the 1750s, and used part of the old house as kitchen quarters. It was bought and enlarged by J. F. Symonds-Jeune in the late nineteenth century, and a later owner, Hon Oliver Brett (later Lord Esher) continued to add to it during the 1920s. In 1954 Major the Hon Lionel Brett, the owner, decided to reduce the house to its former Georgian size, and he demolished most of the nineteenth- and twentieth-century additions, restoring it to the Tilson building.

(4) It is said that Christmas Common received its name in the time of the Civil War, as the truce between Cavaliers and Roundheads for the Christmas of 1643 was agreed near here. The Parliamentarians were in the valley, and the Royalists were up on the ridge. Another possible explanation of the origin of the name is an old medieval word for holly trees which are abundant in this area.

Walk 15 – Nettlebed

Located on OS Landranger 1:50 000 sheet 175 and OS
1:25 000 Explorer map 3.

Length of walk is 9 miles.

Time required is 4–5 hours.

Terrain – no very strenuous sections, but there are
several hills to climb, and sometimes even worse, to
descend.

Starting point is grid ref 703867, alongside the A4130
Oxford to Henley road, which is accessible via the bus
service between these two towns. For motorists there is
a small amount of parking on the eastern side of the
village of Nettlebed, either near, but not in front of, the
gates to the Joyce Grove Nursing Home, or on the
opposite side of the main road along the minor road to
Crocker End, behind the bus shelter and the Pudding
Stones. An alternative starting point could be near the
ruins of St James's Church in Bix Bottom, grid ref
726869.

Nettlebed is an ancient settlement alongside the Henley to
Oxford routeway with old buildings and a former coaching
inn, the White Hart Hotel, which has been mentioned in recent
Egon Ronay guides. The old flint school is next along the road
and a commemorative plaque on the wall mentions Major
Philip Fleming (1889–1971) and Colonel Peter Fleming
(1907–71), who contributed so much to the village. At the far
end of the village is the brick building of St Bartholomew's
church with a large grave yard (containing several Fleming
gravestones) surrounded by a brick wall, and beyond the wall
is a farm complex with large flint and wooden barns, but now

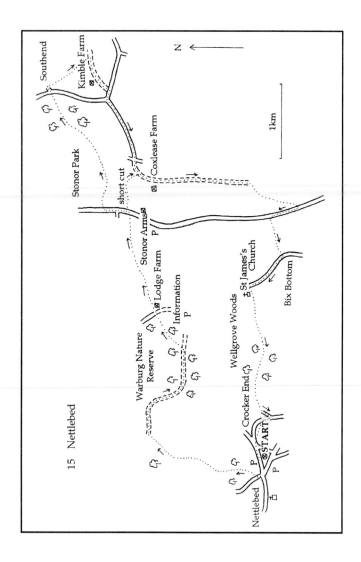

15 Nettlebed

partially modernised and some used as offices. On the road just outside the farm yard is a milestone from the days of the turnpike, with the distances of London 40, Henley 5, Oxford 18.

Nettlebed has a long history of industrial development connected with brick-and-tile making. A few remnants of this can be seen in the surrounding countryside, and in Nettlebed an eighteenth-century bottle kiln is preserved for its historical interest. It was used until 1938, and has been preserved by public subscription and grants from charitable trusts. It was restored 1972–4. The countryside must have been devastated for a time in the nineteenth century with pits, dumps, pools, old buildings, tramways, kilns, quite unlike the present Chiltern scene. The useful information board at the kiln mentions that tiles and bricks have been made in this area since the Middle Ages, using local materials, including the chalk of the Chilterns and the clays from the superficial clay with flint deposits which are found on top of the chalk in places. Reading and London clays are available locally, too. The local woodlands provided fuel for the kilns. One of the earliest recorded uses of Nettlebed materials was for 35,000 tiles made for Wallingford Castle in 1365, and for roofing parts of Abingdon Abbey in 1422–23. Bricks were first mentioned in 1416–17, when Thomas Stonor paid '£40 for 200,000 brykes', and another £15 for transporting them the three miles from the kiln at Crocker End to Stonor House. The Stonor accounts have references to 'Lez Flemyngges', incomers from the Low Countries who brought with them their skill in brick and tile making. The industry declined early this century, especially from the time of the Great War and, although some kilns were adapted for lime-burning, they were not used for long.

On the green between the kiln and the main road are the famous Pudding Stones. The origin of these stones is still uncertain, but they were found in the courtyard of the sixteenth-

century Bull Inn in Nettlebed. They consist of flint pebbles cemented together, as breccia or conglomerate, but the origin of these flints is unknown. One suggestion is that they were part of a line of marker stones from Grimes Graves in Norfolk to Pangbourne.

It is difficult to imagine that Nettlebed was formerly an industrial town, as this walk leads through woods and fields, then into the nature reserve of Warburg, before crossing the magnificent parkland around Stonor House, and then more woods and farmland on the return to Nettlebed, past the old ruined church in Bix Bottom.

Set off along the B481 towards Watlington and Cookley Green, passing the Sun Inn and Nettlebed sub post office. After about 100 m as the road bends left, fork right along the stony track, Mill Road, following the bridleway sign with a blue arrow. When the drive splits, fork left, passing the No Through Road sign, and beginning to ascend. Pass Windmill Cottage on the right and, when the drive ends, go slightly left on to the footpath leading into the woods. Take the right fork shortly after entering the wood, and at a five-ways meeting of paths, take the path going straight ahead (second from the right), leading through to a broad gravelly track. Turn right here and walk along the track until you reach houses. Turn right just before the first of the houses, along a narrow path by the side of the house, passing a telegraph pole, to walk past the small pond in the garden and on to a stile. Beyond this follow the right margin of the field for half the length of the field, then head slightly left, across a small dry valley, to the stile in the far corner of the field. Go over the stile and into the woods, and the path continues along a small ridge with dry valleys down to the left and the right. Descend towards the valley on the right, and at the edge of the wood, go over the stile, turn

The old church in Bix Bottom

right for a few metres, then left along the edge of the field for 20 m to another stile.

Once over the stile, turn right along the track which is leading from Westwood Manor Farm. Where the track splits, take the right fork, ignoring the footpath which turns sharp right to cross the middle of the field, and also ignoring the path which starts from in between the two tracks. Our route leads into the woods and bends round to the right. The woods have an abundance of bluebells and other wild flowers, many butterflies and also a wealth of bird life, for example warblers, including blackcaps and whitethroats, as well as drumming woodpeckers.

Ignore the occasional narrow paths leading off this track, and keep straight ahead, passing a few BBONT Woodland Walk marker posts along our route. The track begins to bend round to the left and then straightens out as it proceeds along the valley floor, with steep slopes both to right and left. Reach a major cross tracks and keep straight ahead, passing areas of cowslips, soon to reach a public footpath sign going off to the right and 20 m beyond this is the left turn which we are looking for. Go left into the Warburg Nature Reserve (1), following the BBONT nature trail sign. Cross a grassy ride, which was formerly a rifle range, and to the right is the Information Centre, which you may wish to visit. The walk round the Reserve Wildlife Walk will take about an hour, and a very informative booklet is available at the Centre if you wish to know more about the fauna and flora.

Beyond the ride the path splits, and we take the right fork to head between silver birch into mixed woodland, with areas of open space and undergrowth, all ideal for a variety of flowers, insects and animals. Climb gently and cross another grassy ride and then begin to climb quite steeply – violets and cowslips are common here, at the appropriate time of year. Other woodland plants around here include bugle and wood spurge, and the twayblade, a green flowering orchid, which is an indicator that this is an ancient area of woodland. Pass an uprooted tree, showing chalk on its roots, and then the path becomes less steep. Cross two stiles in quick succession, to be joined by a path coming in from the right. Continue climbing slightly and then level off to reach the top edge of the wood.

Go over the stile and turn left for a few metres, on a stony track, to reach a small grassy island where three tracks meet. Turn sharp right towards the farm yard, passing through an old iron gate and immediately turn left, along a grassy drive, the Oxfordshire Way, with a bridleway sign and a blue arrow. This passes between Lodge Farm on the right and a small cottage on the left, and leads through to an open field. Our path heads diagonally right across this field, not alongside either of the hedges, and passes to the left of the double telegraph pole out in the field. This leads across to a stile and then on to the path through Park Wood. The clear path soon begins to descend gently, and leads through to the edge of the woods and a stile, from which there are magnificent views of Stonor House and Park. The path is straight ahead, with the margin of the field 30 m to the right. The path leads down to a stile, then across the middle of the next field, which is very chalky at the top but less white lower down. At the bottom of the field, go over a stile and along a narrow path to the road, and to the houses of Stonor village. Down to the right is the Stonor Arms and Upper Assendon Farm, and there is a layby parking space near the farm.

Turn left along the road for 20 m and then by a 40mph sign turn right for a SHORT CUT, if required. It will cut off 2½ miles by missing the section through Stonor Park, which you might wish to visit on another day, and spend time looking round the house and garden as well.

For the short cut, turn right on the bridleway with the blue arrow. Pass between gardens at first and then between woods. On the left is the wire fence boundary to Stonor Park, and the

woods thin out higher up the slope. There may be good views of fallow deer in the park. This is a very steep climb out of a deep dry valley, but the ascent eases higher up. Near the top of the slope on the left is a small pond, and on the right a coniferous wood. The path bends round to the right and reaches a cross track. Turn right along the stony drive and pass the notice saying Stonor Estate, No Public Right of Way.

MAIN WALK
Carry on along the road, passing a narrow road going left to Maidensgrove and Russell's Water, and after a further 200 m turn right before reaching the main entrance into Stonor Park, which is just in Oxfordshire. There is a short stretch of roadside parking here on the left. Also on the left is the cricket pitch in a beautiful setting and on the right is the large iron kissing gate into the park, and a signpost to Southend 1½ miles. Begin to climb up into the park, passing a few trees, including several young ones, planning for the twenty-first century and beyond. The house soon comes into view down to the left near the bottom of the large dry valley. Set in beautiful parkland created in 1395, this is a most impressive house, and well worth a visit. (2)

The path remains on the right slope of the dry valley, giving good views across to the house, with the walled garden on its left and the chapel and stables to its right. Our way leads along the edge of woodland on a clear path to the large iron kissing gate and fence which surrounds the deer park. Go on through Kildridge Wood, still climbing slightly, and a private track comes in from the right, then a narrow path coming up the bottom of the dry valley joins from the left, and we continue ahead on what is now a broad track – the old route from Stonor House to Southend. Many clumps of rhododendron can be

Deer in Stonor woods

seen in these woods, and they are important as cover for game birds, though now the bushes need occasional thinning because they have been very successful. Walking through mainly fir trees, with silver birch alongside the path, the flint-lined track levels off at the top of the dry valley, crosses into Buckinghamshire, and reaches two lovely flint cottages just before the road. This was formerly a drovers' road, and there used to be a pub called the Drovers, a few metres up to the left.

Go straight across and follow a stony track past a small pond, often dry. The track bends round to the right and then, when it bends sharp left as a driveway to a house, go straight ahead over the stile and follow the fence on the right. After about 40 m go right over another stile and immediately turn left to stay near the fence. Then pass a small pond on the left and beyond this veer left to stay close to the fence. Soon go left over a stile and turn immediately right alongside the fence and admire the views across the Chiltern Plateau. There is nothing but delightful countryside all around and there is a feeling of being miles from anywhere, except for Kimble Farm, ahead to the right. At the end of the field, go over the stile and along a path near the right margin of a small wood, leading downhill to the bottom of a dry valley and a cross paths. Turn right here along a track which leads uphill slightly past the modernised and magnificent buildings of Kimble Farm. Pass the duck pond with a good variety of ducks and possibly geese, including a barnacle goose, the last time I walked past.

At the road turn right, and after about 200 m when a road turns right to Southend, keep straight ahead along a single-track road with passing places. There is a wood on the right, but views left are magnificent. Pass the track to Bosmore Farm but just continue along the road until it bends sharp left. Go straight on here, along a stony track, with the tall wire boundary fence of the deer park on the right. This track is signposted as a bridleway to Stonor half a mile, but when a path and the fence turn right to go down into Stonor, keep straight ahead, passing the private notice to the right of the track, which states No Public Right of Way Stonor Estate.

This is where the SHORT CUT rejoins the main walk.

Walk on to the farm buildings of Coxlease Farm, and pass between the barns. Turn right once past the barns, and walk behind the farm buildings on the right, as the track bends left and begins to head southwards. The drive passes between fields and gives good views in all directions. Descending slightly along the fairly exposed ridge, this drive is our route for more than a mile. Many wild flowers, including cowslips, thrive along this drive, which is grassy for much of the distance. It ends by leading into a field and here just bend right to follow the hedge, and descend steadily to a stile leading into the woods. Once over the stile, follow the clear path in this wood, rich in flowers and birds. Fairly horizontal at first, the path stays close to the left margin of the wood, and then gradually descends to emerge from the wood. Keep straight ahead across the middle of the field and drop down to the road.

Middle Assendon is just to the left, but turn right along this road, using the narrow verge where possible. After a quarter mile turn left along the muddy track between hedges, and when this splits take the left fork along the left side of the field. We are now back in Oxfordshire. At the top of a short climb, the hedge bends round to the left, but yellow arrows point straight ahead across the field, and soon two houses can be seen down in the valley ahead. At a corner of the field ahead, turn right to go across the field to the hedge, and then turn left to follow this down to the narrow road. Turn right along the road, and walk along the valley floor, called Bix Bottom. Pass Valley End Farm on the left, with a fine collection of barns. Ignore the footpath signposted left through the farm yard and pass the farmhouse to Crocker End, and proceed along the road to the remains of the Norman church of St James, which was abandoned in 1835.

Parking here is possible if you wish to use this as the starting point of the walk.

Walk along the stony track signposted to Crocker End, with the church on the right. Follow the hedge on the left, climbing slightly and go through the gate straight into Wellgrove Woods. The land to the left of the path is fairly level, but to the right is a steep descent into a dry valley. The trees are mainly deciduous, but a patch of coniferous can be seen to the left. Pass a track going left, and then a track going right but keep straight ahead, with a dark area of conifers to the right of the path. Emerge from the woods over a stile and walk along the left side of the field. The dry valley is visible down to the right, and ahead to the right is a good view of Soundess House. It is believed that Nell Gwynn lived in a house somewhere near the site of Soundess, which only dates from the nineteenth century.

At the end of a large field go over a stile and straight ahead along a stony drive into Crocker End, a former pottery- and brick-making village. Pass a few houses on the left and follow the surfaced drive round to the left. At the T-junction turn right passing an old pub (formerly the Cat), now a house, and a farm on the left with an old granary on staddles. The road bends between houses, and at the green, fork left, past the last house on the left, following the signpost to Nettlebed. This leads through to join the road and, ignoring the turning to the right and to the left, just keep straight ahead to walk back into Nettlebed.

(1) Warburg Nature Reserve is named after Dr E. F. Warburg, an Oxford University botanist, and is the largest of the reserves managed by the Berkshire, Buckinghamshire and Oxfordshire Naturalists' Trust. It was purchased in 1967, covers an area of

106 hectares (258 acres), and employs a full-time warden. Part of the Reserve is an SSSI. In the Reserve is a dry winding valley cutting through the chalk and in the bottom of the valley is a marked frost hollow, where cold air settles and accumulates during calm anticyclonic conditions. Around the valley is a mixture of woodland and grassland, and in the grassy areas sheep are grazed in winter, generally on a three-year rota. Some summer grazing may take place as well, if winter grazing has been insufficient to control coarse grasses. This will allow the wild flowers to flower and produce seed, notably wild thyme, Chiltern gentian and eye bright. The Reserve is especially well known for its flora, having recorded over 450 species.

(2) Stonor House is open from April to September on Sundays from 2–5.30 p.m., on Bank Holiday Mondays and on Wednesdays, Thursdays and Saturdays in the summer. There is an admission charge. The house has been the home of Lord and Lady Camoys and the Stonor family for at least 800 years and is set in a beautiful Chiltern valley. Fallow deer graze in the park and there are many interesting birds to be seen, including red kites which now nest in the park. The first house was built in about 1190, but many additions and changes took place during the following centuries. By the end of the sixteenth century an E-shaped Tudor building had evolved and changes to the present shape occurred in the eighteenth century. The dark red bricks of the facade were manufactured at Nettlebed. The Stonor family prospered for many years, and the chapel was added in the fourteenth century, built of flint and stone, but with a few pudding stones included in the walls. Two hundred thousand bricks from Crocker End were used in 1416 to build the chapel tower. Other estates were acquired in other parts of the country, though this prosperous phase changed with the Reformation. After Henry VIII had broken with Rome in the sixteenth century, the Stonors refused to take the Oath of Supremacy and as a result were subjected to a huge annual

fine. Much of the wealth and all the other estates were lost, but the family managed to maintain Stonor and their Catholic faith. Mass was celebrated in the chapel without a break, one of only three places in England where this was possible. Stonor House supported priests, notably the martyr Edmund Campion who lived in a secret room up in the roof in 1581 and set up a printing press. He was eventually captured and then executed. The house contains many interesting items of furniture, tapestries, sculptures and paintings, and an outstanding collection of Catholic books. The garden is a delight and all around is the park, with a modern stone circle on the site of a prehistoric one.

Stonor garden, back of house and the park beyond

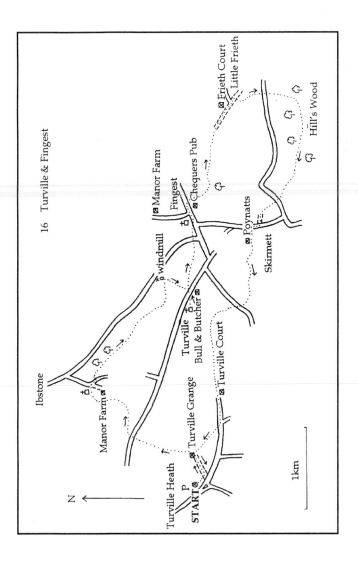

16 Turville & Fingest

Buckinghamshire

Walk 16 – Turville and Fingest

The walk can be found on OS Landranger 1:50 000 sheet
175 and OS Explorer 1:25 000 map 3.
Distance is about 9 miles.
Time required is 4 hours.
Terrain – several steep slopes are encountered up the
sides of dry valleys in the chalk. Three large dry valleys
converge at Fingest and lead southwards as the Hamble
valley which has a stream flowing in it to Hambleden
and the Thames.
Starting point is at grid ref 744909 on Turville Heath
where there is plenty of parking space. To reach this
point, take the minor road from Watlington via
Christmas Common and Northend to arrive at Turville
Heath. Where the road splits and forms a triangle of
roads, take the left fork towards Turville (2¼) and
Fingest (2¼), and at the end of the triangle, the right
turn is signposted to Stonor (1¾) and Henley (6). On the
left are parking spaces on the edge of the common, and
also on the left is a diagonal surfaced driveway leading
away from the Turville road straight towards Turville
Grange.

Set in the midst of the most beautiful Chiltern countryside,
three villages, Turville and Fingest down in the valley, and
Ibstone up on the ridge top, are within easy walking distance
of each other. Valleys, villages, hills, woods and churches, as
well as a windmill, are part of this circuit. Tranquillity and the
feeling of remoteness in these small villages, hidden in their

valleys, and only reached by narrow roads, give an air of inaccessibility quite astonishing within a few miles of the M40 and M25.

Walk along this drive between trees and towards the Grange, a magnificent brick house with some flint, and a warning notice to tell you that alsatians are on the loose. This was the home of Jacqueline Kennedy's sister for a time. Turn right at the house and then immediately left through a gate to pass along the right side of the house. Walk along a track, pass the house and tennis courts on the left, then go over a stile by another gate. Immediately turn left along the edge of the field, with house and tennis court on the left. Heading north, bear slightly left past the corner of the garden fence, and go straight on across the field. The tiny squat tower of Ibstone church might be seen on the next hill. In the middle of the field begin to descend slightly towards the edge of the wood. Go over the stile and on to the path through the woods, descending steeply. Flints and chalk are both exposed on this path. Cross a path, but continue straight on down to the bottom of the wood to a stile and over into the field. Keep straight ahead, with a wire fence on the left. The field levels off before reaching the next stile and you go over on to the road.

Cross the road to the big gate on to the Wormsley Estate (see Walk 11), but fork right here rather than going through the gate, following the public bridleway sign into the woods. When the path splits, fork right, and at the next split fork left. Cross a surfaced track which leads to the farm a few metres to the left and continue to the edge of the woods. Go over a stile and walk along the right edge of the field, climbing uphill alongside a wire fence. At the top of the field, go over the stile and straight on. Follow the path alongside the edge of the wood, until it turns right over a stile into the woods. Cross a track but go straight on, still climbing, to reach St Nicholas Church (1). To the south of the church is the seventeenth-century brick and timber Manor Farm, owned by Merton College, Oxford.

Walk across the churchyard on to the church drive and turn left to walk about 30 m to the narrow road. Turn right here and go steeply downhill for about 40 m until the road bends right and our path goes off left into the woods. Trees are to the left and open fields to the right at first, and then there is a spell with trees on the right as well. A path comes in from the left, but just keep straight ahead, and when the path splits take the right fork along the edge of the woods, with open fields and a beautiful valley to the right. After being joined by a path from the left, we soon reach a stile and pass over into a grassy field. Keep left along the edge of this field, and go over a stile into a patch of scrub with dogwood bushes, wild roses and some grass, with violets in the spring.

Go over a stile on to a grassy track, and turn left, then walk out into an open field. Keep a fairly horizontal route here to arrive at a stile, and go on over this and bear slightly left to climb up to the Ibstone Mill which dates back to the seventeenth century, and is now a private residence alongside the minor road between Ibstone and Fingest. There has been a mill on this site since the thirteenth century, and this particular mill featured in the film *Chitty Chitty Bang Bang*. There is no access to the windmill, so descend the steep slope straight down towards the village of Turville. At the bottom of the hill, go over two stiles and keep straight ahead to the village. There is another stile just before reaching the first houses. A footpath goes left here and this is our way ahead to Fingest, but first go into the village and have a look round. The church of St Mary the Virgin (2), the old houses, the sixteenth-century pub called the Bull and Butcher all contribute to this very picturesque village, surrounded by rolling hills.

There is a cottage in the churchyard, and a tiny village green next to it. Surrounding this are the delightful stone houses which make up the village, with good views to the windmill on the hill top. The village used to be noted for lace and furniture. In the *Shell Guide to Buckinghamshire*, first published

in 1936, and written by the artist John Nash, it states that in Turville, 'the chairmakers are always to be found there working beside their cottage doors.' Many bodgers lived in the surrounding woods.

Leave the village, as though going to the windmill. At the first stile turn right, signposted to Fingest. Follow the fence on the right at first, but then head slightly left towards the stile which is half way up the hedge at the far end of the field. Go over the stile and along the fairly horizontal path through scrub, with open grassy fields sloping up to the left. At the end of this scrub patch, go over a stile, across a narrow road and over another stile. Forty metres beyond this the path splits; take the right fork to go down into Fingest. Go over a stile and turn left along the road, with the Church of St Bartholomew (3) to your left.

On the right is a pub, the Chequers, which dates from the fifteenth century. It has a large car park and garden. Up Chequers Lane, adjacent to the church is the old village pound, and further up the lane the old Manor Farm, just north of Fingest church, with a magnificent flint barn. After detouring to admire this barn, walk on from the pub past a small wooden barn on staddles on the right, and just beyond the last house on the right, turn right and over a stile into a field.

Walk up the right margin of this field to a stile and keep straight ahead, climbing, with Fingest Wood on the right side. Pass a gate leading into the woods and soon reach a seat, where it is well worth pausing to admire the magnificent views back over the village. Go over the stile into the woods, still climbing slightly, and emerge into an open field at the top of the hill.

Go diagonally left across this field, to reach an iron gate and on into the woods. The path splits almost immediately; take

Churchyard, houses and the view up to Ibstone Mill

the left fork, soon with an open field a few yards to the right. Walk along the broad track, which can become muddy, and at the end of the field on the right, turn right to follow the same track. Pass Frieth Court on the left, and keep straight ahead. The track becomes stony and leads on to a narrow surfaced road with a few houses on the right. After about 30 m, follow the footpath sign to the right through a gate, and through a garden (yes, it really is through the garden). Leave the garden through a small gate, go over a stile and turn left, where there is a convenient seat on the right. Follow the footpath, with gardens on the left and open fields to the right, with views across the hills, woods and vales of the Chilterns.

Alongside a small house, Whitefield Cottage, go over a stile, across a narrow road and past the stile into the field. The path immediately splits; take the right fork to walk down towards Hill's Wood through a field where skylarks may be singing.

Go over a stile and into the woods to follow the clear path for half a mile, crunching on beech mast to start with and then passing through a stand of larch. At the end of the wood is an iron gate with metal steps, and a few yards beyond is a T-junction. Turn right along the path between two hedges, with open fields on both sides. We are on a ridge between two valleys and gradually the path descends to emerge on a narrow road by the signpost for Skirmett. Turn left, and after 20 m turn right over a stile and into a field. Follow the hedge on the left side and in the far left corner of the field is a stile. Walk along the drive beyond this stile to the road in Skirmett. A few yards to the left is the Frog in Skirmett, but we turn right to pass several flint buildings. Near the old chapel of All Saints on the right, turn left following the public footpath sign along a private drive with an avenue of trees. Pass the magnificent Poynatts Farm and at the end of the drive go over a stile and straight ahead along a path. Climb quite steeply up to the edge of Poynatts Woods, the name being derived from Poynants, the fourteenth-century owners of Skirmett Manor. Turn right to follow the margin of the woods, with a grassy field and excellent views to the right. The path bends left and then goes a few metres into the woods. Just follow the path, with the edge of the woods not far away to the right. The path becomes fairly level before bending right and descending quite steeply down to the edge of the woods. Leave the woods, cross a narrow field where there are excellent views of the windmill to the right. Go into a small wood, pass the pumping station, and leave the wood via a stile on to the road, where there is space for a few cars to park.

Cross straight over to the stile and on into a large open field. The path leads diagonally up to the right, climbing steadily. Before reaching the far hedge, a path comes in from the left, and we turn right along this for a few yards before going off left to climb steeply up the hill. The hedge is now 20 m to the right and parallel to our route. The hedge gradually becomes further away, to the corner of the field, before turning to come back to the line of the path. We continue alongside the hedge, climbing slightly to the end of the field which is only marked by fragments of a hedge. In the next field the path continues straight ahead, passing just to the left of a telegraph pole, but the hedge bends steadily further away to the right. At the end of this field pass through a small gate and go straight on, to the right of Turville Court, the flint cottages and a large wooden barn on flint walls.

Go along the driveway and then to the road. When the road splits with a left turn, fork right through a gap in the hedge on the footpath going across the field. At the hedge on the far side, turn left and then go over a stile through the hedge and walk along the other side of the hedge. Go over the next stile, with the tennis court seen earlier now on our right, pass Turville Grange between the house and the walled garden, turn right in front of the house and retrace your steps to the starting point of the walk.

(1) St Nicholas church, Ibstone is a little squat church with a wooden shingled cap rather than a real tower, and a wooden entry porch. The porch is nineteenth-century but the doorway dates from the twelfth century. The north door is also from the twelfth century, though this was never used, but just existed to let out the Devil. The font and a window on the west wall of the nave are also twelfth-century and the oak pulpit is early fifteenth-century. The gallery is nineteenth-century. By the church gate is a broken stone coffin, found on a field nearby. The yew in the churchyard is thought to be a thousand years old. The church is isolated from the main part of the village as the school and Manor House are up the lane by the green. There were originally dwellings along this lane, but they were deserted, possibly at the time of the Black Death, and have since been demolished and removed. Dame Rebecca West lived in the Manor House near the school and the green.

(2) There was an earlier church on the site, but St Mary the Virgin, Turville is fourteenth-century, and mainly built of flint, the local material. Stone for the quoins and window and door edgings are limestone or clunch. The tower was built about 1340 and the brick parapet was added in the seventeenth century. The oak roof has retained a rather steep pitch because the walls of the nave were never raised for the insertion of clerestory windows. Many of the windows date from the fourteenth century. John Piper, who lived nearby and helped in restoration work during the 1970s, designed a stained glass window which was made by Patrick Reyntiens at Loudwater and placed in the old Norman doorway opposite the entrance porch. A new north aisle was added about 1733 by the Lord of the Manor William Perry. His daughter married Bysshe Shelley, grandfather of the poet, and records of this family link can be seen in the west windows of the aisle. An old stone coffin, probably from the thirteenth century, was discovered during restoration work in 1901. It contained evidence of two separate burials, and possibly was the relic of a concealed murder. It

must have been used for a tall person, and someone very wealthy to afford such a fine coffin. In the south-east corner of the large churchyard is an area of recent planting, with beech, box, yew, whitebeam and wayfaring trees to replace a row of spruce. This church was used as the parish church in the recent TV series *The Vicar of Dibley*, starring Dawn French.

(3) The twelfth-century fortress type of tower at St Bartholomew, Fingest is very rare, with a saddle-back roof with twin red gables. The walls are 60 ft in height and 4 ft thick, with narrow slit windows peeping out through them. The walls are of flint, with stone quoins. The tower has three storeys, and in the top one is the lone remaining bell. The tower is wider than the nave, as was the case in several pre-Conquest churches. The nave is long and narrow and the low seats emphasise this shape. The fifteenth-century octagonal font still retains the hasp used for locking the cover, which was designed to prevent water from being stolen. In the churchyard are two wishing gates, part of the wall. A brief history of the church and village written by Cassandra (Sir William Connor) the famous *Daily Mirror* columnist who lived here for many years, can be seen on the notice board. The Bishops of Lincoln built a palace here, and the remains can still be seen near to the church.

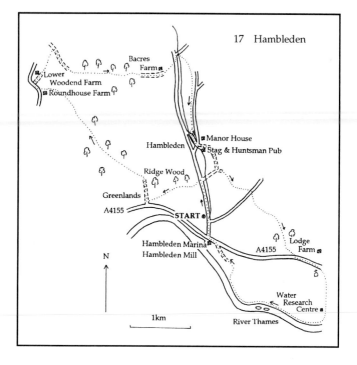

17 Hambleden

Bacres Farm

Lower Woodend Farm
Roundhouse Farm

Hambleden
Manor House
Stag & Huntsman Pub

Ridge Wood

Greenlands
A4155

START

Hambleden Marina
Hambleden Mill

A4155

Lodge Farm

N

Water Research Centre

1km

River Thames

Walk 17 – Hambleden

Located on OS Landranger 1:50 000 sheet 175 and OS
Explorer 1:25 000 map 3.
Length of walk is 12 miles, with a short cut point to
reduce this to 8 if required.
Time required is about 6 hours (or only 4 if the short cut
is used).
Terrain – an undulating walk with several short though
steep hills. It is just possible that the stretch along the
Thames from Medmenham may have flood water
problems in winter.
Starting point is car park at grid ref 785856 just to the
south of the village of Hambleden, and can be most
easily reached off the A4155 Henley to Marlow road.

Considered by many to be the most attractive Chiltern village,
Hambleden makes a good focal point for a walk. This circular
tour of the delightful Chiltern countryside takes in several
woods and the Hambleden valley, and also the interesting
village of Medmenham and a walk alongside the Thames.

Leave the car park and turn left along the road towards
Hambleden. After 300 m and just past the houses on the left,
turn left on the public bridleway which passes behind the
houses, to take the path along the edge of the woods, with
open fields to the left. Skylarks and yellow hammers may be
heard singing on this stretch of the walk.

At a cross paths go left and out of the woods through a small
gate and walk along the field margin with hedge to the left. At
the end of the field turn right alongside an iron fence and walk
towards the farm. Just before reaching the flint wall, turn right
along the track to pass the farm and then Dairy Cottage. This

small cluster of buildings is called Greenlands, and down to the left is a large house by the river which is now the Henley Management College, and was the home of the 1st Viscount Hambleden (formerly called W. H. Smith). During the Civil War this house was the property of the D'Oyley family and was under siege from Parliamentary forces for several days. W. H. Smith purchased Greenlands in 1871 and made several additions to it.

Having turned right along the track, ignore the public bridleway going right, and pass some pheasant pens and then a house on the left. Turn left just past the house, on a public bridleway to climb up to the woods. This is quite a climb up Reservoir Hill and into Pallbach Woods, and there is a beautiful dry valley to the right, looking northwards, which must have been formed by erosion when a stream flowed down to the Thames during colder climatic conditions.

The climb continues in the woods, but gradually levels off. This is a varied wood, with larch, firs, some oaks and patches of silver birch, as well as the usual beech. The variety is partially the result of the soil type, as the roots of fallen trees will reveal. It is not all white from chalk, but has brownish patches from the shallow surface loamy deposits on top of the chalk. It is also rich in bird life and animals. (1)

The route through the woods is fairly straight and is marked by white arrows painted on the trees. In the middle of the woods the path takes a sharp left bend then a right, nothing more than a slight kink in the straight route through. Just before reaching the end of the wood is an area of young larch trees.

Emerge from the wood and the path continues along the edge of the trees with an open field to the left. Like several other paths in the Chilterns this can be muddy in wet weather, and hollows are dug out by the trampling of horses' hoofs. The path goes to the left of a house and then out on to a driveway which leads to a narrow road just after passing Pink Cottage and then the round house, built of chalk, part of Round House Farm.

Turn right along the road, and just before it begins to descend, turn right on the driveway to Lower Woodend Farm and Lower Woodend Barns. When the drive splits fork right by a small pond and pass Persoft Inc and the converted flint buildings before going through a wooden gate and along the right margin of a small field. Keep straight ahead and over a stile and then turn left to walk alongside the wire fence. When the fence begins to bear left, the path cuts diagonally right across the field to a stile in the hedge at the far side. Upper Woodend Farm is over to the left. Once over the stile, turn right along a bridleway between hedges, a very good place for seeing long tailed tits which haunt many of the hedgerows and woodland margins in this area. Arrive at the edge of a wood where the path is sunken and can be very muddy. A drier route has been used, avoiding the muddiest parts in the bottoms of the old sunken route. The field margin is to the right and the sunken track is to the left. Pheasants are particularly numerous in this wood.

Walk on to the cross tracks down in the bottom of the valley, and go straight across to start climbing quite steeply. No horses are allowed here, and this means that the path will be drier. Climb quite steeply and bend left, and as the track levels slightly it is joined by a track coming in from an area of private woodland to the left. Look out for a yellow arrow marking a narrow footpath going off to the left through some young trees in which you may be lucky enough to see fallow deer. Turn right just before the edge of the woods. The field visible on the left soon ends, and the path enters a larch wood. As we emerge from the wood, there is a major cross tracks, where we keep straight ahead, following the white arrow marked on the tree. The driveway to Built Farm goes to the left.

Walk on, close to the edge of Barnwood, with an open field to the right and a wooded deep valley to the left. The track is surfaced and leads steadily downhill, and just beyond a sharp left turn passes alongside Bacres Farm. Do not turn right along the drive by the flint buildings but go straight ahead and into the field, following a path diagonally right leading down to the road at a T-junction.

Go straight across, and just beyond the small bridge over Hamble Brook, turn right over a stile following the footpath signs. Cross the very small field and then go over another stile, an impressive ladder structure, and turn right here to go diagonally across this field to a stile in the far corner.

Turn right alongside the hedge, and soon reach another stile beyond which the hedge is on the left. At the end of the field pass through a kissing gate and keep straight ahead to a small gate by a house on the right. Cross the narrow road and continue ahead along a narrow footpath between gardens, some of which slope down to the stream on the right. Pass through a small iron gate and a wooden kissing gate and out into a field, and then over a stile and through a kissing gate to get into the next field, and still keep straight ahead. There is a narrow road over the hedge to the left, you will see traffic on the main road across the stream over to the right, and straight ahead is Hambleden church, partially hidden by trees. Pass through another kissing gate and straight on at first, then bend slightly right to reach a kissing gate near the flint and brick bridge. Go through the kissing gate and out on to the road, turn left and walk into Hambleden.

In the village the route ahead is left past the church and straight on passing the Stag and Huntsman pub and free car parking area. Before this have a good look round Hambleden. (2)

The village contains flint and brick houses, built by the Estate around 1870, and around the small village green with its pump are old buildings such as the Old Bakery, now a private house, and the post office. A stream flows through the village, and it also has a cricket pitch. All the essential requirements of a picturesque English village can be seen in Hambleden, including the magnificent Manor House. (3)

Leave the village between the old flint cottages and the Stag and Huntsman, and go along the private road to turn right at the first track. This passes the sports field and gives good views over the cricket pitch back towards the church. To the left of this track is Kenricks, the former Rectory, built in 1724 for the Reverend Scawen Kenrick. This fine Georgian house looks out over the village, and was probably the site of the original Manor House. In the Middle Ages the Manor was the property of the Scrope family.

When the track reaches the T-junction, turn left where we can see one of the typical big old Chiltern barns down to the right. When the track becomes a private way at a wooden gate, turn right here and walk along the field margin with a hedge on your right. This path leads to North Cot Wood and a stile. Once over the stile the path splits. Take the left fork leading inside the margins of the wood rather than right into the field. The path climbs gently and then bends left to go into the heart of the wood, though it is quite open because of recent clearance and planting of young trees. Pass a simple wooden bench which might be useful for a picnic if you have not eaten in Hambleden, and just after the path has levelled off, reach a stile beyond which is a narrow sunken road.

SHORT CUT. For a walk of 8 miles rather than 12, turn right along this road which will lead down to a T-junction, and the car park starting point is just a few yards to the right.

MAIN WALK

If continuing ahead, go straight across the road and over another stile. After 20 m join a track and turn left. Pass through a few trees and after about 30 m, turn right alongside a fence, with a field on the left and Chalkpit Wood on the right, and a carpet of bluebells here in the spring. Turn left over a stile and continue along the path which is now between two wire fences. Over to the left are the magnificent flint buildings of Burrow Farm in a totally rural setting, though there are likely to be noises of planes overhead.

Reach the edge of Binfields Wood, and turn right into the woods. There is a steep valley down to the left. These woods are rich in bird life and wild flowers in the spring. Walk on the fairly horizontal path, with some pheasant pens to the left. As the noise of traffic begins to be heard, the path drops steeply downhill, passing a path coming in from the right, and descends Killdown Bank to the A4155. Notice the good view up the dry valley to the left, as you descend.

Turn left along the road and cross over to make use of the footpath to enter Medmenham. Up on the left at the top of the field is a magnificent flint barn (NT), and alongside it is a fine house which becomes visible further along the road. This is Lodge Farm, rebuilt about 1750 on its commanding position. On the right is the Water Research Centre, with its frog sign, and then on the left is the Old Dog and Badger, formerly a church house, dating from about 1390, although the present building is sixteenth-century. Part of its car park is in a former chalk quarry. A cannonball was dug out of the walls of this pub when the walls were being reconstructed.

Opposite the Old Dog and Badger are the church cottages, built around 1400, and just past those is the church with its flint and chalk walls and chalk tower. At the cross road turn right on Ferry Lane where the sign for Medmenham has a drawing of a Viking-style boat. This is a memorial to the first settlers here in about AD 550 whose descendants built the first church in about 640.

Walk into the church of St Peter and St Paul (4) before carrying on down Ferry Lane past several delightful old houses. On the right-hand side is another entrance to the Water Research Centre (5), and on the left is the site of the former Medmenham Abbey (6), with grounds stretching down to the river.

The road ends at the river where there is a slipway (and one of those imaginative road signs with a car falling over into the water). To the left is a wonderful garden with lawns sweeping down to the river, but we turn right over a footbridge on to the riverside path. A notice tells us that fishing is for Medmenham Angling Club members only.

Go through a gate and out on to a huge field, the flood meadows, and walk on westwards following the river bank. Boats of all sorts will be seen on the river and a variety of birds too, ducks, geese, coots, moorhens, great crested grebes, with skylarks singing in the riverside meadows. Over to the right is the wetland area of Rodbed Wood. (7)

A 1.5 mile walk along the bank passes a small island (eyot) used by birds, and then the magnificent Culham Court on the other bank. This Georgian mansion, dating from 1770, has terraced gardens down to the river. Our path finally reaches a white house where we turn away from the river. At the end of the field go left over a stile and on to the driveway used by local residents. Pass a large house with a tennis court on the left, and beyond this is a huge black and white house close to the river bank. The driveway becomes a narrow road and continues between open fields, with the river away to the left, and the main road to the right, and the houses of Mill End straight ahead, where some of the houses have the Hambleden crest as they were built for workers on the Estate.

At the main road turn left, and use the narrow verge on the left until the pavement begins on the right side of the road. Pass the road turning right to Hambleden, and the signposts to Chiltern Vinery and Brewery, and Car Park 500 yards. Cross over to the left side of the A4155 and pass the gated entrance to Hambleden Marina. Between the next two buildings is a footpath which leads through to pass Hambleden Mill, which is now residential, but was grinding corn until 1958. This footpath continues built out on top of the weir, enabling walkers to cross to the lock and thence to the other bank of the

Thames. There has been a mill here since before the Domesday Survey, and the weir is thought to date from 1376. On the other bank is the Thames Path going upstream to Henley and downstream to Hurley. Just have a look at the lock, with the likelihood of seeing some boat traffic, before retracing your steps and walking along the road towards Hambleden. This leads past several fine flint buildings on the left, and a narrow road coming from Rotten Row to the right, which would have been used by anyone cutting the walk short to 8 miles. And then on the left is the car park.

(1) The bird life in these woods includes up to five varieties of tits, three or four types of warblers in summer, greater spotted woodpecker, robin, chaffinch, and occasionally nuthatch. If you get a good view of one of these last birds you will notice that, unlike woodpeckers and tree creepers, they run down as well as up the tree trunks. Spring is a good time for seeing the birds before the greenery hides them away, and also this is the time when they are singing and at their noisiest and tell you of their existence.

The commonest animals are the grey squirrels, but deer are also numerous, both the small muntjac showing their white rump and upturned tail when they run away, and larger fallow deer.

Notice that the noisiest of wild life are not the most exciting. For example wood pigeons crash out of trees looking like an air transport Hercules with heavy undercarriage, and then they flap madly in their attempts to fly away, but often only just circle before returning. Grey squirrels are scurrying around on the floor as well as overhead, crunching or crashing.

(2) An earlier Saxon church in Hambleden was replaced by a Norman church in the twelfth century, though the nave was rebuilt in the fourteenth century and the chancel and south transept were enlarged. The original central tower was replaced by the present western tower in the early eighteenth century.

Note the four weathercocks on the tower, made by local iron workers. The oldest part of St Mary's church is the north transept, from about 1230, in which is the D'Oyley monument, and near this is the oak muniment chest which belonged to James Brudenell, the 7th Earl of Cardigan. Other interesting old relics in the church include the font, which is twelfth-century or earlier, the oak Wolsey altar in the south transept and a sixteenth-century panel which is thought to be the bed head from Cardinal Wolsey's bed. The south wall of the tower has a memorial to a former rector, Ralph Scrope (1572), and there are other Scrope memorials in the brasses in the north transept. In the churchyard are many ancient graves on the south side, but fewer on the north which was regarded as the area of darkness and evil in the Middle Ages. W. H. Smith is buried in this churchyard, as also is Major George Howson who began the tradition of wearing poppies on Armistice Day.

(3) Across the road to the east of the church is the flint and red brick Jacobean Manor House which dates from 1603, but was modernised in the nineteenth century. It was the birthplace of the 7th Earl of Cardigan who led the Charge of the Light Brigade at Balaclava in 1854. It became the home of W. H. Smith and his descendants.

(4) St Peter and St Paul, Medmenham is a delightful and well cared for church with lovely kneelers. It was founded in 650 when it was a wooden church on the old route following the Thames Valley. It was rebuilt mainly of chalk blocks and flint rubble around 1150 under the patronage of Hugh de Bolebec, and then much restored in 1844. The nave walls and the south door are Norman. The early sixteenth-century tower contains three bells, two dated 1624 and 1691. Legend says that the fourth bell was sold to help ransom Richard I in 1189. The church was expanded in the early fifteenth century during the religious revival following the Black Death. Amongst other interesting features inside the church are several windows; one in the south nave shows the Feeding of the Five Thousand.

(5) The Water Research Centre is an independent company with offices in Europe and the USA, and specialises in environmental toxicology and research in inland waters. Recent projects have included aquatic toxicology, industrial discharge to sewers, river water quality, and studies of drinking water. Research on fast growing willows at the Medmenham site is part of a study on producing energy by burning willows as fuel, whilst sewage sludge is used as a fertiliser to aid the rapid growth of the trees.

(6) Medmenham Abbey was built on this site in 1204 on land granted to the Abbey of Woburn by Isabel de Bolebec, Countess of Oxford. Little history of the Abbey remains. At the dissolution, which took place before 8th July 1536, it was made part of the new Abbey of Bisham. There was only one monk left, a sign of it not being very successful! The Abbey was built by Normans in the thirteenth century, rebuilt in 1590 and restored by the Hell Fire Club around 1760. Sir Francis Dashwood lived here for a time in the 1760s and it is rumoured that orgies and mock religious ceremonies were held here. The stories grew and a political campaign developed against Dashwood. The motto of the Hell Fire Club was 'Do what you will' ('*Fais ce que tu voudras*' was written over the door). One of the best stories is that Sir Francis released a baboon at one meeting, and his friends are said to have fled, believing that it was the Devil.

(7) Rodbed Wood is an SSSI noted for its wetland plants. Willow and alder are the main trees, with some ash, while yellow flags and marsh marigolds grow well beneath these trees. There are also summer snowflakes, known locally as Loddon Lily, which have white flowers with green tips, and are at their best in May.

Walk 18 – The Chalfonts

Located OS Landranger 1:50 000 sheet 176, OS
Pathfinder 1:25 000 map 1139 and OS Explorer 1:25 000
map 3.
Length of walk is about 7 miles.
Time required is 3–4 hours, but the addition of several
hours may be necessary if visits to the Open Air
Museum or to Milton's house are included.
Terrain – is mostly gentle, with only occasional
gradients.
The starting point is at the Chiltern Open Air Museum
next to the entrance to Newland Park Campus, part of
Brunel University, near Chalfont St Giles. Grid ref
009937. This can be reached from either Chalfont St
Giles or Chalfont St Peter on the A413, by following the
brown signs with the Museum symbol. There are also
signs off the A412 for anyone leaving the M25 at
Junction 17. Either of the Chalfonts can be reached by
bus. Information is available from local Tourist
Information Centres.

A line of towns at the lower eastern margin of the Chilterns, including the Chalfonts and Amersham, are adjacent to the A413 and the M25, with easy access to London for the commuters who live here. This walk is through the two Chalfonts and the surrounding countryside, passing many fields used for grazing horses. We can visit two contrasting museums, the Chiltern Open Air and the Milton, and walk along the valley of the River Misbourne between Chalfont St Peter and Chalfont St Giles.

A visit to the Open Air Museum (1) is well worth while,

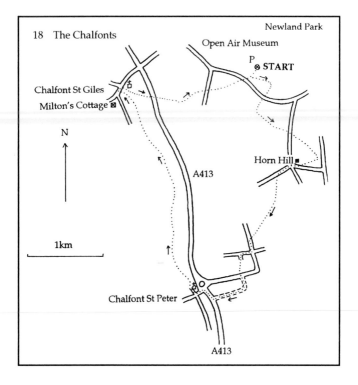

18 The Chalfonts

Newland Park

Open Air Museum

P
⊗ START

Chalfont St Giles

Milton's Cottage ⊠

N

↑

A413

Horn Hill ■

1km

Chalfont St Peter

A413

either at the beginning or the end of the walk. Probably about 2 hours will be needed to look at all the buildings and much more time can be happily spent in the 18 hectares (45 acres) of parkland.

Walk from the car park back to the driveway with its avenue of chestnuts and turn right towards the road. At the road turn left, but take great care along this narrow road. Pass the entrance to Rowan Farm Nursery and then turn right, over a stile and along a narrow path between a fence on the right and a hedge on the left. To avoid walking on this road it may be better to take a slightly longer alternative which can be followed for this first section. In order to do this, walk down the drive from the car park and about 100 m before reaching the road, turn left over a stile. The direction of the walk from this stile is like an upturned V. Head diagonally left across this field to its far corner, towards the extreme right-hand end of the buildings, passing the clump of trees and a small pond in the middle of the field. Go over a stile and turn immediately right along a fence for about 30 m, before turning right again for the second leg of the upturned V. Head across the field to a stile in the hedge, and this leads through a few trees and out to the narrow road. Up to the left is the Chalfont Shire Horse Centre, but we go across the road, over a stile, to follow the footpath between fence and hedge.

Pass the greenhouses on the right and at the next stile turn immediately left and go over two stiles. Walk along the left margin of a field, which may contain shire horses, and after about 200 m, where the hedge bends left, keep straight ahead for another 200 m to a stile in the corner of the field. Go over this, along the right margin of the field to another stile and out on to the narrow road, next to the entrance to Brawlings Farm and Riding Centre.

Cross the road, and pass to the right of the house and follow the path leading diagonally through the middle of the field which is the top of a low hill, Horn Hill. Wild flowers and skylarks may add to the pleasure of this walk here, though M25 noises may detract slightly. Head to the far corner of this very flinty field towards a couple of houses. At the end of the field, do not go on to the road, but turn sharp right to go westwards back across the field towards a wood, just to the right of a few houses. Pass through a small patch of woodland, and at the road turn right to walk along the path. Just before the cross roads on the right is St Paul's Church, Horn Hill. It was built in 1865 as a chapel of ease for the hamlet of Horn Hill. This hamlet was part of the Newland Park Estate, owned in the 1920s by the Harben family who endowed the village hall across the road from the church.

Proceed straight along the road beyond the cross roads, with the church on the right and the village hall on the left. The path is on the left of the road at first and then crosses to the right, but after a further 50 m turn left at the footpath sign along a stony track to a stile and a track along the field margin, with Robert's Wood to the right. Go through a gate at the end of the field and continue straight on to a cross paths by a gate on the right. Go through this fairly new kissing gate into the woods, and after 40 m at the cross paths, fork left. Do not follow the path which is descending but bend round to the left and go slightly uphill between some holly bushes. This path soon levels off and then begins to descend and approach the right side of the woods. Go over a stile and across a field to another stile in the corner and then across to the far right corner of the next field. Beyond here is a narrow path between two lines of trees, leading to a drive and then out to a road.

Turn left along the road, pass a school on the left and turn right along Copthall Lane. Take the first left turning, Ninnings Road, and then go right along Ninnings Way to a narrow path between the gardens of the bungalows. At the next road turn left and then right into Chalfont Heights, passing Private and No Through Road signs. After about 200 m the surfaced road turns right and becomes Chiltern Hill, which gradually begins to descend, passing a GR letter box, to cross over the main A413. Shortly beyond this road, turn right along High Street and walk into the centre of Chalfont St Peter. (2)

Leave the town from the church on the road passing the car park on the right and the school on the left, to find the path along the valley to Chalfont St Giles. This is the South Bucks Way and leads alongside allotments, passing the football pitch and on to the cricket pitch. Keep straight ahead, beyond the pavilion and to the left side of the tennis courts. Pass through a few trees, and over a stile and along a narrow path between fields. Pass through an old metal gate and out into an open field, where the noise of the A413 may be heard to the right.

Go over a wooden stile and straight on, passing a footpath going off to the right, but we just keep straight ahead. At the end of a large field is a stile and a yellow arrow pointing ahead, and we go over the stile and into the next field where there is an old orchard, looking a delight with blossom in the spring. The path leads through a dense growth of blackthorn and hawthorn at the lower end of the old orchard. Ignore the stile off to the right, but go over the stile straight ahead, and then right over another stile and across a garden to reach a surfaced path.

Our onward route is really to the right here, but before proceeding, turn left, passing the church for a visit to the main street of Chalfont St Giles. At the main street, turn left and walk along the road to visit Milton's cottage. (3) Across the road are a pub and restaurant both using the famous name of Milton.

Another famous name associated with this area, though not on the line of the walk is William Penn, the Quaker, who founded Pennsylvania. He is buried 2 miles away at Jordans, together with his two wives and five of his children.

From Milton's cottage, walk down the main street, noisy with traffic. On the right is a row of eighteenth-century cottages, and over on the left is the Rectory. Stonewells Farm on the right dates from the fifteenth century and is the oldest house in the village, and shortly beyond this on the left is the old Reading Room, a seventeenth-century building and the first village school. Near the end of the village is the small green, with the village sign depicting St Giles, the patron saint of cripples, beggars and travellers, and beyond that is the pond near which are two sarsen stones. (4) Just beyond the pond is the stream bed which is normally dry at present, though efforts are being made to restore water to the channel. The word *font* in the village name is derived from Old English for a spring, one reason for the creation of the village in this location. There was a mill on the River Misbourne but it is thought that well-digging has dried it up by lowering the water table. When it ran, the river rose in Mobwell Pond near Great Missenden. Retrace your steps, passing Merlin's Cave, to visit the church as we leave the village. The parish church (5) is reached from the main street through an alley between shops, leading to the unusual swivel lych gate which swings on a centre post.

The onward walk is along the right side of the church and over a footbridge across the non-existent stream. Walk across the meadow and through a kissing gate and up the narrow path between fences to the main road. Beware of traffic as we cross straight over and take a path just to the left of the driveway between a hedge and fence. Houses and gardens are on both sides at first, and then gardens on the left and two small paddocks on the right. The path splits and we take the left fork over a stile. Go diagonally left to the far side of the field to a stile in the hedge, and diagonally right across the next field to a stile in the corner. Cross over two stiles here and turn right along the hedge to another stile and out on to a road.

A few metres to the left across the road is a broad track leading through the woods which are part of the Rowan Farm. The track emerges from these woods directly opposite the entrance driveway to the Chiltern Open Air Museum and the Newland Park Campus.

Newland Park was the home of Sir Henry Gott, the son of George IV's head gardener who rebuilt the Manor House in 1770. It was owned by Henry Harben from 1910–21, when it was used as a sanctuary for suffragettes.

(1) The Open Air Museum was founded in 1976, with the aim of rescuing and preserving buildings which would otherwise have been demolished and lost for ever. The museum is a registered charity with no regular grants towards running costs and depends heavily on volunteer assistance. It is open from April to October; Saturdays, Sundays and Bank Holidays from 11 a.m.–6 p.m.; Tuesdays to Fridays 2–6 p.m., and from 11 a.m. on Wednesdays and throughout August. There is an admission charge.

The old buildings preserved range from a barn to a public convenience, and there is also a High Wycombe chair factory and a farm yard. The chair factory is the firm of James Elliott and Sons from Shaftesbury Street, and was given to the museum by Wycombe Borough Council in 1978. It mainly made Windsor chairs. Behind the factory is a bodger's hut from which the Nature Trail begins, and passes through chalk pits in the bluebell woods to the Iron Age house. This house has been based on a seventh-century BC house from Puddlehill near Dunstable, and was constructed on this site between 1978–81. Adjacent to this house is the medieval fields project which began in 1987, where a three-field rotation has been created, attempting to use original techniques and old varieties of crops. A nineteenth-century farm has been recreated around the farmyard, with barns, byre and stables of that period. A recent addition to the collection is Skippings Barn which was rescued for the museum from the National Centre of Epilepsy in Chalfont St Peter, and now contains information on the Hawk and Owl Trust. Henton Mission room is not in the guidebook. The ground at Henton was let by Magdalen College Oxford for the mission to be built. It was known as the little tin

church, as can be easily imagined. The old Caversham public convenience won the Loo of the Year Award in 1991.

(2) Chalfont St Peter developed as a small village in the Chiltern foothills in the valley of the river Misbourne, a tributary of the Thames. It was mentioned in the Domesday Book and during the Middle Ages was part of the land controlled by Missenden Abbey. In the town centre is the church of St Peter, a brick structure which has seen much restoration and extension work during the last two hundred years. The present tower replaced a medieval tower which collapsed after a storm in 1708. The five bells in the tower are still rung on Wednesday evenings and on Sundays. There are other interesting buildings in the town, and the Greyhound pub dates from the sixteenth century, though there has been an inn on this site since 1407 or earlier.

(3) Milton's cottage is open from 1st March–31st October, Wednesday to Sunday, 10 a.m.–1 p.m. and 2 p.m.–6 p.m. It also opens on Bank Holiday Mondays. There is an admission charge.

John Milton moved to this sixteenth-century half-timbered cottage from London in 1665 to avoid the plague. While here he completed *Paradise Lost* and started on *Paradise Regained*. There was much misery in his life but he found a certain amount of peace at Chalfont, with his third wife. As soon as possible however he went back to London, which he preferred, and died there in 1674. His friend Thomas Ellwood who found the house at Chalfont for him, and who used to read to Milton when he was blind, died here in 1713. The cottage was owned by the Fleetwood family, who also owned The Vache (where there is a memorial to Captain Cook), and have a family tomb in the chancel of the parish church. The house was bought by public subscription in 1877 to avoid it being dismantled and

An open barn showing methods of construction

shipped to the USA. It is now a museum, with three rooms of interesting and priceless exhibits, including a lock of Milton's hair and first editions of *Paradise Lost* and *Paradise Regained*. There is a lovely garden with a mulberry tree outside the main door.

(4) The sarsens or greywethers are blocks of sandstone which were found on top of the chalk. They are about 55 million years old and are hard remnants of much softer sandstones which have been eroded. Tiny scratch marks on one of the stones suggest that they may have been transported to this location by ice during the Ice Age.

(5) The oldest parts of the flint church of St Giles date from the thirteenth century and the doorway of the church is decorated with carved flowers, which are 600 years old. There are fourteenth-century wall paintings inside, and fifteenth-century angels on the roof. In the churchyard is the burial place of Bertram Mills, the circus owner.

Walk 19 – Burnham Beeches

> Located on OS Landranger 1:50 000 sheet 175 and OS Explorer 1:25 000 sheet 3.
>
> Total distance is 9 miles.
>
> Time required is 4–5 hours.
>
> Terrain – mostly flat or gently undulating.
>
> Starting point is at grid ref 957851 on Egypt Lane, reached by driving southwards along the A355 from junction 2 of the M40, for nearly 2 miles before forking right on to Egypt Lane.
>
> No dogs except guide dogs allowed in Egypt Woods.

This is a walk where the thick and thin of landscape have to be taken together, as it crosses some of the finest and most famous woodland areas of England, but also passes areas of industrial land use and near dereliction associated with motorway construction and sand and gravel extraction. We also visit a nature reserve, cross an area of common land and pass through the delightful village of Hedgerley.

Burnham Beeches are the remnants of much larger woods and are located partly on gravels and partly on Reading Beds. They extend over 220 hectares (540 acres) and are owned and managed by the Corporation of London, the first 162 hectares (400 acres) having been bought in 1880. At that time the land was all grazed. The woods were named after Viscount Burnham who donated 36 hectares (88 acres) in 1921. This ancient woodland is the home of a large range of plants and animals and contains about 800 of the famous old oak and beech pollards. Many of the older trees are now dying off. A famous old pollard, known as His Majesty, fell in the storm of October 1987. It had a girth of 8.9 m (29 ft 1 in) and was the largest

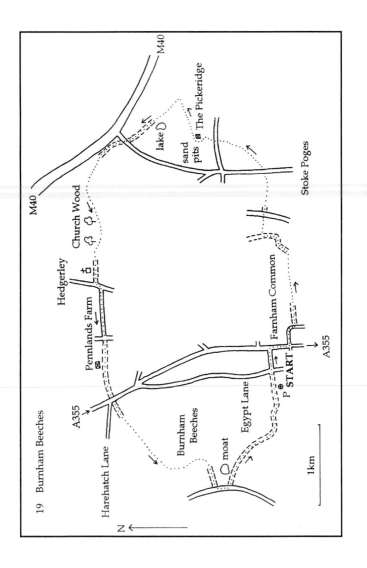

19 Burnham Beeches

pollarded tree in the British Isles. The timber poles were used for firewood, but pollarding stopped when coal became much cheaper in the early nineteenth century. The Corporation of London has reintroduced some active management practices, such as pollarding and grazing on the old pasture and heathland. Burnham Beeches are managed by the Corporation to preserve the ancient woodlands and also to provide recreational areas for the public. They certainly achieve the latter, as there are miles of driveways and footpaths suitable for providing enjoyment and exercise for large numbers of people, as well as their dogs. An estimated three quarters of a million visitors come each year. Horse riding is also popular, although only allowed on the surfaced driveways. This ensures that footpaths do not become too muddy and churned in wet weather. Parts of the wood may be used for shooting from October to February.

Walk along the driveway, Lord Mayor's Drive, to the road and the notice board giving information about the Burnham Beeches East and Burnham Common. Cross over the road and follow the signposts to Farnham Common and Beeches Way. At the T-junction with a major road, turn right on the A355 towards Slough, pass a few shops, and the Stag and Hounds which dates from 1799. At the Foresters turn left along Victoria Road and about 30 m after it bends sharply to the right, go left along a public footpath with the Beeches Way sign.

The narrow path passes between fences and gardens and goes through into the woods, with a fence continuing along the right side. A notice mentions that this wood is managed by the Woodland Trust, and contains many beech trees, with some holly and laurel. Cross a small stream and keep going, climbing slightly. This is a woodland area, though called Farnham Common. There is not much undergrowth in the mainly beech areas, but in some hollows, former chalk or gravel pits, there is a denser growth of vegetation. The many birds to be heard or seen in these woods include tits, warblers in summer, and woodpeckers.

Pass a lone house to the right, and the path joins a driveway. Where the drive splits, the right turn is signed Beeches Way, but take the left turn following a blue arrow. Pass a bungalow, South Lodge, on the left, and walk along the edge of the woods with open fields to the right. The broad path bends right, then left, and at a stile on the right, turn right, following a yellow arrow, and a sign for Beeches Way. The Beeches Way is a 16-mile walk from the River Thames to the Grand Union Canal developed by the Buckinghamshire County Council, together with the Iver and District Countryside Association.

Walk alongside the wire fence and at the end of the field go over a stile, cross the road, and straight ahead over a stile and along the edge of the woods. Pass through an old gate, along the margin of a small field, and through a modern kissing gate. This is the Beeches Way still and leads into a woodland of small trees, with birch, gorse and undergrowth. Walk straight ahead alongside a recently cleared patch and, where the path splits, take the left fork even though about 20 m along the right fork is a marker post for the Beeches Way. Go through a gap at the side of a wooden gate and cross over the road, Gerrards Cross Road.

On the other side is Stoke Common (1), with areas of small trees and more open land, where an ongoing programme of management tries to preserve a wide range of habitats for plants and animals. Much of the original common was changed by enclosures in the early nineteenth century, but in spite of that, a small amount has survived. The present day problem is to maintain it, as without any management the scrub and then trees would gradually take over and all the more open commonland would disappear. The so-called natural heathland can only survive with man's assistance.

After about 100 m, at a cross paths where the main path goes straight ahead as Beeches Way, turn left along a narrower but still gravelled path. The gravel path soon becomes a grass and mud track, crossing a large area which was cleared in 1995–6 to allow small plants to grow. At a broad stony cross track, turn right for a few metres and then left to walk through to Stoke Common Road.

Cross this road towards a large driveway and walk along the concrete drive used by lorries arriving at the old sand pits. On the right is the entrance to the head offices of BFI, Browning Ferring Industries UK Limited. The path goes on to the left of the old farm buildings which include a fine grain store perched on stone staddles. Once past the building turn right to pass behind the farm and the large white building of Pickeridge. There are several sand pits to the left of the path. The grassy path is between fences and gradually descends, with views of the lake ahead down in the hollow, with the M40 beyond. Go over a stile by an old iron gate and carry on downhill, with woodland to the right, and open field to the left.

At the bottom of the field turn right through a new kissing gate, and then immediately left, and after a few metres reach another kissing gate. A pond with ducks and geese on it is to the right, but turn left, along the footpath which is between two hedges and fences. The motorway is up to the right. The relics of sand pits and the noise of the motorway make this seem very remote from the quiet valleys in the heart of the Chilterns. It is difficult to picture what this area must have been like before the sand pits and motorways appeared on the scene.

Go over a stile and keep straight ahead. To the right is a hedge and to the left is another lake with ducks, coots and swans, though vegetation is filling in this lake to create a wonderful wetland nature reserve. Walk beneath the overhead electricity wires and move on over a stile. The path goes on between two fences and fields, then past some orchards on the left. This area may undergo changes during the next year or two with sand pit developments and, as at Stoke Common, some parts of this walk may be different by the end of the century.

Emerge on a road and turn right along the pavement, but after about 30 m turn left along Mount Hill Lane. A good shrubby embankment is on the right alongside the motorway, helping to encourage wild life. The lane is blocked by an iron gate, but go over the stile and continue straight ahead. When the drive ends, fork left slightly over a stile by an iron gate, and follow the hedge on the left and the signpost to Hedgerley. Pass beneath the power cables again, and at the end of the field go over a stile at a cross paths. Turn left across the middle of the next field, towards the telegraph poles and walk away from the motorway.

At the end of this field is a stile and we continue straight ahead along the field margin. To the right of the path is Church Wood (2), a nature reserve. At the end of the next field go over a stile and keep straight ahead, and just before the end of this field is the entrance to the nature reserve on the right. Have a walk round this RSPB nature reserve. Once through the gate you can see the map.

Leave the wood through the kissing gate and turn right. After about 15 m at the end of the field, climb over a narrow stile and walk straight on along the track. Pass Church Meadow and the village church on the right, just before reaching the village road. Here there is a small pond and the sign saying that Hedgerley was the best kept village in Buckinghamshire several times in the 1980s and again in the 1990s. Before turning left, which is the onward route, turn right to visit the church of St Mary the Virgin, built in 1852, though there had been earlier churches on this site. The wooden pulpit comes from a church in Antigua, destroyed in an earthquake of 1843. Beyond the church is a pub and at the end of the village are Shell House and Quaker House, two of the interesting old houses in this very old village. Retrace your steps past the pond and the parish notice board and at the cross roads turn right. On the right here, is the Brickmould pub, the name being an indicator of one former activity (3) in this area.

Follow the narrow Kiln Lane out of the village, pass Yew Tree Cottage on the right, with its yew tree, and go on to a small group of houses just before a T-junction. Keep straight ahead here along the public bridleway, through the small wooden gate by the large metal gate. At Pennlands Farm, the site of a brickworks until 1936, there are paths which go off to right and to left, but keep straight ahead. Pass between the barns and farm on the right and a large house on the left, just beyond which is an old granary on staddle stones, designed this way to keep out the rats and also to allow air to circulate beneath the barn. The surfaced drive climbs and bends left, passing Pennlands Kiln, a grand house on the right, and then a few old sheds. Walk on until the driveway reaches the main road, A355.

Cross over to the minor road, Harehatch Lane, and after about 20 m fork left along the path into the woods, following the Public Footpath and Circular Walk signs. This is the area known as Egypt Woods, once the haunt of gypsies. The word gypsies originated in the sixteenth century, as though they had come from Egypt. In fact they were groups of wandering people who called themselves Dukes of Little Egypt.

The path soon splits but either branch will lead through to a gate and a stile and a yellow arrow pointing straight on. After about 40 m the path splits, and take the right fork which is really straight on, signposted with a yellow arrow. Mainly conifers grow in this section of wood, with a line of silver birch alongside the path. Many large wood ant nests (4) can be seen around here, as well as in many places later on in these woods.

As the path descends slightly, the wood becomes more deciduous in composition. At a cross paths keep straight ahead, still following the yellow arrow. There is an open field to the right of the path at this stage, and much evidence of coppicing on the left. At a junction of paths the circular walk we have

been following now turns left, but we just turn right for about 20 m to where the path splits. We do not go straight ahead here, but turn left into the heart of the woods.

A broad grass and mud track leads southwards through deciduous woodland, mainly silver birch, as well as beech and oak, with the oak being the largest trees. Patches of heather can be seen in the late summer. At a cross paths, with yellow arrows pointing in all directions, go straight on along a permissive path, where no dogs are allowed, except for guide dogs. The path soon bends left past a post with a yellow arrow, going east for a short distance, and then the path bends round to the right for a long straight which is heading almost in a southerly direction. Silver birch and holly are the main trees to the left and beech and oak to the right, with fir trees beyond. There is little undergrowth on the right, but the ground is covered by layers of leaves, whereas on the left, grass grows beneath the silver birch. Soon there are also silver birch and grass on the right of the path.

The path bends slightly right to a bearing of 200°, and comes to a cross paths with a wooden post and a yellow arrow pointing right. There is a footpath going straight on here, but we turn right along a track, to follow the direction of the yellow arrow, heading west with a bearing of about 270°. This leads to a wooden stile by a wooden gate and beyond this is a narrow road, Park Lane. Turn left along here and soon reach a large Corporation of London noticeboard giving the information that this is Park Lane. Burnham Beeches is a SSSI.

About 100 m beyond this noticeboard, where there is a stile on the right, turn left through a small car parking area, and go over the embankment at the back of this space to an old driveway which is partially covered by leaves. This leads

Gnarled pollard in Burnham Beeches

through rhododendrons which are magnificent in May. Walk along McAuliffe Drive for about 30 m and on the left is the corner of the moat, with a plaque giving information about its history. (5)

The walk from now on is along the surfaced driveways through the Burnham Beeches, with massive rhododendron bushes (6) lining parts of the way, including the very scented yellow *rhododendron luteum*.

From the moat walk along Halse Drive from the junction with McAuliffe Drive, soon passing the end of Dukes Drive which goes off to the left. The drive descends and at the bottom of the valley, the unsurfaced Victoria Drive comes in from the right, and Burnham Walk is to the left, but just continue ahead, as the road climbs and bends left. Some remarkable old trees can be seen along here, with a variety of weird shapes. (7)

At the cross roads called Victory Cross, there are several areas of parking space. Coming in from the right is Lord Mayor's Drive and we turn left along this to walk back to the starting point. At the cross roads is a notice saying 'Welcome to Burnham Beeches Nature Reserve'. Described as a wood pasture, this is the ancient form of land management where animals graze and trees are grown in the same areas. From the ecological viewpoint, pollarded oak and beech trees are useful and valuable for supporting many insects and fungi found only in ancient trees.

(1) Stoke Common is being managed to maintain a variety of habitats. Reviving heathland has been one major target and this involves clearing many trees which would otherwise dominate and prevent heathland from surviving. Part of Stoke Common has been designated an SSSI for its heathland habitat. In 1993 the District Council took over responsibility for maintaining the common and its wild life. Help and advice are obtained from ecological groups and also from English Nature. The principle of grazing has been discussed and it is possible

that grazing may be introduced on the common as part of the management process. Stoke Common is in the parish of Stoke Poges where the parish church was the setting for Thomas Gray's 'Elegy in a Country Churchyard', with those famous lines:

> The curfew tolls the knell of parting day,
> The lowing herd wind slowly o'er the lea,
> The plowman homeward plods his weary way,
> And leaves the world to darkness and to me.

A monument to Gray, designed by James Wyatt, was erected in the churchyard in 1799.

(2) Just inside the entrance to Church Wood is a useful map. The main path soon splits, but take the left fork going uphill. Flowers in the wood change with the seasons, but in spring there will be bugle, vetch, violets, yellow archangel, herb Robert and masses of bluebells. There are many nesting boxes in this wood for the tits and also larger ones for owls. Turn right at the seat, a memorial to John Hennel 1918–88, and after 15 m turn right again to follow the path parallel to the telegraph poles down to the hut. In this are a few chairs if you have time to sit around, and lists of what has been seen in these woods. The variety of birds is amazing and includes nuthatch, bullfinch, greater spotted woodpecker, green woodpecker, sparrow hawk, wood pigeon, wren, pheasant, song thrush, tawny owl, tree creeper, jay, magpie, four types of tit, and in summer there are blackcaps and chiffchaff. Several mammals live in this wood and the summer sees a good selection of butterflies such as brimstone, gatekeeper, large white, meadow brown, orange tip, peacock, red admiral and several others. The hut, which is located nearly in the middle of the wood, also contains a book for visitors to record their comments and what they have seen during their visit. From the hut walk straight across from the door along a narrow path leading back to the path you came along earlier. Turn left and walk back to the edge of the wood.

The wood is mixed deciduous and contains many silver birch as well as beech.

(3) Hedgerley has an ancient history of brick-making, even as early as Roman times. Pottery as well as bricks were made in this area, using the suitable loams which are derived from the Reading Beds of rock. The peak years for working were in the eighteenth and nineteenth centuries.

(4) The wood ant nests may be up to 70–80 cm in height. The wood ant, *Formica rufa*, is Britain's largest ant, the workers growing up to about 6 mm in length, while the queens and males reach 10 mm. The workers gather leaves, small twigs and pine needles to build the nest, and there may be 300,000 of them in one nest, or half a million in one colony which may consist of several nests. In late summer they can be seen everywhere and often cover the paths. Long columns of them will be rushing about their business, whatever that is, so do take care where you sit down if you pause for a rest or a picnic. They are omnivores and about half their food is honeydew they collect from aphids, and most of the remainder is insects which they can kill with a small spray of formic acid from a gland at the rear of the abdomen. They will all defend the nest, and can squirt formic acid on any invaders. Try this by sticking a pencil into the nest, not your fingers. The ants can often be seen dragging caterpillars back to the nest. Ants will eat anything they can find, and they forage widely in summer, searching for food at ground level, and also right up to the tops of the largest trees. They are great scavengers and important for keeping woodland pests under control. Winged males and winged females fly out at breeding time, and some fertilised females return to the nest, lose their wings, then settle down to breeding.

(5) Hartley Court Moat is also known as Hardicanute's or Harlequin's Moat, the alternative names probably derived from the wood at Hertleigh, the name for this part of the land of Burnham Abbey. This moated homestead consists of two

enclosures. The inner enclosure of 0.6 hectares (1.5 acres) is secured by a sub-rectangular moat to protect the homestead and cultivated ground from livestock. The outer enclosure of 3.7 hectares (9 acres) is surrounded by a ditch and bank which would have been surmounted by a pale as a fortification and a defence. It dates approximately from the twelfth to the fourteenth century.

In the seventeenth century the Moat belonged to the Eyres of East Burnham, whose family owned most of what is now Burnham Beeches. A well has been located in one corner of the homestead, and there were probably buildings used for animals, and for baking and brewing. The Moat is a scheduled ancient monument. All around the Moat are large rhododendron bushes which were planted at the beginning of the century. These are cut back to prevent them from growing too large, as the root systems might easily damage the old earth works.

(6) In places the rhododendrons have grown very successfully and are being removed as part of the overall management plan. They were originally planted at the beginning of the century as cover for game, but have become too numerous. In order to allow other bushes and trees to grow and thrive, the cutting is aimed at removing rhododendrons from many areas of the woodland, but retaining them alongside the roads.

(7) Some of the pollards in Burnham Beeches are at least 400 years old. Pollarding involves cutting the trees at 2.5–3 m (6–7 ft) above the ground and was introduced here in the mid-sixteenth century. It enabled the foresters to grow the trees for timber, animals could graze beneath them, and it also prolonged the life of the trees. They were cut every twelve to fifteen years. There were approximately 3000 pollards in the seventeenth century, and probably 547 remain today. They have not been pollarded since about 1820, though some pollarding has been reintroduced as part of the management of the forests. Trees are ideally spaced to enable grass to grow

between them and, without pollarding, the pasture will become overgrown with birch and holly, which are unsuitable for grazing. As part of the modern management plan some of the pollards are cut to reduce their size and weight in order to reduce the danger of wind damage. The areas which are being grazed have been fenced, to keep animals in, but not to keep visitors out, as there are gates to provide access for walkers.

Oxfordshire into Berkshire

Walk 20 – Goring

Located on OS Landranger 1:50 000 sheet 175, though the start is on sheet 174, and on Pathfinder 1:25 000 maps, most of the walk is on Explorer 3 Chilterns South and number 1172, but small sections are also on numbers 1155 and 1171.

Length of walk is a circuit of 8 miles, but this will become 10 if the detour into Whitchurch and Pangbourne is added.

Time required is 4–5 hours.

Terrain – this walk begins along the river bank and then passes through farmland and woods. The flat riverside path is followed by some undulations in the latter half, with a few gentle climbs but no steep scarp to be climbed.

Starting point is grid ref 599806 in Goring, which can be reached by crossing the river from Streatley on the A329 Wallingford to Reading road, or along the B4409 on the east side of the Thames. Car parking is possible in the centre of the town. Goring can be reached by train, as it is located on a very busy line between Reading and Didcot. It has its own station though most trains do not stop, merely passing through at great speed.

Goring is a charming Georgian town, with several old flint houses along the High Street. Situated on the River Thames, Goring is at the old fording point used by early travellers from flint mines in East Anglia, or from Stonehenge and Avebury. There is now a wooden bridge link with Streatley, but there

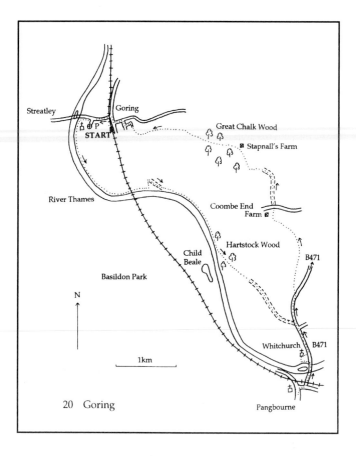

Streatley

Goring

Great Chalk Wood

P

START

Stapnall's Farm

River Thames

Coombe End
Farm

Hartstock Wood

B471

Child
Beale

Basildon Park

N

Whitchurch   B471

1km

20   Goring

Pangbourne

was only a ferry crossing here until the nineteenth century. Goring is at the southern tip of the Chilterns, and some delightful chalkland scenery can be seen on both banks of the river, travelling downstream towards Marlow and Maidenhead.

Walk along the High Street towards the river bridge. From here the lock and weir can be clearly seen, as well as the boat traffic which is likely to be very active in summer and at weekends. Pass a few old flint houses, as well as the Old Mill, now an antique shop, to get on to the river bank where a useful information board has been placed. This mentions the ancient importance of Goring as a crossing point of the Thames, as well as a little of the geological history. (1) The old Icknield Way crossed here (see Walk 1) and the modern long-distance Ridgeway path still crosses here (see Walk 5).

This is a lovely place to start a walk, with the river and the boat activity to look at. Set off downstream, passing boats tied up at the free moorings. The church can be seen on the left, and then the public moorings end. The path becomes narrower but continues along the bank, passing a few old boathouses just to the left.

The river is rich in bird life, with kingfishers, great crested grebes, ducks, swans, heron, coot and moorhen. The banks are lined with bushes and trees, ideal for the many small birds flitting to and fro. Butterflies and dragonflies can be quite numerous on warm days.

The main road is just across the river over to the right, and the far bank contains a few magnificent houses, with gardens sloping down to the river. Parked cars may be seen at one large imposing building recently being used as the Institute of Leisure and Amenity Management.

Pass through a zigzag gateway, and out into an open field, but still continuing along the river bank. Good views to the left reveal a typical chalk landscape rising to low hills, and the main railway line with frequent speeding trains passing along

it. After two fields, go through a kissing gate and head on towards the railway bridge, with a small pill box adjacent to it.

Several patches of reed are found on this stretch of the river, and sedge warblers will be noisy here in the summer months. Yellow water lilies grow here. Pass beneath the bridge and straight along the river bank, then go through a small wooden gate and along the path, with a fence to the left and the river to the right.

The public footpath soon turns away from the river at Ferry Cottage and crosses over a wooden footbridge following a permissive sign. We are on the Thames Path, the country's newest national trail (which diverges from the river here as far as Whitchurch). Walk away from the river for just over 100 m, and Gatehampton Manor is to the left. After passing a paddock on the right, turn right on the Thames Path, a public bridleway. The broad path leads between fences, with the river to the right and the sloping chalklands to the left. Continue on into Hartslock Wood, a mixed woodland with patches of under-growth, and very rich in wild life, and the path soon begins to climb slightly. Occasional views to the right and across the river towards the Berkshire Downs open up, especially in winter. For nearly half a mile climb gently and move slightly further away from the river, but notice the ponds down on the plain on the other side of the Thames. They mark the site of the Child Beale Wildlife Trust, and further west on the hillside is Basildon Park (NT).

Reach the edge of the wood and walk along a narrow path between hedges and fields. After a short descent, climb up some steps, to reach a gravelled driveway. Walk along this for half a mile, as far as the B471, passing a few houses. At the road a Thames Path sign tells us that we have walked 3½ miles from Goring, and very nice it has been too.

Boats at Goring

The route onward from the T-junction is by crossing over the road and turning left, to walk along the raised grassy path parallel to the road. Before doing so it is interesting to turn right along the road, still following the Thames Path, and walk into Whitchurch.

DETOUR INTO WHITCHURCH

Walk into Whitchurch between walls of houses on a narrow stretch of road which soon widens out, and we pass a collection of delightful old houses. Go downhill slightly, pass between Manor House on the right and the house with the herringbone brick pattern on the left. Swanston Cottages on the left are very old, Swanston House is behind the big wall on the left, then comes Whitchurch House and the diminutive flint building, Flint Cottage. Pass Walled Garden House on the right, and on the left are Duchess Close, the Old Forge, and the Greyhound, with the village school up the lane alongside the Greyhound.

On the right is the driveway to the church and private drive to Mill Cottages. We turn right here, as does the Thames Path, and go to visit the church of St Mary. Inside is a memorial to Sir John Forbes of Swanston House, the Queen's Physician who died in 1861, and also memorials to the Whistler family on the church floor. There are bare wooden beams up in the roof of this flint church. In the churchyard is a pink granite memorial to Sir John Forbes, and we pass this as we take the footpath going diagonally across the churchyard to the far left corner and through to the mill and the river. Turn left along the drive which leads back to the road, very close to the toll bridge. Turn right over this (2) and walk into Pangbourne, and the Royal County of Berkshire. The Thames Path turns left to follow the river, Purley 2½ miles, but we just go on ahead.

Stroll round Pangbourne, which has several old buildings including interesting pubs, and at the main road, notice that Beale Park (3) is 1¼ miles away, and Basildon Park (4) is 2, if you wish to visit either.

Across the road and to the left, is the eleventh- or twelfth-century church of St James the Less (5), and next door to this is Church Cottage, where Kenneth Grahame lived.

Retrace your steps from Pangbourne, over the river and through Whitchurch, to continue the circuit back to Goring.

MAIN WALK

Continue along the elevated path, climbing slightly, on the right side of the road. When this path ends, at the entrance to Fir Hill, cross over to the war memorial to the men of Whitchurch who died in World War I. There is a seat here, if you need a rest or a picnic. Continue along the left side of the road for about 30 m and where the road begins to bend right, take the narrow path going off to the left through the trees, passing a signpost to Coombe End 1 mile. It soon splits but take the left fork, as the right fork just goes back to follow the road, and at an iron kissing gate go through to walk along the left margin of a field. There is woodland to the left, and open field to the right, with a line of telegraph poles running parallel to our route. At the end of the field go through a metal kissing gate and straight ahead along a grassy track between a hedge and a fence. Thatched houses visible over to the right are part of Whitchurch Hill.

The track begins to descend towards an impressive farm building with Wealden-style hung tiles, and the path bends right and then goes through a metal kissing gate to pass along the right side of the farm complex and converted farm buildings of Beech Farm. Cross over the concrete driveway to a small wooden gate and along the left margin of a field. In the far corner is an iron kissing gate and beyond this is a narrow path into the woods, passing holly trees at first and then more beech. At a marker post the path splits and our route is the left fork, which is more or less straight ahead. At the end of the wood, go over an old wobbly stile and across the field towards the far corner, heading to the right of the farm buildings. Go

over another wobbly stile and across a small field towards a gate. Just before the gate to the farmyard, go right through a holly hedge and over a stile. Turn left and pass to the right side of the farm, which includes some old flint buildings, and over another stile on to the stony drive. The main farmyard at Coombe End Farm is to the left, but turn right here and follow the drive to a narrow road.

Cross straight over and continue along another stony drive to pass between a tile-hung house on the right and a flint and thatch house on the left. The stony drive reaches a surfaced track, where we turn left on the private road to Stapnall's Farm, following the signpost and blue arrow to Goring, 3 miles. Just before reaching the farm buildings, turn left through a large iron gate, and walk along the right margin of this field. In the far corner is a small gate and beyond this the path leads through a narrow wooded area, with a house to the right. Pass through an old gateway into the main part of the woods, Great Chalk Wood.

About 20 m into the wood the path splits and we take the right fork, a fairly level stretch through conifers. The path begins to descend slightly and leads to a wooden gate, but turn left just before reaching the gate and following a yellow arrow. After about 40 m, when the path splits, take the right fork. There are occasional yellow arrows on the trees. Soon cross a track and go straight on, but after about 15 m, when the path splits, take the left fork, more or less straight on and fairly level, following yellow arrows marked on trees. The wood opens out a little and a broad grassy path goes gently downhill. Fir trees are still to the right, but small silver birch and a few beech trees are on the more open area to the left.

The path closes in with fir trees on both sides, and the descent continues. An open field becomes visible 20 m to the

Herringbone patterned brick in Whitchurch

right, and then an open field can be seen on the left as well. Wild honeysuckle is common just before reaching the end of the wood, where a stile leads into a tunnel of dense growth of blackthorn, beyond which is another stile. The path leads straight on beyond this stile, following the right margin of a field and climbing quite steeply. At the top of the climb bend left, but still following the field margin. To the right is a narrow wood and over to the left are good views of characteristic chalkland scenery. The wood ends and beyond the hedge on the right is a small cemetery; straight ahead and down on the valley floor is the River Thames and also the railway line, with the wooded slopes of the Berkshire Downs beyond.

At the end of the field go over a stile and straight on. Skylarks and yellowhammers may be heard here and wild flowers grow in profusion along the field margin. Goring can be seen down on the plain as we descend to the bottom corner of the field. Go through a gap in the fence on to a playing field. Walk across to a small wooden gate and then on to a short stretch of path, before reaching the road of a smart housing development. Turn left along the first road, and then right at the T-junction, along Whitehills Green. At the next T-junction and a major road, turn left and walk on past the cul de sac with the old railway cottages. Next is the Queen's Arms, with the station across the road. Turn right here for a few metres and then we turn left over the railway bridge to walk back into the centre of Goring.

Visit the eleventh-century parish church of St Thomas of Canterbury, Goring on Thames. The church was surrounded by an Augustinian nunnery on three sides during the Middle Ages, and for a time the nuns had their own church, but this was removed after the Dissolution of the Monasteries. Virtually no trace of the nunnery remains, except the corbels supporting the roof of the cloister on the south wall, a few tiles now in the clergy vestry, and the mark of a gable over the west door. The church has an old lych gate and the yard is surrounded by a flint wall. The chalk tower has a stair turret protruding, an unusual addition to a Norman tower. One of the oldest church bells in England, dating from about 1290, can be seen inside the church, hanging on the west wall. Two of the brasses are for the Whistler family who lived at Manor House, Gatehampton, and are also remembered in Whitchurch.

(1) The Goring Gap is a famous landscape feature, where the Thames cuts through the ridge of chalk which is known as the Chilterns to the north and the Berkshire Downs to the south. The gap was enlarged at a time when the river was made bigger than at present by the addition of melt-water. During the melting phases of the Ice Age when the climate was warming up, vast quantities of melt-water would be flowing downstream. The enlarged river had extra powers of erosion for long periods. The river is now the county boundary, with Streatley being in Berkshire.

(2) The crossing point at Whitchurch was a ferry until the first bridge was constructed in about 1792. The proprietors were given the right to charge a ½d for every person crossing on foot. For a horse or a bull the charge was 2d, but only a ½d for a sheep. A carriage cost 2d for every wheel. A replacement wooden bridge was built in about 1852, and in 1902, when this was showing signs of age and deterioration, the present iron bridge was built. The toll house dates back to 1792. The toll bridge collects tolls from 7 a.m.–10 p.m., and the fee for a car is now 8p, but walkers go free.

(3) Beale Park is popular for fishing, and has many birds and animals, including rare breeds of sheep and goats, and a pets' corner. There is a willow maze, a steam railway, and a model boat collection, as well as boat trips on the Thames and riverside walks, all contributing to a good day out.

(4) Basildon Park contains an eighteenth-century Georgian mansion and a magnificent garden set in a delightful park overlooking the Thames. The house is most noted for its

Octagon Room, but also has a fine collection of pictures and furniture. There is a formal garden, as well as walks in the surrounding woodland. The house is open Wednesdays to Sundays (and Bank Holiday Mondays) from Easter till the end of October and, in addition, the garden and park are open throughout March.

(5) The church of St James the Less is of flint and clunch and much repair work was done in the 1860s. The tower was built in 1718, with clunch walls faced with small red bricks. The east window by Karl Parsons is a World War I memorial given by Sir George and Lady Armstrong. The part of it showing the Archangel Gabriel holding lilies was used by the Royal Mail as the design for the 18p Christmas stamp in 1992. Church Cottage next to the church is where Kenneth Grahame lived until his death in 1932. Like his hero, Ratty, he loved to go messing about in boats. The village sign in Station Road shows King Burtulf with the village charter dating from AD 844, a Saxon ship, and Kenneth Grahame's book, *The Wind in the Willows.* Another author with a Pangbourne link is Jerome K. Jerome, who featured the Swan Hotel, which is close to the weir, in his famous book, *Three Men in a Boat.*

Whitchurch church and the quay

Index